Y0-EEF-300

# Language, Learning, and Deafness

## Theory, Application, and Classroom Management

# Language, Learning, and Deafness

## Theory, Application, and Classroom Management

**ALICE H. STRENG**
University of Wisconsin–Milwaukee

**RICHARD R. KRETSCHMER, JR.**
University of Cincinnati

**LAURA W. KRETSCHMER**
University of Cincinnati

MADONNA COLLEGE LIBRARY
Livonia, Mich.

HV
2430
.S915

**Grune & Stratton**

A Subsidiary of Harcourt Brace Jovanovich, Publishers

New York • San Francisco • London

79907

**Library of Congress Cataloging in Publication Data**
Streng, Alice H
  Language, learning, and deafness.

  Includes bibliographies and index.
    1. Deaf—Education.   2. Children, Deaf—
Language.   I. Kretschmer, Richard R., joint
author.   II. Kretschmer, Laura W., joint
author.   III. Title.
HV2430.S86        371.9'12        77-18196
ISBN 0-8089-1060-4

© 1978 by Grune & Stratton, Inc.

All rights reserved. No part of this publication may be reproduced or transmitted in any
form or by any means, electronic or mechanical, including photocopy, recording, or any
information storage and retrieval system, without permission in writing from the
publisher.

Grune & Stratton, Inc.
111 Fifth Avenue
New York, New York 10003

Distributed in the United Kingdom by
Academic Press, Inc. (London) Ltd.
24/28 Oval Road, London NW 1

Library of Congress Catalog Number 77-18196
International Standard Book Number 0-8089-1060-4

Printed in the United States of America

# Contents

**Preface**                                                                                                      ix

**Chapter 1**   From Then to Now                                                                1

**Chapter 2**   The Learning Process                                                        15

**Chapter 3**   Establishing and Maintaining Communication            45

**Chapter 4**   Language, the Basic Tool                                               69

**Chapter 5**   The Learning Environment in the School Setting        99

**Chapter 6**   Developing and Stabilizing Language through an
                        Experience-Based Integrated Language Arts Program   109

**Chapter 7**   Reading and Writing in the Curriculum                     129

**Chapter 8**   Assessment and Planning for Language Growth         167

**Chapter 9**   Beyond Deafness                                                          187

**Appendix A**   Grammar I                                                                 209

**Appendix B**   Grammar II                                                               213

**Index**                                                                                                 217

# Tables

1-4  Transformational Operations Possible in Spoken English

2-4  Possible Semantic Relations Expressed through Sentence Patterns I through V

1-6  Suggested Sequential Acquisition of Syntactic Structures for Expressive Purposes for Hearing Impaired Children

2-6  The Fitzgerald Key with Illustrations of Sentences Written in the Key

1-7  Syntactic Complexity Formula

1-8  Work Sheet for a Structural Analysis

# Figures

1-1  American Manual Alphabet

2-1  Cues for English Vowels and Consonants

1-7  Pages from a Child's Dictionary

1-8  Samples from an Assessment Record

# Preface

The steady but gentle winds of change that blew through the first century and a half of our national life have suddenly become a hurricane. The education of hearing impaired children has been caught in this storm. During our early history, a paternalistic attitude toward the hearing impaired contributed to their seclusion in segregated schools and society in general. Today, hearing impaired adults, together with other groups of handicapped persons, are vigorously demanding social changes that will give them a share in the bounties of our society. They are asking for our willing cooperation as well as for government mandates to assure them their due civil and educational rights.

Along with societal changes, educational policy is also changing. Federal legislation now guarantees handicapped children the right to public education in schools where they can receive instruction most appropriate for them in the least restrictive environment. It also provides for parent participation in the educational process.

An increase in local education programs for handicapped children, including the hearing impaired, has also created a special need for information and material that will help update the educational process and make it more thorough and effective. This book purports to meet many new demands on our schools by providing the educator with a framework for setting instructional goals and by suggesting remedial strategies that could ensure their fulfillment.

Although we are aware that the education of the hearing impaired child involves considerably more than language instruction, the focus of this book is on language. We see the central mission of any educational program for children who cannot hear to be the establishment of language and communication. In the past, teachers of the deaf, like their pupils, were segregated from the mainstream of education and depended largely on their own creativity to devise procedures for teaching language. Fortunately, during the third quarter of the twentieth century, a flood of linguistic information became available to heighten our understanding of what language is and how it is learned. In this book we try to apply contemporary ideas derived from developmental psycholinguistics to the instruction of hearing impaired children.

This text is the result of the collaboration of three people with diverse but complementary backgrounds. One has been involved in the education of deaf children for 50 years; the second is the son of deaf parents and a teacher of deaf children; and the third, his wife, is an educational audiologist and also a teacher of the deaf. We have all been engaged in teacher education for many years. This book grew out of our intense desire to share our hopes for future change with teachers, professional support persons, parents, and students who are about to become involved in the compelling, fascinating, and sometimes frustrating world of educating hearing impaired children.

We take responsibility for all the opinions expressed in our book, but we challenge each reader to join us in discussion, in contemplation, and in action to ensure that every hearing impaired child will be able to understand and communicate effectively, and will be able to assume his rightful place in society and take responsibility for his own future.

Many people have assisted in the preparation of this book and we wish to thank them for their help: Jane Schoen and Margaret Peterson, our typists; Dr. Roberta Truax, University of Cincinnati, for reading and evaluating the manuscript; and these members of the Department of Exceptional Education at the University of Wisconsin–Milwaukee for their generous sharing of materials and advice: Nissan Bar Lev, Kathleen DeFever, Leo Dicker, Mary Beth Fafard, Richard Fox, Susan Gruber, Paul Haubrich, Margaret Kyllo, and Arthur Willans.

# 1

# From Then to Now

## FROM 1817 TO 1977

Very early in the history of our country, concerned men felt the need to provide education for children who were shut off from the hearing world because of deafness. The only other handicapping condition that was conspicuous enough to merit attention of educators in those long-ago days was blindness. Dunces, of course, sat in school corners because they could not learn, but hardly anyone thought of them as children who needed understanding and guidance or special education. Deaf children were indeed fortunate to find their advocate in Thomas Hopkins Gallaudet, who was instrumental in founding the first permanent school for the deaf in the United States in Hartford, Connecticut, in 1817, the American Asylum for the Deaf and Dumb, today known as the American School for the Deaf (Brill, 1974). This semiprivate school accepted and still accepts pupils from all sections of the nation. Even though deafness has always been a low-incidence handicap, difficult travel in the early 1800s impelled most existing states to establish their own residential schools for their scattered populations during the first half of the nineteenth century. As urban areas developed and grew, local educational agencies, with the support of the state, began to develop day school programs by the turn to the twentieth century (Am Ann Deaf, 1969). Early in the 1900s concern for children with lesser degrees of hearing impairment began to emerge. In some localities these children were taught in isolated special classes as deaf children were, but in others teachers traveled from school to school to give them special help when needed. The establishment of local programs was effective in lowering the age of admission to schools for the deaf from 12 years in the nineteenth century to 4 or 5 in the 1970s. Many

1

states now make provision for education of children from 3 to 21 and some from birth onward.

In the days before the discovery and use of antibiotics in the 1940s, childhood diseases such as measles, mumps, scarlet fever, and diphtheria destroyed the hearing of many children who made up the bulk of the population in schools for the deaf. Many became deaf after their language had been established and many were hard of hearing. Theirs was a communication problem rather than one involving the acquisition of a first language. But because there were no readily available hearing aids until the late 1930s, these children found their way into schools for the deaf. Today such children can wear powerful, reliable, individual hearing aids and remain in regular classes with the support of special teachers.

Genetic factors, such as that found in familial deafness, account for about half of the cases of deafness among school children. With a few still uncontrollable diseases, they are responsible for most of the hearing deficits that currently affect the school population. It is thought that the frequently encountered "cause unknown" appearing in the health records of hearing impaired children may have a genetic origin, but only future basic research will substantiate such a hypothesis.

Many of these children have been severely or profoundly deaf since birth. Better prenatal care and intervention have saved many babies who might otherwise have died. Yet children are still being born with multiple handicaps such as cerebral palsy and deafness, cleft palate and depressed hearing, retinitis pigmentosa, which causes both visual and auditory impairment, and minimal brain damage with a hearing component. Children with multiple handicaps may make up as much as 25 percent of the population in classes and schools for deaf children today (Am Ann Deaf, 1973). In Chapter 9 we shall shed some light on their educational problems and offer some solutions.

Education of the deaf in the United States is deeply rooted in European tradition, a tradition which developed over several centuries prior to the establishment of the first American schools. At that time deaf children in England and Germany were taught to lipread, speak, read, and write, while in France they were taught to sign, read, and write (Bender, 1960). Gallaudet reached France via England in his quest to learn how to teach deaf children. He decided that sign was the natural language of the deaf and so introduced this mode of communication in his new school. Until Clarke School for the Deaf in Northampton, Massachusetts, was established 50 years later as an oral school, sign was used almost exclusively as a mode of communication in state residential schools. In the middle of the 1800s the oral approach depended on lipreading and print for input, and speech and writing for expression. Hearing aids as we know them were nonexistent at that time.

The International Congress of educators of the deaf, convened in Milan, Italy, in 1880, strongly endorsed oralism and a natural approach to teaching language. This important Congress set trends that influenced the rise of oralism in American schools beginning in the early twentieth century. Because some educators were not entirely satisfied with a "pure" oral approach, they sought support systems for lipreading and speech. Two of these used hand signals. The older of the two, the Rochester method, coordinates fingerspelling with speech. Every letter of every word is spelled out as a person talks (Fig. 1-1).

The second is Cued Speech, developed in 1966 by Cornett (1967). It consists of a series of standardized hand signals. Eight configurations and four positions of either hand are used in synchronization with speech to differentiate visually similar lip patterns from each other (Lykos, 1971). They are illustrated in Figure 1-2. Since none of the signals is meaningful in isolation, they must be seen in relation to a cluster of lip movements. Both approaches are combined with auditory input and deliver their messages in standard English.

Ear trumpets were the only hearing aids available to deaf persons until the 1930s when heavy-battery driven individual aids and crude electronic group aids made their way onto the market. Yet auditory training had been

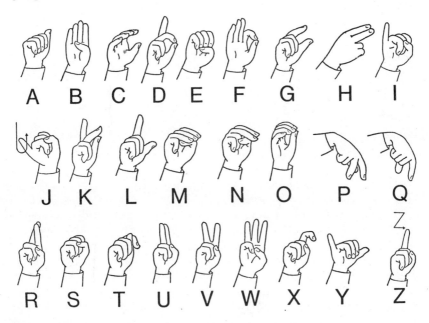

Figure 1-1.  The American Manual Alphabet. (Courtesy Gallaudet College Press.)

## CHART 1
### Cues for English Vowels

|  | Group I (base position) | Group II (larynx) | Group III (chin) | Group IV (mouth) |
|---|---|---|---|---|
| open | [a:] (fäther) (gŏt) | [a] (thăt) | [o:] (fôr) (ought) | |
| flattened-relaxed | [Λ] (but) [ə] (the) | [i] (ĭs) | [e] (gĕt) | [i:] (fēet) (meat) |
| rounded | [ou] (nōte) (boat) | [u] (gŏŏd) (put) | [u:] (blue) (fōōd) | [ə:] (ûrn) (hêr) |

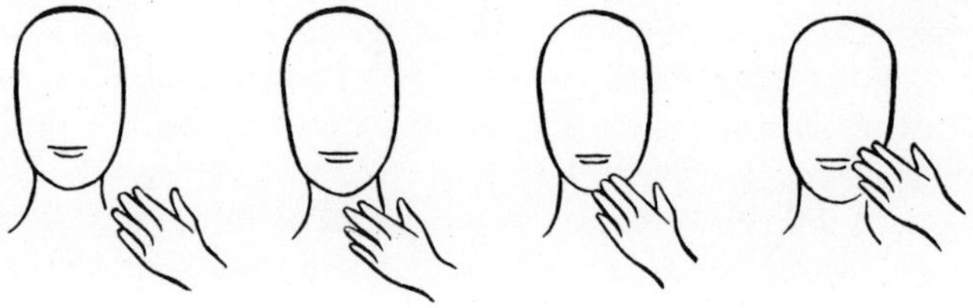

## CHART III
### Cues for English Consonants

| T Group* | H Group | D Group | ng Group | L Group | K Group | N Group | G Group |
|---|---|---|---|---|---|---|---|
| t | h | d | (ng) | l | k | n | g |
| m | s | p | y (you) | sh | v | b | j |
| f | r | zh | ch | w | th (the) | hw** | th (thin) |
|  |  |  |  |  | z |  |  |

*Note: The T group cue is also used with an isolated vowel—that is, an initial vowel not run in with a final consonant from the preceding syllable.

Figure 1-2.   Cues for English vowels and consonants. (Courtesy R. O. Cornett.)

promoted by Dr. Max Goldstein of Central Institute for the Deaf in St. Louis from the time he established his school in 1914. Even with the most severely impaired pupils he consistently used ear trumpets and mechanical devices in conjunction with lipreading and tactile impulses to support speech reception and language growth. He devised specific sets of exercises to train residual hearing and called his approach the Acoustic Method (Goldstein, 1939). Only after World War II were individual hearing aids of sufficient fidelity and size for children really to profit from their use. Group aids tied children to their seats and restricted their use as a consequence. Some educators, such as Pollack (1970), began to advocate a unisensory approach to teaching language and speech to the very young hearing impaired child through hearing alone. They believed that hearing had to be exploited to the fullest without distraction of other sensory stimuli in order to condition the child to listen to language, for it is through hearing that language is learned. Most programs today devoted to oralism give priority to the use of residual hearing but do not exclude speech reading and print as a child learns to understand and speak English. This approach is identified as the "aural-oral" approach.

With the advent of hearing aids, those educators who preferred the manual approach could not ignore the impact of auditory stimulation in the learning of language, so they too began to integrate the use of a child's hearing into their communication mode. This mode, popularly known as "total communication" has had wide acceptance in American schools in the 1970s. A child receives stimulation simultaneously through signs and fingerspelling, and lipreading and hearing. Children are expected to understand and produce all systems simultaneously.

American Sign Language (ASL) is a bona fide language but one quite different from English. Efforts are being made today to bring sign language into conformity with spoken English, although no concensus had been reached as to which of the manually coded systems should be universally adopted for instructional use. Schools may choose from among *Seeing Essential English* (Anthony, 1971), *Signing Exact English* (Gustason et al., 1972), *Signed English* (Bornstein et al., 1975), and *Linguistics of Visual English* (Wampler, 1971). In "total communication" the message a child gets may or may not be English depending on the skill of the sender as well as on the receiver. The impact of ASL and its derivatives on the acquisition of English follows in some detail in Chapter 4.

An important aim of all of all communication systems is to ensure the best possible input to the deaf child in learning language. Studies undertaken in the United States on the various communication approaches indicate that the sign component alleviates frustration of both child and parent in early communication and promotes better personal adjustment. It is still an open question as to whether sign does or does not interfere with ability to lipread or whether it inhibits the use of speech. When it comes to influencing the acquisition of language, neither it nor any other approach stands out as being superior. Thus, the controversy over communication modes seems to be a nonissue as far as language acquisition is concerned. In this book our goal will be to set forth ways in which language can best be learned. It is *what* goes into a child's mind and not *how* it goes in that is our greatest concern. Chapters 1 through 8 deal with this matter.

## FEDERAL LEGISLATION AFFECTING THE DEAF—1819
## TO 1970

By looking back in time we saw that the education of the deaf had a long history, longer in fact than that for any other disability. Services and practices have evolved within the social context of our country's development from a rural to a technological society, from the concern of private individuals to public responsibility. Although education is still vested in the state, the federal government has not stood idly by during the past 150 years. It has initiated and supported programs to the great benefit of deaf persons throughout the nation.

Federal involvement in the education and welfare of the deaf began as early as 1819 when the American School in Hartford received a land grant from Congress. The sale of these lands assured the development of its campus and its financial stability (Bender, 1960). In 1857 federal legislation established the Columbia Institution for the Deaf, Dumb, and Blind, which in 1864 became Gallaudet College, the first college in the world for deaf persons (Brill, 1974). Gallaudet College, which grants a 4-year liberal arts degree and masters and doctors degrees in teacher education, and the masters degree in counseling and in school psychology, still receives most of its financial support from federal funds. In 1966 Congress authorized a Model Secondary School for the deaf in the District of Columbia to be located on the Gallaudet campus and to serve as a model for all secondary education for deaf youth in the United States. This school began operation in a modern new facility in 1977. In 1974 Kendall School, which has been a unit of the college since 1894, was designated as a model elementary school for deaf children.

Deaf persons have profitted from federal legislation providing vocational rehabilitation services to handicapped persons age 16 and over. Since 1946 the Vocational Education Act, subsequently amended and improved, allows physically or mentally handicapped persons to receive training, guidance, job placement services, and financial assistance for securing prostheses in their search for employment. In 1967 the federally supported National Technical Institute for the Deaf was established on the campus of the Rochester Technical Institute, New York, for the purpose of providing postsecondary training in technical and vocational pursuits. In 1968–1969 three additional vocationally and technically oriented programs came into existence at Delgado College in New Orleans, at Seattle Community College, and at the St. Paul Vocational Institute in St. Paul, Minnesota. More than 40 such facilities are scattered throughout the country now (Rawlings et al., 1975).

Several Acts between 1958 and 1970 provided for the captioning and free distribution of films and other visual materials to groups involved in the cultural enrichment of the deaf. Creation of media centers for the production and free distribution of materials and the training of personnel in the use of media added impetus to the use of visual aids in schools and classes for deaf children during 1962 to 1972 (Brill, 1974). Chapter 5 contains additional comments on this subject.

To alleviate a critical shortage of well-qualified teachers of the deaf, Congress was persuaded to provide federally funded grants-in-aid to institutions of higher learning offering approved programs of teacher education, and scholarships to students. This legislation, implemented in the academic year of 1962–1963, changed the manner in which the majority of teachers of the deaf had been educated in the United States for 150 years: it moved the responsibility for the training of teachers from in-service types of programs in residential schools for the deaf to their education in universities and colleges, thereby eliminating an obvious anachronism that had existed all too long.

Much of the federal legislation passed in behalf of the deaf concerns the establishment of separate, and hopefully equal, facilities for their education at the secondary and postsecondary levels. Only in the technical area was an effort made to integrate deaf persons into programs for the hearing. Most of the recent legislation affecting the deaf and hard of hearing has been centered in laws based on a growing awareness of the needs of all types of handicapped children. We survey this legislation in the following section of this chapter.

## PUBLIC LAW 94-142—THE EDUCATION OF ALL HANDICAPPED CHILDREN ACT OF 1975

Under the broad cover of the Elementary and Secondary Education Act (ESEA) of 1965, Congress enacted legislation that was far-reaching for special education. ESEA attempted to strengthen public school programs where large numbers of handicapped children were concentrated (Weintraub et al., 1976). As with many laws, this one was soon found wanting, so it has been amended and its amendments amended until today we have a definitive federal law which ensures (1) that all handicapped children between the ages of 3 and 21 are to receive free and appropriate public education designed to meet their unique needs; and (2) that the rights of parents and children are to be protected through due process hearings if there is dissatisfaction with the education provided. The law also calls for assisting states and localities through federal grants in establishing programs for their handicapped children and for assessing their effectiveness.

This act is basically a civil rights law. As a condition for receiving financial assistance, a state must demonstrate that handicapped children are guaranteed certain basic rights and protections, namely, the right to free and appropriate public education, due process for placement in the least restrictive environment, and nondiscriminatory testing. Even if a state does not elect to receive grants, it must meet basic rights provisions if it received any financial assistance whatsoever in its other federally funded education or civil rights programs. Undoubtedly, your state now has laws which are in compliance with PL 94-142. Regulations implementing the act were developed through public hearings, but they are conceived of as evolving rather than as being final (Federal Register, 1976). Every teacher should become familiar with both federal and state laws and their current regulations since these will influence what goes on in the classroom if not minute by minute at least month by month and year by year.

## EDUCATION AND SUPPORTIVE SERVICES

Deaf and hard of hearing children are included in the eight categories of handicapped children for which the law provides. Each category is broadly delineated from the standpoint of the impact of the handicap on education. The deaf child is described as one whose hearing is nonfunctional for purposes of educational performance and the hard of hearing child as one whose impairment, whether stable or fluctuating, adversely affects his educational performance. In this regard the act is not very specific. It does not attempt to define these two categories of children in terms of objective audiological measurement, but rather leaves that to the professionals in the field. For more comprehensive definitions you may want to refer to books by Brill (1974) and Davis and Silverman (1962).

The law is addressed only to those children who by reason of their handicap need special education and related services. Among them, the children to receive priority in program development are, first, the handicapped children who are not receiving an education and, second, the very severely handicapped who are receiving an inadequate education. Incentive grants are available for school systems that provide services for handicapped preschoolers. Their education would encompass specially designed instruction to be carried on in special class placement or special programs carried out in a regular class setting, in hospitals, state schools, and institutions, or in a home setting. A child placed in a private school at the request of a state or local education agency must be provided an education and services that meet the standards of the federal law. However, the law specifies that a child be placed in the least restrictive environment. In other words, the procedures for placing children must assure to the maximum extent appropriate that handicapped children are educated with children who are not handicapped. Special classes, special schooling, or other removal from the regular educational environment is to be considered only when the nature or severity of the handicap is such that education in regular classes, with the use of supplementary aids and devices, cannot be achieved satisfactorily. This facet of the law has tremendous implications for regular education programs, as well as for those special educators who are striving to provide the best possible environment for the handicapped child. It means that all teachers must be prepared to work with each other in behalf of all children. To this end the act requires each state to develop and implement a comprehensive system of personnel development that includes the preservice and in-service training of general and special education instructors and support personnel.

Broad supportive services, including transportation at no cost to parents, are assured under the law. However, only services that are required to assist a handicapped child to benefit from special education are to be covered. Brief summaries of these services are listed below. Those uniquely applicable to the deaf and hard of hearing are included (Federal Register, 1976).

1. Audiological services provide for identification of children with hearing loss; determination of range, nature, and degree of hearing loss; formulation of plans for finding children at all ages but especially at the earliest possible age; medical referral and other professional attention for the habilitation of hearing; creation and administration of programs of hearing conservation.

2. Professional services for habilitation of hearing cover such activities as "language habilitation, auditory training, speech reading (lipreading), hearing evaluation and speech conservation."

3. Counseling and guidance of pupils and parents or parent surrogates by certified counselors include assisting them in understanding child development and the needs of their own child. All counseling is to take place in the native language of the parent or, where necessary, interpretive services are to be provided. In the case of manually communicating deaf parents, sign language can be requested.

4. Psychological services include the administration and interpretation of educational and psychological tests in the child's native language; interpretation of information about child behavior; working with other staff members in school programs indicated by psychological testing; and psychological counseling of parents and children. The law stipulates that all testing must be nondiscriminatory when used for placement purposes. No single test or evaluation procedure may be the sole criterion for determining an appropriate program for a child. Moreover, parents or guardians have the right to examine all relevant records with respect to the identification, evaluation, and placement of a child. If they are not satisfied they are entitled to obtain an independent evaluation.

5. Physical education includes development of physical and motor fitness,

individual and group games and sports, and dance and movement education.

6. Vocational education includes educational programs directly related to the preparation of careers not requiring a baccalaureate or advanced degree.

## THE INDIVIDUALIZED EDUCATION PROGRAM

The competence of all support personnel must be assured through rigorous training and through experience if they are to participate in making educational plans mandated in PL 94-142. Perhaps the most critical portion of this act for teachers and children alike is the one which requires each local education agency (LEA) to initiate and conduct meetings for developing, reviewing, and revising every child's Individualized Education Program (IEP). This plan must be created through state or local education agencies by the time a child is ready to enter a program or before the school term begins in September. It is to be reviewed and if appropriate revised periodically but not less than once a year. The gathering of relevant data about each child is but the first step in the development of the IEP. This is the responsibility of a multidisciplinary team (M-Team) consisting of a person other than the child's teacher, one or both of his parents, the child where appropriate, and other individuals or specialists at the discretion of parents or the agency (Federal Register, 1976).

For children with hearing impairments, the M-Team might consist of (1) a specially designated teacher, or supervisor, who has a broad perspective on the education of deaf children, and who is responsible for assessing a child's speech, language, ability to communicate by manual methods, and academic achievement; (2) the school psychologist; (3) the child's teacher; and (4) his parents. Audiological reports would certainly be an essential part of the child's records. Additional reports of social workers and speech pathologists could be useful in some cases. On the basis of the data gathered, general goals for the child are formulated and recommendations made for placement. Consultation with parents at this level provides for the necessary give and take required to reconcile parental values and goals with those of the school. If parents feel they have a genuine role in formulating plans and view it as part of a cooperative venture, they can become an invaluable asset in the education of their hearing impaired children. Some parents are reluctant or unwilling to assume such a role. If they do not do so of their own volition or if they cannot attend meetings where decisions are made, they must be apprised of the action through correspondence, telephone calls, or home visits. At that time their approval of the plan for their child is requested. Chapters 3 and 9 contain suggestions for involving parents in the education of their children. Other suggestions for organization and delivery of services are found in recent publications (Tracy et al., 1976).

Plans to implement the recommendations and long-term goals of the M-Team become largely the responsibility of the child's teacher(s), his parents, the child, and appropriate supervisors designated by the LEA. The IEP must contain (1) a statement of the child's present level of functioning, including academic achievement, social adaptation, prevocational and vocational skills, psychomotor skills, and self-help skills; (2) a statement of specific educational services needed by the child regardless of their availability, including physical education, instructional media, the extent to which he will participate in regular education programs, and justification for placement; (3) a statement of short-term instructional objectives which must be measurable intermediate steps between present level of functioning and more general annual goals; and (4) objective criteria, evaluation procedures, and schedules for determining whether short-term objectives are being achieved. Although the written IEP is a definite requirement set by law, it is not to be considered as being a binding contract by the school, children, or parents (Federal Register, 1976). The school will not be held in violation of the law if the child does not achieve the growth projected in the annual goals set up for him. The IEP is an essential guide to a child's growth and development but not a guarantee of it.

Although the IEP contains the child's total program, the aspects with which we are concerned in this book are those related to language acquisition by hearing impaired children. The annual goals must, of necessity, be stated in somewhat general terms and cannot possibly contain the fine details necessary to guide a child in learning language. Unless a teacher herself knows what a child knows about language she cannot plan adequately. She must assess his language in order to gain this knowledge. Assessment and planning are two interrelated functions that must be part of an ever-continuing process. Chapter 8 contains some techniques for assessing and planning for language growth for hearing impaired children.

## FULFILLING A HOPE

PL 94-142 has unlimited potential for ensuring that all hearing impaired children receive an education unique to their needs, but without sincere dedication to the spirit of the law by administrators, teachers, support personnel, and parents, it could fail in its grand vision. This law does not and cannot legislate cooperation or excellence of performance, two ingredients that will prove the real bulwark of its strength. It is easy to see how conflicts of interest could arise between school and home, between regular class teachers and special teachers, between residential schools for the deaf and local education agencies vying for attendance of hearing impaired children—and indirectly for dollars, between LEAs desiring to provide for a few local residents rather than bus children to well-established regional centers, between professionals who hold differing philosophical views on the subjects of communication modes, mainstreaming, and the interpretation of "least restrictive environment." In the open participatory system designed for the delivery of services and mandated by the law, a deliberate effort has to be made to bring about a concensus among the many factions and personalities involved in the implementation of the law. Good leadership, open discussion, and a willingness to learn from one another can fulfill the hope that a better day has dawned for all handicapped children.

## REFERENCES

American Annals of the Deaf, Directory of Services for the Deaf in the United States 114:3, May 1969

American Annals of the Deaf, Directory of Programs and Services 118:2, April 1973

Anthony D: Seeing Essential English. Anaheim, Ca., Anaheim School District, 1971

Bender R: The Conquest of Deafness. Cleveland, The Press of Western Reserve University, 1960

Bornstein H, Hamilton LB, Saulnier KL, and Roy HL (eds): The Signed English Dictionary for Preschool and Elementary Levels. Washington, D.C., Gallaudet College Press, 1975

Brill RG (ed): Education of the Deaf, Administration and Professional Developments. Washington, D.C., Gallaudet College Press, 1974

Cornett RO: Cued speech. Am Ann Deaf, 112:3–13, 1967

Davis H and Silverman SR: Hearing and Deafness. New York, Holt, Rinehart and Winston, 1962

Education of Handicapped Children and Incentive Grants Program, Assistance to States. Federal Register Part IV, December 30, 1976

Goldstein MA: The Acoustic Method. St. Louis, The Laryngoscope Press, 1939

Gustason G, Pfetzing D, and Zawolkow E: Signing Exact English. Rossmoor, Ca., Modern Signs Press, 1972

Lykos CM: Cued Speech—Handbook for Teachers. Washington D.C., Gallaudet College Cued Speech Program, 1971

Moores DF, Weiss KL, and Goodwin MW: Recommended Policies and Procedures: Preschool Programs for Hearing Impaired Children. Washington D.C., Department of Health, Welfare and Education, US Office of Education, Bureau of Education for the Handicapped, 1976

Pollack D: Educational Audiology for the Limited Hearing Infant. Springfield, Ill., Charles C. Thomas, 1970

Rawlings BW, Trybus RJ, Delgado GL, and Stuckless ER (eds): A Guide to College Career Programs for Deaf Students. Washington, D.C., Gallaudet College and NTID, 1975

Tracy ML, Gibbons S, and Kladder FW: Case Conference: A Stimulation and Source Book. Bloomington, Ind., Department of Public Instruction and Developmental Training Associates, 1976

Wampler DW: Linguistics of Visual English. Suison City, Ca., Solano Community College, 1971

Weintraub FJ, Abeson A, Ballard JE, and LaVor ML (eds): Public Policy and the Education of Exceptional Children. Reston, Va., The Council for Exceptional Children, 1976

# 2
# The Learning Process

There is nothing more intriguing than trying to unravel the mystery of what learning is and how it takes place. For centuries philosophers and psychologists have theorized about the subject. As a result modern learning theory has many faces. Some psychologists focus on changes that take place in the nervous system itself when an organism learns. Others describe learning as a series of mental events with the learner expecting something to happen or hoping for some satisfying or useful outcome. Still others conceive of learning as a dynamic processing of information derived from sensory input which is then synthesized with prior knowledge and stored in memory. As we explore these theories for information relevant to the teaching of hearing impaired children, we may be able to recognize how bits and pieces of the various theories have influenced educational practice in the past and how we can translate the most cogent aspects of modern psychological theory into our own teaching.

There are two major approaches to the study of learning: one, the behavioral or stimulus-response approach, and the other, the cognitive. We will look briefly at the behavioral approach first.

## BEHAVIORAL LEARNING

The behavioral approach to learning has dominated American psychological thinking for most of the twentieth century. It attempted to establish lawful relationships between behavior and its determinants (Green, 1962). Be-

15

haviorists acknowledge the dependence of learning on the environment, but believe it does not just happen. They hold that it can be altered and controlled. Learning is considered to be change in behavior which is simply not ascribable to maturation. This change refers to more than a momentary one and results in increased capability of performance and in human beings may also result in altered attitudes and values (Gagne, 1970).

The early behaviorists conducted meticulous experiments with animals in which responses were observed under controlled stimuli. Thorndike (1931) formulated several "laws of learning," one of which proposed that learning was influenced in a positive way when a satisfying state of affairs was attained by the human learner. Experiments with animals verified this premise. For a hungry pigeon satisfaction might consist of receiving grain as a reward for the completion of a simple learning task. In the 1930s Skinner (1938) introduced the idea of *reinforcement* as central to his view of stimulus-response learning theory. The response of Skinner's pigeon was contingent on certain stimulus conditions which, in turn, brought about another response. This is referred to as *operant conditioning*. The pigeon might be expected to peck at a particular geometric figure before a door would open to release a food cache. The pigeon had to learn that the final effect of its effort was contingent on several other aspects in the learning sequence.

When a teacher of a young deaf child attempts to teach him the name of an object, such as *ball*, by placing a ball on the table and saying, "This is a ball. Show me the ball.", she is creating a stimulus-response type of learning situation. The word *ball* on the lips or in "sign" is the stimulus which is expected to evoke a response such as pointing to or picking up the ball. However, the child can not do this until the tutor has demonstrated nonverbally what response is expected of him. His reinforcement is contingent on his correct response. This may be a nod of approval, a smile, or a pat on the head. In subsequent lessons when a child is presented with another object, he is expected to make a verbal association and react according to the specified directions. His responses are conditioned by the situation. Every teacher of the deaf using this approach learns that many trials and constant repetition are necessary to fix the verbal association in the child's mind.

The practical application of the concept of reinforcement has resulted in school practices known as *behavior modification*, which reinforces the learner for responses contingent on expected performance. This may take the form of verbal approval, social approval, and use of tokens. Tokens may be exchanged for money, food, prizes, or pleasurable activities. According to practitioners of behavior modification techniques, reinforcers provide a powerful basis for establishing motivation for a learner. When you use behavior modification techniques you are basing your practice on stimulus-response (S-R) theory.

## A SKINNERIAN VIEW OF LANGUAGE

According to Skinner (1957) all verbal behavior is under stimulus control. Stimulus, response, and reinforcement are contingent on each other. A child is said to acquire verbal behavior when his relatively unpatterned vocalizations are selectively reinforced. This behavior is not elicited by anyone, but when a given response does occur, the parent reinforces the child. For instance, if a thirsty child says "wawa," he is reinforced by getting a drink of water. Later the parent reinforces him with a drink only when he articulates the word *water* correctly.

In learning the morphemic aspects of language, the behaviorist might explain the acquisition of the spoken form of the past tense of weak verbs as in *looked, wished, burned, grabbed,* and *acted, added* in this way: a child exposed to these words would try to imitate his tutor. After innumerable trials the child would have been reinforced by the tutor for appropriately applying the final sound of /t/, /d/, or /id/, depending on the previous contiguous final consonant in the verb. After these associations had been formed between the ending of a word and the past tense response, the correct endings would be expected to occur when a new word was encountered (Schumacher and Sherman, 1970). This abbreviated and simplistic presentation certainly does not do justice to Skinner's lengthy exposition of language learning. What is included here is meant only to provide background for the discussion of other theoretical points of view to follow in this chapter.

## EXTENSION OF S–R LEARNING THEORY

Stimulus–response learning theory, like most theories, has been continually evolving. Among those contributing to broadening its concepts were psychologists who worked on problems of training and education in the military and in industry. Gagne (1970) has tried to bridge the gap between laboratory scientists and educators. Although he does not discard the behaviorist point of view, he suggests that there are many kinds of human learning. One of these is learning to classify. This results in concept learning, a very pervasive type of learning. A child in preschool may view a collection of objects as individual items and pick out a football and a helmet to play with, or he may classify or group the objects into sets of *toys, clothing,* or *dishes* as the case might be when he is called on to help put them away in the cupboard. Ability to see higher level order among objects or events is the basis for the development of concepts. Concrete concepts such as *toys* and *clothes* have a physical referent, whereas abstract concepts such as *volume* and *temperature* depend largely on verbal representation. Behaviorists believe that there is danger of verbal superficiality if a person does not know the concepts represented by the words he uses or is expected to read. If he is unable to use a word in an appropriate stimulus situation, he really does not know that word. A teacher may assume that if a child can pronounce a word, he knows its proper usage. It would be safer to test such an assumption rather than to take all the child's concepts for granted. However, not all higher level concepts have words attached to them. What would you call the class of things that consists of a toothbrush, toothpaste, dental floss, and disclosing tablets? It would be most convenient to have a word such as *dencares* for them, but we don't. Even though we do not have names for all higher level concepts, most of our thinking is done with concepts.

Thinking is conceived of as combining rules into a higher order set of rules. According to Gagne (1970), rules are inferred capabilities that enable a person to classify a stimulus situation with a set of predictably related performances. These rules apply to language as well as mathematics. If a child has learned that two plus three equals five $(2+3=5)$ and that three plus two equals five $(3+2=5)$, he can then apply the rule to other combinations such as $3+4=7$ and $4+3=7$. In learning phonic rules, he learns that a vowel in a CVC syllable, as in *fin*, is pronounced with one kind of sound and that adding a final *e* to the word changes the sound of the vowel. He further learns that *pan* becomes *pane* and *cop* becomes *cope*. When presented with the word *frame*, he will give the vowel sound its proper pronunciation if he has learned the rule that governs the sound change. In passing, it must be said that most phonic rules have exceptions, so that a child might not really know how to pronounce the word *have* the first time he sees it in print if he applies the rule he has just been taught!

Behaviorists view rules of syntax and punctuation as having organized sets of rules. A learner may be unable to verbalize the rules but he can demonstrate them. The simplest rule for constructing a sentence contains two concepts as in *birds fly*. A child who knows the rule will be able to produce other sentences, for example, *airplanes fly* and *kites fly*. There are many types of rules besides those for pronunciation and those for constructing sentences. In the subject of science, a child may have to learn rules having the form of a defined concept such as *temperature* and *degree* (Gagne, 1970). To solve the equation Fahrenheit temperature = 9/5 Celsius + 32, he would have to understand many complicated sets of concepts that have been developed in hierarchical order over a period of time. These concepts involve higher order verbal terms and mathematical operations that have to be acquired before the equation can be understood and solved. Later in this chapter we will present another definition of a rule, one that modern linguists use in discussing the grammar of a language. The word *rule* has many meanings.

Behaviorists are mainly concerned with how the environment can control and affect behavior, whereas another group of psychologists, the cognitive psychologists, focus on characteristics of the mind as determining human behavior. They propose that human beings are the products of their experience, that they are curious and can self-direct their learning. They think that what a child has chosen to extract from the environment cannot be dependent on external reinforcement because only when a learner informs the reinforcer of his internalized knowledge can it be reinforced. And by that time he already knows it. What the child has learned reduces his uncertainty, and that in itself may be all the reinforcement he needs. We will now look further at what cognitive psychologists and psycholinguists have to say about learning in general and language learning in particular.

## PIAGET AND COGNITIVE DEVELOPMENT

Jean Piaget, the Swiss biologist turned research psychologist, has perhaps done more than any other person in the twentieth century to give us insights into the development of a child's mind and thought processes. His voluminous publications, begun in 1924, included studies of language, logic, and origins of intelligence as well as morality in the young child. His works, translated from the French, are replete with terms uncommon to the vocabulary of American teachers, but the concepts they represent are far reaching for educators, including teachers of hearing impaired children.

Piaget was more interested in studying the structure of the child's thought than the mechanics used to achieve it, which is principally what concerns S-R psychologists. His goal was to chart the intellectual activities of the mind from birth to adolescence. He observed his own and other children systematically for many years and developed cognitive tasks to help him understand how children think, perceive, and generalize. His is a genetic theory of intellectual development, a development that he describes as being ongoing, intentional, anticipatory, and flexible (Pulaski, 1971).

A child is endowed with capacity to organize his environment and adapt to it from the day he is born. He does this through the two complementary processes of assimilation and accommodation. The child takes in, or assimilates, aspects of his environment into his own activities. He incorporates the features of external reality into his psychological structures, which in turn are modified or changed to meet the conditions of the environment. To assimilate knowledge a child must act on it and transform it in some way just as his body does the food he eats. He must decide what he thinks about it if he is to accommodate his new knowledge to what he already knows (Lavatelli, 1973). When a child engages in symbolic play, as when he acts out being the mother or father in a "play house," he is not only assimilating information about sex roles, but accommodating to them in the manner in which he executes his role in the situation. He is also learning to classify and organize information about objects in the play house, and perhaps discovering that cups and spoons are not usually stored in a doll buggy. He may still believe in Santa Claus even though he sees a Santa on every corner during the holiday season. He will eventually reconcile his internal world with that of the real world and restructure his knowledge accordingly. He tries to strike a balance between assimilating the environment and accommodating to it (Pulaski, 1971). When a child encounters new knowledge, his prior knowledge is likely to be modified, especially if there is a discrepancy between old and new. As he matures this is accomplished through logical thinking which has its sources in interaction with the environment (Morehead and Morehead, 1974). ➤

## PIAGET'S PERIODS OF INTELLECTUAL FUNCTIONING

➤ Piaget divided the development of intellectual functioning of children into four periods to which he ascribed approximate chronological ages, but made it clear that there was not a one-to-one correspondence between chronological age and mental growth (Furth, 1970). Development within periods or across stages is not to be thought of as linear. One child might traverse a stage more quickly and another might proceed more slowly, but both would go through the evolving constructs as outlined in the following four periods:

1. Sensory-motor (approximately birth to 2 years)
✗ 2. Preoperational (approximately 2½ to 7 years)
3. Concrete operational (approximately 7 to 11 years)
4. Formal operational (approximately 12 years to adulthood) ⌐

### Sensory-Motor Period

﹣ In the sensory-motor period a child is described as being completely immersed in his own self but is becoming aware of others in a social sense (Lavatelli, 1972). Until about age 1½, the infant knows only what he does. He acquires rudimentary ideas about space by crawling about, about time through routinized schedules of eating and sleeping, and about simple causality through attention he receives by crying or smiling. He lays the foundation at this time for later representational thought. By age 2 he has begun to view objects in the physical world as having stability or permanence, or in Piaget's terms, he develops the idea of object constancy. He knows his mother is in the house even though he cannot see her. He looks for a favorite toy which is not in sight. This is his first step beyond the sensory-motor stage and it forms the basis for the development of a symbol system, of which language is the most important manifestation. Piaget believed that a child had to see, touch, smell, hear, climb, run, and explore before he could be expected to understand the world about him (Piaget, 1926).

## Preoperational Period

In the latter part of the sensory-motor period, language is just beginning to emerge. In the early part of the preoperational period it comes into full bloom. At this stage, the child begins to use words as well as images in his thinking. Language and thought are becoming interrelated. Nevertheless, the child still copes with the physical world largely on the basis of sensory-motor experiences.

Piaget uses the term *operations* to describe the activities of the mind—actions which the child performs mentally (Ginsburg and Opper, 1969). In this period the child makes judgments on the basis of how things look to him, how he perceives them, rather than on any logical judgment. To him the world still revolves around him alone and is still interpreted quite differently from that of an adult. He thinks as he observes. He usually centers on one variable and lacks ability to coordinate several variables. In his drawings during this period, a doorknob may occupy half the area of the door. His perception of the door is quite different from that of an adult. He would find it difficult to understand that a red toy truck could belong to several classes of objects at one time, as a class of red things, a class of vehicles, and a class of toys. What is perceptually appropriate for him is what he knows.

Piaget devised a number of interesting tasks which illustrate how a child develops the concept of invariance of quantities, substances, weight, and volume during this period. They illustrate a child's ability to visualize a particular quantity as being equivalent to another when it assumes a different shape from that of the original. Piaget refers to them as *conservation* tasks (Ginsburg and Opper, 1969). We adults frequently face problems of conservation, as when we try to estimate the size of a jar needed to store the soup left in the kettle. First we judge the amount of the liquid, and then because we know something about standard measures, we can correlate in our minds the amount in the kettle with the size of the container into which to pour it. We can do this, although not always precisely, because we know that the quantity itself does not vary when it is moved to occupy a different space, but children do not understand this until they are about 7 years old. They perceive a ball of clay to be of a different quantity than a sausage rolled into that shape, or juice to be different in amount when poured from a short fat glass into a taller thinner one before their eyes. It is difficult for young children to reverse an operation in thought. They cannot compare the starting point with its present state, as when objects first bunched together are spread apart. They believe that the number changes in the operation. In the next stage their thinking becomes less bound to immediate perceptual restraints.

## Concrete Operational Period

In the concrete operational period, the child begins to develop ability to operate logically in thought on concrete objects and situations or their representations as in dreams, drawings, and symbolic play (Pulaski, 1971). During this time, he is able to focus on several aspects of a situation simultaneously and can change the direction of his thinking. He centers not only on one aspect of an object or situation, but takes into account several other aspects and incorporates them into a more accurate whole, although he still is oriented to concrete characteristics. He can place objects in series and combine structures into new relationships, as arranging dolls in order of size and also fitting appropriately sized hats to them. He understands classification, categorization, serial arrangements, and set relationships as in mathematics. He can range forward and backward in time and space on a mental level and can think logically within the framework of his limited concrete experiences.

## Formal Operational Period

In the period of formal operations, ages 12 to adulthood, the young person can think about thinking itself and can deal with hypothetical concepts. Through the processes of assimilation and accomodation and self-regulation, intellectual development proceeds gradually from genetically regulated behavior to the construction of logically regulated behavior. At each level what is already known is incorporated into the child's behavior.

## A PIAGETIAN VIEW OF LANGUAGE

Piaget had definite views on the relation of language to thought. He did not believe that language as it emerged in the young child organized or directed his experience, but rather that language served to translate what he already understood through his sensory-motor experiences. He suggested that word meaning depended on representation based on internalized actions. He thought that as the structures of thought were refined, the more language was necessary. He further believed that knowledge and language had to be coordinated or a person could not function at an adult level. In the process of coordination, he proposed that new forms of language designated old cogni-

tive content while new knowledge initially appeared in old forms of la
(Lavatelli, 1972).

During the preoperational stage when language is rapidly developing,
children are full of questions. Why____? questions are especially numerous,
followed in frequency by What____?, Is____?, and other yes/no questions,
and less so by How____?, When____?, Where____?, and Who____? Between
the ages of 3 and 7, Why____? is used for multiple purposes. (Piaget, 1926).
For instance, a child may ask, ''Why is this so heavy?'' when all he wants is
a physical explanation, such as ''Because there is a watermelon in the box.'' If
he asks, ''Why are we going to the store now?'' or ''Why can't I go outside?''
he wants the motive or the justification for an event or activity. The truly
causal meaning of the word *because* is not really understood by a child
before the age of 7 or 8. Neither is the child interested in the *how* of phenomena
during this period. But in the next period he is, and his *why* questions then
become causally oriented.

Sinclair-de-Zwart (1969) conducted research on the relation of language
to the child's ability to deal with conservation tasks—tasks that require ability
to visualize transformation of material such as solids or liquids into different
shapes or sizes. She found no differences between children who could do the
conservation tasks and those who could not in their ability to comprehend the
language she used in her tests. She found that the children used language that
reflected their understanding of the operations involved. Linguistic structuring, she concluded, depended on the child's grasp of the intellectual task, and
instructing a child to use words in sentences did not ensure making him more
logical. However, supplying lexical and syntactic information could support
the child's logical structures as they emerged. Sinclair-de-Zwart agrees with
Piaget that language is not the source of a child's logic, but is structured by
what he knows.

Teachers of children with language deficiencies should also become
aware of these precepts. The language a child is exposed to and taught must be
based on what he comprehends. Matching language to the child's knowledge
and concepts is the name of the game. Constant observation and informal
testing are essential if instruction within the normal day's activities, especially
in the early stages of a child's schooling, is to fit the child and his need to
know. By becoming familiar with and using some of the tasks that Piaget so
cleverly designed, teachers can increase their knowledge about the cognitive
abilities of their pupils. Although this book will not be able to go into details
of how this can be implemented, we recommend highly that teachers of young
hearing impaired children explore what some early childhood programs based
on Piaget's work are accomplishing and use them as models in their own
teaching (Sharp, 1969; Lavatelli, 1973; Kamii, 1971).

Many psychologists share Piaget's ideas even though they may view learning from a different vantage point. We will now attend briefly to the views of a group of psychologists we will designate as perceptual psychologists. They, like psycholinguists, look at learning as a dynamic process, one in which information is being continually processed by the learner.

## THE PERCEPTUAL PSYCHOLOGISTS' VIEW OF LEARNING

This group of psychologists (Gibson, 1969; Lindsay and Norman, 1972; Gibson and Levin, 1975) views learning as perceptual in nature. Essentially, perceptual learning consists of extracting relevant information from the myriad environmental stimuli which, when processed by an individual, cause modification of behavior. Perceptual learning is described as being active, adaptive, and selective (Gibson and Levin, 1975). Young children use their senses actively to search for useful information from the time they are born. Nobody teaches them to do this, but their own discovery through sensory-motor activity allows them to function with less uncertainty in what is still a very unstructured world for them.

Children learn to adapt to their environments by observing distinctive features and the contrastive as well as the invariant characteristics of the physical environment. Early in life they perceive that sizes, shapes, and locations are constant despite movements of the observer or the observed. Incidentally, movement is very important in the processing of visual information and is especially effective when the observer is doing the moving (Lindsay and Norman, 1972). Parents of a deaf child often notice that after he has learned to walk, the child tends to by physically very active, running about seemingly aimlessly. Because he is deprived of his most important distance sense, hearing, he is impelled to explore space actively with his eyes and his other senses. Kretschmer (1972) noted in a study of the play and social relationships of 71 preschool children that the hearing impaired were more active, displayed more scanning behavior, and engaged in little actual play when compared with the normally hearing children in his population.

A deaf child obviously takes more time to acquire less information when he has to explore with his eyes alone. As a consequence there is a real question as to whether he will organize his world in the same way as a child who hears does. It is hoped that he will be supplied with a hearing aid and with a rich environment in which to grow. Despite his sensory handicap, he does become more selective in what he extracts from the environment as he grows older. He integrates into his behavior what has utility for him. The tendency to attend to and selectively to organize sensory data is a general characteristic of perceptual learning.

A child gradually becomes aware of the differences among things—toy cars and trucks, cats and dogs, baloons and balls, oranges and apples, edible and nonedible items—through having noted their distinctive features. For instance, he discovers that oranges have their own peculiar odor, taste, texture, weight, size, and color. He uses distinctive features to aid him in organizing his knowledge.

## The Role of Attention

Active attention is essential if a child is to become aware of likenesses and differences among things and events and to notice the relevant and to exclude the irrelevant. Attention of the young child wanders and he is easily distracted, although ability to ignore the irrelevant improves with age. In general, incidental learning is typical before attention comes under conscious control at about age 7 or 8. It is not known if this trait can be trained or if it is a factor of maturation (Gibson and Levin, 1975).

Psychologists have been interested in analyzing the processes involved in directing attention to one of more signals reaching a person and trying to determine how much of either signal gets into the memory. Research has centered mainly on two competing verbal auditory signals. The main message which is to receive attention and to be remembered is fed through a receiver into one ear while a different message is fed into the other ear. The subject is asked to repeat the substance of the main message as best he can but also tries to pay attention to the unattended message (Lindsay and Norman, 1972). What interests psychologists is how much of the unattended message gets through. A person can usually identify the gross features of an unattended message such as the sex of the speaker or any environmental sounds in it, but he cannot remember anything about what was said. As we listen to a lecture or a sermon with eyes or ears or both, it is relatively easy to drift off into our own thoughts or even doze for a short time. We seem to hear what is going on, yet we do not remember any details of the message.

Attention is selective. It appears that we have a built-in monitoring device to alert us to events to which we are not attending. This processing device could be likened to the volume-attenuation dial on a radio or television. We hear only the sound or ''noise'' when a signal is unattended, but when it contains significant information we can respond to it, as when we hear our name called in a busy airport. Our monitoring mechanism allows us to separate out irrelevant aspects and also to interrupt our attention from one event in order to concentrate on another. What seems to happen is that the rejected message is analyzed for its gross features, stored in short-term memory, and then synthesized with the main message to allow us to pick up salient aspects of the rejected message (Lindsay and Norman, 1972). The relevant message alone is actively processed, and the only signals in the unattended channel that are analyzed are those whose features are consistent with the ones expected by the active analysis.

## Attention in Simultaneous Communication

In communication among deaf persons using oral language and signed language simultaneously to receive a message, there are two channels to which to attend, either the lips or the hands. Only one channel at a time can receive attention and active processing. If the lipreader takes his eyes off of the lips for even a second, he misses the message, but if he has the added channel of manual sign he can switch to that and back again, synthesizing the two in terms of their expected meaning. Deaf persons who prefer the oral channel report that they are able to use the information in the unattended channel without directly looking at it. Research in this area has not substantiated this observation, but it is possible that such observation is valid because of the close coordination of the two channels through the unitary meaning of the message. For the individual concentrating on the manual channel, lipreading seems to offer little in supplementing the meaning of the message.

## LANGUAGE FROM A PERCEPTUAL POINT OF VIEW

Perceptual psychologists, along with Piaget, believe that language is the coding of meaning that the child has already gained, but they differ from him somewhat. They think that much of meaning has roots in perceptual understanding, whereas Piaget lays stress on sensory-motor experience as basic to furnishing meaning. There are many words in a language such as English prepositions and conjunctions that do not have concrete referents since they state relationships. Some adjectives, for example, *fair* and *true*, and even *long* and *short*, involve fairly abstract concepts and cannot be directly related to sensory-motor experiences as *ball*, *bottle*, and *break* can. Other concepts such as the negative and the conditional have no visual perceptual representations and are thought to be introduced into the cognitive structure through language itself.

Seeing relationships between parts and wholes, as in fingers on a hand, and between whole and parts, as in a bushel of apples, enhances a child's ability to structure his knowledge. Although deaf children may be perceptually aware of these relationships, they are often unaware that parts of things have names. All they know is that an apple is an apple, but they do not know that it has a peel, seeds, or a core. Awareness of relationships, combined with the language that expresses these relationships, is important in the education of hearing impaired children.

Between the ages of 7 and 10 a child gains ability to organize his thoughts at a higher order level (Gibson and Levin, 1975). Here language becomes very important. The language used in this kind of mental operation goes beyond the touchable and the movable. It deals with abstractions and is not easily picturable. Higher level organization depends on finding relationships between distinctive features. It also depends on cognitive development. For instance, a child learns that boys and girls are *children*, that children can be *brothers* and *sisters*, that mothers and fathers are *parents*, and that children ... *family*. He knows he has a grandmother, grandfather, u les, nd a nts. cause that is what he calls them. He does not understand t r others such as *husband, wife, cousins,* or *brother-in-* der of birth in his own family until he is 7 or 8 years rds but he does not really understand them. When he le to restructure his prior knowledge and deal with it

ew of perceptual learning differs somewhat from the response theories in relation to concept development. S-R s on repeated exposure to specific stimuli as the basis of acquiring nation. Perceptual psychologists, think that as a child gains information through self-directed exploration he adds to his store of knowledge. This knowledge continually evolves through a restructuring of what he knows. As more and more knowledge is stored in memory, all of his past experience is brought to bear on the understanding of new events. As a corollary to this statement, it is easy to see how individual differences among people arise. If understanding is the product of experience and subsequent mental operations in rearranging new information, each person generates his own view of the world, even though his experiences seem to be similar to those of another (Lindsay and Norman, 1972). When teachers of a deaf child try to help him attach language to his experiences and concepts, it is important to be aware of the status of his internalized knowledge. His concepts may not be those of his teacher, so they must be identified in order to bring meaning to his language.

## PSYCHOLINGUISTICS AND LANGUAGE LEARNING

Psycholinguists have proposed their own cognitive theories about language and language acquisition. Lenneberg (1967) and some of his contemporaries believe that the human brain is genetically programmed to learn language. If this is true there is no reason why any child, deaf or not, should be unable to acquire language. But since nobody can actually prove this by direct observation of the brain, psycholinguists have looked instead at language and language acquisition to explain its relation to brain mechanisms. They have observed that certain cognitive universals appear common to all languages. All have functions of asserting, denying, and requesting (Slobin, 1973). They have a grammar of which the whole carries greater meaning than the sum of its parts. Most commonly used words are short and have multiple meanings, and all languages require ordered rules.

When a child first begins to learn his language, he can process no more than two or three terms, perhaps because of limited memory capacity. These combinations are words displaying semantic rather than grammatical relationships. One of the earliest semantic relationships to develop in all languages is that of verb-object, as in *want cookie*. When a toddler begins to organize his utterances grammatically, he uses simple sentences before he uses complex ones. He makes statements about place before he does about time. There seems to be a common sequence of acquisition of difficult linguistic features. Ends of words, or suffixes, are acquired earlier than prefixes. Structures requiring transposition of elements first appear in unpermuted form as in *I can go?* Sentence-final relative clauses develop earlier than relative clauses after the subject. When several morphemes and/or changes in word order are required to produce a particular structure, as in the English passive, it is much more difficult to conceptualize than when a simple marker alone is required. Arabic children learn to use their passive at an early age because it has one easy marker (Slobin, 1973). Information of this kind can be very valuable to teachers of the hearing impaired. They must be aware of the many fine structural details of language as well as its meaning aspects when they plan a language program for a child.

Noam Chomsky, with his publication *Syntactic Structures* (1957), was most responsible for a resurgence of interest in linguistics early in the 1960s. He described grammar as being generative in nature and consisting of a system of rules that assigned structural descriptions to sentences in an explicit and well-defined way (Chomsky, 1965). This system of rules makes it possible to generate an infinitely large number of grammatical structures from a few base structures. For instance, the rule for a base structure says that a sentence consists of a noun, an auxiliary, and a verb, as in *Jane can run*. By applying specified transformation rules, we can convert the base structure into a question or a negative statement. To create a yes/no question, the rule says that the auxiliary is shifted to the beginning of the sentence to produce *Can Jane run*? To create a negative statement, *not* is inserted between the auxiliary and the verb, as in *Jane cannot run*. There are many rules governing transformations, all of which have to be mastered before a language is learned. We will be using the terms *rule*, *rules*, and *rule learning* throughout this book with meanings ascribed to them in psycholinguistic literature.

All of us have mastered the rules of the language we speak, though even as adults we may be unaware that any such rules exist. When we learned language initially we gained knowledge of a generative grammar through intuition, not through a conscious knowledge of the rules of syntax. We must keep this in mind when we deal with the problem of how we will guide hearing impaired children into learning language. Will it be by insisting that they learn rules consciously or by giving them opportunities to deduce them by demonstrating their internalized knowledge of the rules through creative expression? It is hoped that the answer to this question will be made clear in the succeeding chapters in this book.

Chomsky states that the grammar of a language includes a semantic component and a phonological one besides the base and the transformational components. But he believed that syntax was the central element in language and equated it with logic as central to thought. To Chomsky, the semantic and the phonological components played only an interpretive role (Chomsky, 1965). Like other theories, Chomsky's has undergone revision and is still being refined. Many psycholinguists now believe that the acquisition of meaning has as important a role in language as that of syntax. Along with the Piagetian point of view, they believe that a new formal grammatic structure serves only to code a cognitive function which the child has already understood and expressed implicitly. Once cognitive abilities have developed, an active search for acquisition of new grammatic forms appears (Slobin, 1973).

Fillmore (1968) has tried to reconcile syntactic and semantic relationships in his "case grammar." He emphasizes relationships embodied in propositions set forth in sentences as being responsible for carrying meaning. His case categories include *agent, experiencer, instrument, object, source, goal, place,* and *time* (Perfetti, 1972). In the sentence, *The grass was mowed with our new hand-mower by my son, son* is the agent; *mower* is the instrument; and *grass* is the object. In the traditional syntactic analysis, *grass* would be the subject, and *son* and *mower* the objects of prepositions. In case grammar, relationships such as *agent, action, experiencer,* and *instrument* are keys to meaning. The ultimate manner in which words can be combined seems to depend more on semantic selectional restrictions than on syntactic restrictions. For instance, the next sentence is syntactically correct but semantically not acceptable: *The worm decided to eat the bird.* The field of semantics is receiving a great deal of attention with a view to formulating a theory as precise and elegant as Chomsky's transformational grammar was for syntax.

The early psycholinguists thought that in gaining multiple meanings of words, a young child attended only to one or two features of a word rather than to an entire set as adults do. The word *father* might first be learned as having the features ⟨+animal⟩ and ⟨+human⟩ and only later those of ⟨−human⟩ and ⟨+masculine⟩. The child does not at all conceive of *father* as a verb at this point. Now linguists are beginning to think that although it is possible to store features in our memories, it is more likely that we process words in relation to their semantic aspects. For instance, it is easier to respond to *How tall is Mark?* than to *How short is Mark?* They believe that features are less important in gaining knowledge of words than personal experiences with the words themselves. These words, then, must appear in the frameword of linguistic structures to bring to them a totality of meaning (Bowerman, 1973). In the following sentences the word *show* derives its meaning from the experiences that an individual has had with the word as well as with its position in the sentence: *We saw a funny show. Show me your hands. He's a show-off. He didn't show up.* A child must store thousands of word meanings in his memory and be able to retrieve them and use them in situations that are coordinated with his experiences and his structural linguistic capacities. For a hearing impaired child, rehearsal of his vocabulary in appropriate structures is most important in order to make his language functional. Learning lists of words is less than fruitful in helping him acquire a usable vocabulary. Rehearsal within structures must be consistent over time if vocabulary is to be retained and used.

Researchers such as Brown (1973), Bloom (1970), and Menyuk (1969, 1971) have observed the emergence of language in young children and in doing so have contributed to refining the views of the early psycholinguists. Their research has used the concepts of transformational grammar as well as case grammar in analyzing child language. A great deal of valuable information has come from this research. It made clear how transformational grammar can serve as a rational base for observing syntactic development. It also confirmed that there are consistent stages in the development of grammatic structures in early language learning. Bellugi and Klima (1972) have observed that deaf children learning "sign" as their first language follow the same steps as those learning to speak. In short, the brains of young children the world over work in the same way in regard to language acquisition. Rule-generating capacity that results in the use of simple and complex sentences peaks at from 18 months to 4 years.

Deaf children and those with language learning disabilities do not usually reach competency even with simple syntactic structures by age 4. Theirs is a long road to mastery. Unless their teachers are well grounded in the fine points of English syntax as delineated by modern transformational and case grammarians, they will be handicapped in guiding the establishment of language in their pupils. Modern psycholinguistics has much to offer to teachers of hearing impaired children.

## DEAFNESS, COGNITION AND LANGUAGE

Most modern psycholinguists share Piaget's views on the relation of language to cognition. If Piaget is correct in proposing that cognitive growth is independent of language, it seems safe to assume that children born with severe or profound hearing deficits would exhibit the same cognitive characteristics as normally hearing children. Studies of the intelligence of deaf children between the years 1930 and 1967 based on standardized nonlanguage performance tests of intelligence as the Pinter Non-Language Test, the Grace Arthur Performance Scale, the performance section of the Wechsler Intelligence Scale for Children, the Hiskey-Nebraska Test of Learning Aptitude, and the Chicago Non-Verbal Examination indicate that the distribution of intelligence among the deaf is essentially the same as that of the hearing (Vernon, 1969). These IQ tests are norm-based tests and tell only how a child performs in relation to a large group. They do not clarify the basic factors involved in thinking, nor how a child reacts cognitively to his environment.

Other research has focused on certain aspects of intelligence, as visual perception, memory, abstraction, concept formation, generalization, and problem solving in deaf children. Furth (1973) and his co-workers presented Piaget-type tasks over a period of several years to deaf children and youths. They substituted "sign" or visuals for spoken or written language to clarify the task requirements. Furth reported the deaf group to be equal to the hearing on many tasks, but inferior on several. For instance, he found them delayed on short-term memory for digits and deficient in conceptualizing *opposites* and on transfer tasks where verbalized rules were of help, but not on tasks where verbalization was not a factor.

Furth (1973) ascribes this deficit to impoverished experiences rather than to linguistic limitations. Hearing children have considerable practice in remembering digits by practicing with telephone numbers, but hearing impaired children do not. On the opposites task, in which even the oldest deaf children did not perform as well as the youngest hearing children, Furth suggests that language may play some role in giving the hearing an advantage. This research seems to raise questions about the relationship of language to cognitive performance in deaf children.

In a conservation task in which a clay ball is transformed into a sausage in view of the observer, deaf children improved their performance when nonverbal directions were clarified for them. In a previous similar experiment, none of the 10 year olds had succeeded even when pretrained with a particular set of directions, whereas at least 25 percent of the 8 year olds and 67 percent of the 11 year olds did so when directions were made clear to them (Furth, 1964).

Even in tasks involving formal operations of symbolic logic, some deaf students with great language deficiency succeeded in comprehending logical operations in a training task, although, not surprisingly, others did not. On performance of tasks of probability, the deaf were strikingly similar to the hearing. Furth tested some older nonverbal deaf persons on tasks in which the group had shown retardation at an earlier age, but with maturation they did as well as their hearing counterparts.

Furth has decided as the result of his extensive research that in the concrete operational period, deaf children function about as well as hearing children from low-motivation educational environments. In this period he feels that language is not necessarily a condition for operating effectively cognitively, although it is likely that language does have an indirect effect for concrete operations. Language has a definite and direct effect on formal operations in which logic, hypothesizing, and problem solving require symbolization. Deaf adolescents in Furth's studies showed a general representational deficit and failed to develop the kind of abstract thinking expected from adults (Furth and Youniss, 1969). The message that comes through is that language must support cognitive development at all periods if a deaf person, or any other with poor linguistic skills, is to function more fully throughout his life as a thinking human being.

Rosenstein (1961) reviewed the literature on cognitive abilities of deaf children and found some disagrement among the research findings largely because of lack of clarity in the definitions of terms such as cognition, concept formation, and generalization. One researcher might find the deaf as a group functioning with severe perceptual and conceptual restrictions, whereas another might find them operating much the same as hearing children. Rosenstein concluded, like Furth, that there is no difference in conceptual performance between deaf and hearing children when linguistic factors are eliminated and that abstract thinking is not closed to them.

Templin (1950) studied the reasoning in young adolescent children with normal and defective hearing. They were matched for sex, age, grade placement, and on performance based IQ tests. She used Piaget-type questions such as *What makes shadows?* and *What makes clouds move?* and evaluated responses according to Piaget's classification of causal thought. The defective-hearing children used more phenomenistic explanations than the hearing. In phenomenistic explanations, two facts can be related causally with no relation other than contiguity in space or time, as in *The smoke moves; the clouds move, too.* The deaf resorted to magical explanations more often than the hearing, but both groups were equal in their mechanical explanations, as in *The wind pushes the clouds.* At age 18 years, 44.5 percent of the hearing and 20 percent of the deaf used logical deduction. Retardation of several years in the deaf population persisted even when intelligence was controlled. Templin concluded that defective training, especially in language-related areas, was responsible for the discrepancy in the responses of the two groups.

Furth's suggestion that some of the deaf child's handicap lies in impoverished experience may have some validity. Since the auditory channel is the most effective one for processing distant stimuli, the child gets little or no practice in attaching labels to things not seen. If a hearing child hears a noise, in order to react he must decide if what he hears is the slamming of a door, an object falling, or someone throwing a rock on the roof. His auditory experiences sometimes demand quick responses and increasingly accurate thinking. He gets many opportunities to practice abstracting information from his environment beyond the limits of his visual field, whereas a hearing impaired youngster may retain a concrete symbol system just because he is deprived of experiences that promote seeing relationships beyond the immediate and the concrete. To avoid unnecessary delay or retardation in cognitive growth, Furth recommends a school curriculum in which thinking is one of its major goals. Templin recommends a language program that supports the deaf child's cognitive development. What we need is a curriculum in which both elements have priority and are coordinated if hearing impaired children are to live up to their potentials.

To round out the discussion of the subject of this chapter, we will now consider several other aspects of learning, namely, memory, motor learning, and social and attitudinal learning, all of which have implications for educators.

## MEMORY AND LEARNING

We use memory in our thinking, to make logical deductions, to understand ideas, and to memorize facts. All the information we possess is interconnected for use in retrieval and interpretive processes. Smith (1975) defined memory as a complex system concerned with selection, acquisition, retention, organization, retrieval, and reconstruction of all of our knowledge including past experience. Such a definition excludes the concept of memory as a single entity located somewhere in the brain. Psychologists have identified three aspects of memory: sensory storage, short-term memory, and long-term memory. Sensory images—visual, auditory, and the like—can be placed in sensory storage for a part of a second and can then be processed either in short- or long-term memory. Information in short-term memory is readily accessible for a minute or two. Long-term memory is what its name implies. Anything that goes into long-term memory is said to be there forever (Lindsay and Norman, 1972).

Short-term memory deals with transient information. We do not remember most of what we see, hear, or do during a day: the number of degree-days reported for Zone 11 on the morning weather report; where we put that note for Jimmy's mother; all the items we bought at the supermarket only half an hour before; or what we had for dinner 2 weeks ago yesterday. The ability to hold information in short-term memory is brief and limited. Short-term memory persists only as long as we pay attention to it, but it can be gone forever if we are distracted.

What we have in short-term memory can be put into long-term memory by rehearsing it and relating it to already acquired knowledge. All of us have been introduced to groups of strangers. Suppose we are at a party and have met Patti, Marcy, Al, Paul, and Derek and are still to be introduced to a dozen or more other party-goers. By that time we have already lost all but the last name we heard. To commit the names to long-term memory we must hear them again, pay attention to them, say them, and focus on some features of the person to associate with his name. For instance, we learn that Patti and Derek are husband and wife; both are wearing blue jeans and gorgeous American Indian jewelry; and both have long straight blonde hair. In fact, they look like brother and sister. For that evening we have no difficulty in remembering their names. But are their names really in our long-term memory? I doubt it.

It takes a relatively long time to get information into long-term memory. Once it gets in, getting it out when we want the information becomes the problem. Psychologists tell us that the ease of getting information out of long-term memory depends on how it is integrated with prior knowledge (Smith, 1975). The more relationships that can be established and the more ways that the new information is integrated with that knowledge, the more likely it will be remembered. Not only verbal associations and sensory-motor experiences, but perceptual memories—visual, tactual, olfactory, gustatory, and certainly auditory—represent knowledge that can be called on to help integrate the new with the known. Visual memories undoubtedly play a considerable role in the integrative processes of hearing impaired children. A child who has seen camels at the zoo may store a picture of them in his mind, and later recognize on the television screen animals walking through the desert or charging an enemy with their riders in a desert battle as being camels. Later he may call up these images when he is expected to read and understand a selection about desert life. The more perceptual experiences and the more knowledge a child has when it becomes necessary to organize thinking at higher conceptual levels, the easier it will be to form new categories, and to retrieve information when he needs it.

There is evidence to support the contention that young children do not lack memory capacity, and that preschoolers do not differ much from fifth graders in this respect. Fifth graders use better strategies for remembering, however (Gibson and Levin, 1975). The ability to use categories is the most efficient way to remember, and this is what older children do better than younger ones. Sequential naming or pointing and rehearsal are used more by younger children until they develop categorizing techniques for remembering. Teachers could promote categorizing for remembering by being aware of its effectiveness. Imagine that a class of deaf six year olds is about to prepare some jello as a class exercise. The teacher starts the lesson by saying, "We're going to make jello today and we'll need a bowl, jello, a cup, a kettle, some water and a spoon. Who can remember what we need?" The children will perhaps remember the last item and the first item, but not those in the middle of the list. The teacher repeats the list as she gave it the first time in the hope that the children will now remember it. She names the items sequentially, and rehearses them with the children. Of course, no teacher could conduct a lesson this way. If she really wanted to help the children remember this list, she might present it by saying, "We'll need jello and water; a cup, a kettle, a bowl, and a spoon"—naming the ingredients first and the utensils second and writing them on the chalk board, or by saying, "We'll need a bowl for the jello, a cup to measure the water, a kettle to heat the water, and a spoon to stir the jello." Actually, sequential rehearsal interferes with categorizing. Rehearsal keeps memory alive but it cannot increase the memory system as categorizing can (Gibson and Levin, 1975). All strategies become more purposive with age.

To behaviorists, remembering is the outcome of learning, but it is also subject to reduction or decay. Forgetting is described as a complex combination of processes involving possible lack of stimulus support, possible extinction by presence of distracting activities, possible interference of subsequent learning with earlier learning and perhaps with just the passage of time itself. Imagine yourself in a theater lobby and seeing a blonde young woman wearing a long black dress with her hair in a chignon. You know that you have met her before, but who is she and where have you seen her? She approaches and says, "I'm Patti. Remember me?" According to behaviorists, perhaps you needed the stimulus support of the party scene where you had met her three months before, the beautiful Indian jewelry and the presence of Derek, her husband, to remember her. Remembering information such as telephone numbers, names, and addresses, or the aisle in the supermarket where you can find anchovies cannot be attached to enough information to allow it to get into long-term memory easily. If information is not rehearsed frequently and if it cannot be integrated with prior knowledge, it is easily forgotten.

Schools are heavy on asking children to remember facts. Do you recall how to complete this simple algebraic equation: $(a+b)(b+c) = ?$ Or can you name three battles of the Revolutionary War with their dates? When was the Federal Reserve Bank established and why? Undoubtedly you knew the an-

MADUN
LIVONIA, MICHIGAN

swers to these questions once upon a time. Teachers more often than not ask children to remember facts that they are bound to forget, facts that are important for answering teacher's questions but useless to the pupil. High school or college students themselves labor under the misconception about remembering facts when they study for exams half the night before their tests. They try to cram a host of facts into their long-term memories in too short a time. The result is an overload on the memory with not many facts getting into it, and fewer getting out of it. If a conscious effort is made to memorize facts from a book, comprehension will suffer (Smith, 1975).

If a child has not learned the facts a teacher thinks important, no amount of suggestion to "think, think harder" will promote memory. It becomes necessary to analyze why the child has not remembered the facts. Did he depend only on rote memory for learning the facts? Did he merely try to match answers in his book with the teacher's questions? Did he have enough background information to which the facts could be related? Does remembering the facts make sense to him? Has he had time to assimilate the facts and integrate them with his present knowledge?

Learning facts can be exciting if they enrich a child's understanding of the world around him. A child will normally seek information that makes him less uncertain about his environment. If the facts are important to him for his own reasons, he will remember them and assimilate them into his cognitive structure. There are simply too many facts in the world to commit to memory. A child must learn where to locate them but he must not be expected to memorize them. The school can play a vital role in helping children to discover what facts he needs to know.

## LANGUAGE AND MEMORY

Teachers of children with language handicaps are very much concerned with the effect of memory capacity on language acquisition, especially on the morphemic aspects of language. They frequently complain because their pupils do not seem to remember the language they have been taught for more than a few minutes, to say nothing about overnight or over the long summer vacation. In order to determine what part memory played in language development of hearing children, Menyuk (1969) studied the syntactic structure of sentences that preschoolers, ages 3.0 to 5.11, produced under conditions described as typical language situations. The study confirmed that the basic structures used by adults were used by some children, but that grammatical development continued beyond the first-grade level. Follow-up studies attempted to determine whether certain structures were memorized or generated by a child's grammatical rules. Children were asked to recall immediately sentences presented orally. None had difficulty in repeating sentences even nine words long when the utterances were meaningful. When a child understood a sentence, its repetition might not always be verbatim, but was modified according to his comprehension of it. In other words, information in the sentence was stored but not the words themselves.

When word order was reversed or scrambled, even though the utterances were presented with normal phrasing and intonation, children had difficulty in repeating them. Here short-term memory definitely played a part. Some not completely well-formed sentences were also presented. The children were directed to correct them or did so spontaneously. Even three-year-old children were able to do this within the framework of their ability to generate their own sentences. Menyuk concluded that repetition was dependent on a child's structural rules rather than on imitation up to the limits of memory capacity. She believed that children stored rules of grammar but first had only enough capacity to store a subset of rules. With increase in the number of rules they acquired, reorganization took place and they then became able to generate completely well-formed sentences, and to remember them. Research with older subjects points out that syntactic word groups within a sentence also serve as functional memory groups (Jenkins, 1973).

Responses of children described as language deviant, although not hearing impaired, were also evaluated by Menyuk (1969). Even though some of the children used idiosyncratic rules, they did use grammatical rules and were able to repeat sentences spontaneously. However, many times only the last word in a sentence was repeated. This led Menyuk to speculate that the difficulty might lie in short-term memory storage. The questions raised by this study still need to be resolved.

On the basis of current psycholinguistic research, it seems safe to conclude that rule-generating capacity rather than memory alone is what eventually determines how a child masters language. We know that deaf children can and do learn language and that they can and do generate rules, deviant though some of the rules may be. The big challenge for teachers is helping children acquire standard rules for the construction of standard English sentences and their constituent parts. Memory, of course, does play a role in language acquisition. A child must acquire a vocabulary and remember it. At first a young deaf child, like all children, can process only one or two word sentences. In the preschool, teachers try to guide him into internalizing rules that create simple, basic sentence patterns. Ample opportunity to practice these patterns is essential before children advance to more complex structures if they are to use them independently and automatically.

Memory load for producing sentences is greater than for understanding them since semantic and syntactic information is available when someone else is doing the talking. Yet, when a lipreader is trying to get meaning from spoken language without using his hearing, he is dealing with a less redundant form than the auditory one, since many phonemes look alike and cannot be differentiated on the lips without auditory support. Sentences seen on the lips can also be highly ambiguous because many more words look alike than sound alike. For instance, a lipreader may think that a speaker has said "Do you have a dime?" when what he really said was "Do you have the time?" If sentences are to be read from the lips they must not only be formulated with vocabularly and structures familiar to the lipreader, but must be couched in language that is visible on the lips and as unambiguous as possible. A more visible and less ambiguous query about the time of day might be "Is it after four o'clock? What's the time please?" or "Do you have a watch? What time do you have?" Anybody who has contacts with hearing impaired lipreaders has to learn how to phrase his sentences to incorporate all of these features. It takes practice to learn to talk in visible language.

Frequently a teacher does ask a deaf child to repeat a sentence in order to check on whether he has been paying attention or if he has understood what she said. If he cannot comply, she may repeat the sentence several times in the hope that he will, although repetition does not ensure that the child will understand it any better the third or fourth time than he did the first. A child looks for meaning when he reads lips, just as a child does who hears a sentence, and if he finds none on first or second hearing, he will have difficulty in repeating it. The teacher must analyze why the child was unable to respond. Has he failed because the sentence was not visible? Does the sentence contain vocabulary with which the child is unfamiliar? Does the child's repertoire of language rules include those she used? If the child does attempt a response which is not verbatim, this may serve as an excellent clue as to what rules the child is using. An alert teacher can use such information to clarify whatever misconceptions a child has about the use of particular structural or morphemic rules.

Some aspects of language learning for hearing impaired children will likely require rote learning. Suppose a deaf child seems not to remember when to use a past tense form, always substituting a present tense form for it. This does not necessarily mean that he has a faulty memory, but rather it may mean that he lacks information to control the morphemic aspects of the past tense. Even as the number of verbs increases in his vocabulary, he can find no simple rule which governs the formation of the past tense. The past of *buy* is *bought*, the past tense of *go* is *went*, and the past tense of *put* is *put*. This means that the child may have to learn by rote the principal parts of our weak and strong English verbs. To get this information into long-term memory will require frequent rehearsal within the framework of meaningful sentences in which the verbs are appropriately used. A child will learn language by using it, and will remember it when he knows the rules that govern it.

## MOTOR LEARNING

Children learn to walk, throw a ball, ride a bicycle, swim, skate, and ski by walking, throwing balls, riding bicycles, swimming, skating, and skiing, and not by listening to parents or teachers talk about how to perform these activities. As a child gains increasingly greater mobility with advancing age, his sensory-motor experiences continue to contribute to his intellectual development as well as to his motor control. Some linguists have even theorized that a child begins to babble when he can sit up, develops a crude vocabulary when he begins to crawl, and uses syntax when he can run. Many motor skills and cognitive skills are closely interwoven.

Learning a motor skill requires timing and coordination, and if one part of the activity is performed at the wrong time, the skill is disrupted. Even walking is not a simple motor activity but a series of coordinated muscular skills learned over a period of time. A child usually takes many tentative steps and many tumbles before he becomes a competent walker.

Whereas learning to walk, like learning to talk, is regarded as a natural development in the life of a normal child, learning to swim is not. Children as young as 18 months can learn this skill and many four and five year olds do, but they require instruction. A good swimming teacher breaks up the act into simple steps. As a child masters each step it is combined with a previous one, and coordinated with it, until the child can actually swim. In the process, the child's brain was busy organizing the sequences into a total plan. When once the sequence was started it triggered the whole act.

A beginning swimmer may know when he is not achieving a smooth performance, but he may not know why. The feedback that he gets from his muscles does not give him precise enough information to perfect his performance. His teacher can provide verbal feedback by pointing out how he can change it. Here is where language actually plays a part in learning complex motor activities. But all the words in the world will not make a champion swimmer. A champion works at swimming better by swimming better. He practices under the verbal guidance of a coach to gain power and precision. He is a highly motivated person who values achievement above all.

Learning to speak is not usually thought of as a motor skill since it is a natural event in the lives of most children. Yet speaking is an extraordinarily complicated motor activity superimposed on a complex cognitive skill. To master the sounds, or more precisely the phonology of his language, a child must use a special set of sounds that are linked to its semantic and syntactic aspects. Hearing children to this through their ears. They hear the sounds in the oral language of others and check their own production through auditory feedback. If the auditory system fails to function completely, a child actually has to be taught to speak, or to use oral language. When this happens, the motor aspects of speech become only too evident. The child must then depend on the tactile and visual senses rather than hearing for input and must rely on kinesthesia for his feedback, a sense not closely related to those he uses for input. As we noted above, the muscle sense is an imprecise one and cannot be expected to furnish enough information to the speaker to guarantee the kind of mastery that is achieved through auditory feedback.

The movements of the articulators require very fine adjustments, many of them dependent on the special environments created by the flow of oral language. For instance, the two *k's* in *kicked* are produced quite differently. The first is followed by an aspiration, whereas the second is not even exploded, and in the word *screen* the *k* actually becomes a *g* in American speech. Movements of tongue, lips, and palate have to be coordinated with the muscles of the larynx, diaphragm, and rib cage, supported by adequate breath in order to produce well-articulated speech. These are motor skills. Beyond that, phonology has to be coordinated with linguistic structure and meanings if oral language is to serve a deaf child in communication with the hearing world.

Oral language does not emerge full blown in a hearing child, and for a deaf child, learning to use oral language may become a lifelong task. For many severely handicapped children, a hierarchical order encompassing a series of simpler speech acts may have to be established before he can get it all together. But if a child does not know what he is practicing or why he is doing it, it may not make sense to him. He may rightly reject efforts to go through speech drills day after day if he sees no purpose in them. Speech development and improvement must be directly related to communication needs. Just as in learning to swim, learning to speak implies conscious practice. Yet speaking intelligibly in an uncontrolled situation is difficult for beginners. When a child is thinking about *what* he is saying, he may not be able to attend to *how* he is saying it, for he can attend only to one thing at a time. He must possess well established motor speech skills in order to speak automatically. Unless he receives feedback from the listener in the early stages of learning to talk, he may not reach the desired criterion which is intelligibility. His ability to communicate depends on his language, and thus these two aspects of oral communication become inseparable partners.

Fortunately, children with no functional hearing for speech, with or without the use of a hearing aid, are relatively few in number. Hearing only a small amount helps greatly in establishing good voice quality, rhythmic speech, and normal intonation patterns. Nevertheless, most hearing impaired children require the guidance and support of knowledgeable teachers and parents to help them reach the stage where their oral language becomes functional. If no time is provided for children to use their speech skills, or if a low priority is placed on development of intelligible speech in meaningful situations, the probability that they will develop and be used independently will greatly diminish. Every child needs to be guided, encouraged, and, yes, reinforced for using good speech. It must be kept in mind that a child learns to speak by speaking, not by swimming or signing or watching the teacher talk. Our champion speakers are usually those children who have seen a real purpose for talking, who talk incessantly, and who are motivated to speak intelligibly because they realize its importance in communication.

This text will not go into the details of how to guide children in gaining intelligible speech for it would require a book in itself. The following references should prove useful to those who desire specific details about teaching speech to deaf children (Haycock, 1933; Ewing and Ewing, 1954; Calvert and Silverman, 1975; Vorce, 1974; Ling, 1976).

## SOCIAL, ATTITUDINAL, AND CULTURAL LEARNING

Thus far we have dwelt mainly on the importance of cognitive learning and its relation to language development. But learning is much more complex than even this complex relationship. Man is a social creature and during his lifetime his full range of learning encompasses not only the sensory-motor and the cognitive, but also its interpersonal and attitudinal aspects, all highly integrated in real life. Social learning takes place from the time a child is born. He soon discovers how to manipulate people in his environment by cooing, smiling, kicking, and screaming. Some children learn that to gain attention they must be "bad" according to the standards set up for their behavior. Others learn that to be "good" gets them pats, hugs, and kisses, and some learn quickly how to get their own way. Children perceive these interpersonal relationships in their families without being taught them. They imitate familial behavior and integrate it into their own. In the same way, the broader social environment—school, church, and other social institutions—contributes to their concepts of societal values. Adults may eventually learn to be "good" citizens by supporting themselves and their families and not stealing or violating traffic laws; or they may feel alienated by what they consider the hopelessness in governmental participation, stop voting forever, sit and watch TV, and let the world take care of itself; or they may aggressively fight the so-called power structure through law, or even become urban guerillas to show their discontent. Social learning takes many directions.

At the same time that social learning and cognitive learning are taking place, the child is developing feelings about himself in relation to the other persons in his environment. For a child to develop positive feelings about himself, psychologists agree that he must feel liked, wanted, and accepted (Combs, Avila, and Purkey, 1971). He learns this not by being told so, but by perceiving how others treat him. If he has a positive view about himself, it will be easy for him to feel successful. Unfortunately, many children develop negative feelings about themselves and find it difficult ever to feel successful at home or at school.

Social psychologists differ about whether basic changes can really occur in personal and emotional learning that a child acquires early in life. Some hold that early experiences exert a lasting influence on a child's personality, whereas others believe that continuous conditioning takes place as a response to cultural and social forces. Case histories of well-adjusted children reveal the same traits throughout life, modified only a little by insights acquired over time (Langdon and Stout, 1951). Although personality may stabilize early in life, participation in school life and in the society of one's peers can and does influence behavior and value systems. In the school setting, teachers often feel the need to establish limits for pupil behavior. Some report success in changing the conduct of maladjusted children through behavior modification techniques when other approaches seem to have failed. In Chapter 5 you will find additional comments on this subject.

Cultural diversity exists in the United States despite our claim to be the world's greatest melting pot. Blacks, Spanish speakers, native Americans, and Orientals as well as numerous other ethnic groups all have their own unique identities. Perhaps the manually communicating deaf should be included in a census of minority cultural groups. Although they may originate in families of diverse cultures, they tend as adults to form a close-knit social subculture as the result of their education in residential schools generally isolated from the mainstream of the hearing world. Each cultural group has developed its own values and attitudes, such as motivation for learning, morals and ethics, status of women, gratification of needs, punishment, self-discipline, and the like. They pass these attitudes and values on to their children. If we believe that cultural pluralism adds strength to a nation, the schools will find it necessary to provide programs to support diversity. If we believe that all of our people must conform to the standards of the white middle class, programs will continue to reflect this culture in curricula and textbooks as they have for decades. Although it is not within the province of this book to settle the matter, it is our hope that teachers will become aware of the differences in the backgrounds of their pupils and try to understand them when they set out to provide meaningful educational programs for the children they are teaching.

## REFERENCES

Bellugi U and Klima E: The roots of language in the sign talk of the deaf. Psychol Today 6:60–64, 1972

Bloom LM: Language Development: Form and Function in Emerging Grammars. Cambridge, Mass., MIT Press, 1970

Bowerman M: Structural relationships in children's utterances: syntactic or semantic? In Moore TE (ed): Cognitive Development and the Acquisition of Language. New York, Academic Press, 1973

Brown R: A First Language—Early Stages. Cambridge, Mass., Harvard University Press, 1973

Calvert DR and Silverman SR: Speech and Deafness. Washington, D.C., A. G. Bell Assoc., 1975

Chomsky N: Syntactic Structures. The Hague, Mouton, 1957

Chomsky N: Aspects of the Theory of Syntax. Cambridge, Mass., MIT Press, 1965

Combs AW, Avila DL, and Purkey WW: Helping Relationships: Basic Concepts for the Helping Professions. Boston, Allyn and Bacon, 1971

Ewing IR and Ewing AWG: Speech and the Deaf Child. Washington, D.C., A. G. Bell Assoc., 1954

Fillmore CJ: The case for case. In Bach E and Harms RT (Eds): Universals in Linguistic Theory. New York, Holt, Rinehart and Winston, 1968

Furth HG: Research with the deaf: implications for language and cognition. Psychol Bull 62:145-164, 1964

Furth HG: Piaget for Teachers. Englewood Cliffs, N.J., Prentice-Hall, 1970

Furth HG: Deafness and Learning, A Psychological Approach. Belmont, Ca., Wadsworth Publishing Co., 1973

Furth HG and Youniss J: Thinking in deaf adolescents: language and formal operations. J Commun Disord 2:195-202, 1969

Gagne R: The Conditions of Learning. New York, Holt, Rinehart and Winston, 1970

Gibson EJ: Principles of Perceptual Learning and Development. New York, Appleton-Century-Crofts, 1969

Gibson EJ and Levin H: The Psychology of Reading. Cambridge, Mass., MIT Press, 1975

Ginsburg H and Opper S: Piaget's Theory of Intellectual Development, an Introduction. Englewood Cliffs, N.J., Prentice-Hall, 1969

Green EJ: The Learning Process and Programmed Instruction. New York, Holt, Rinehart and Winston, 1962

Haycock GS: The Teaching of Speech. Washington D.C., A. G. Bell Assoc., 1933

Jenkins JJ: Language and memory. In Miller G (ed): Communication, Language and Meaning. New York, Basic Books, 1973

Kamii C: Evaluation of learning in preschool education: socioemotional, perceptual-motor and cognitive development. In Bloom BS, Hastings JT, and Madaus GF (eds): Handbook on Formative and Summative Evaluation of Student Learning. New York, McGraw-Hill, 1971

Kretschmer RR: A Study to Assess the Play Activity and Gesture Output of Hearing Handicapped Preschool Children. Final Report. Washington, D.C., Bureau of Education for the Handicapped, USOE (ERIC 071-247), 1972

Langdon G and Stout IW: These Well-Adjusted Children. New York, John Day Co., 1951

Lavatelli CS: Piaget's Theory Applied to an Early Childhood Curriculum. Boston, Mass., A Center for Media Development, Inc.; Book, American Science and Engineering, Inc., 1973

Lavatelli CS: Teachers Guide to Early Childhood Curriculum—A Piaget Program. Boston, Mass., A Center for Media Development, Inc.; Program, American Science and Engineering, Inc., 1973

Lenneberg E: Biological Foundations of Language. New York, John Wiley, 1967

Lenneberg E: Prerequisites for language acquisition by the deaf. In O'Rourke TJ (ed): Psycholinguistics and Total Communication: The State of the Art. Washington, D.C., American Annals of the Deaf, 1972

Lindsay P and Norman D: Human Information Processing. New York, Academic Press, 1972

Ling D: Speech and the Hearing Impaired Child: Theory and Practice. Washington, D.C., A. G. Bell Assoc., 1976

Menyuk P: Sentences Children Use. Cambridge, Mass., MIT Press, 1969

Menyuk P: The Acquisition and Development of Language. Englewood Cliffs, N.J., Prentice-Hall, 1971

Morehead DM and Morehead A: From signal to sign: a Piagetian view of thought and language during the first two years. In Schiefelbusch RL and Lloyd LL (eds): Language Perspectives—Acquisition, Retardation and Intervention. Baltimore, University Park Press, 1974

Perfetti CA: Psychosemantics: some cognitive aspects of structural meaning. Psychol Bull 78:4, 241–259, 1972

Piaget J: Language and Thought of the Child. New York, Harcourt Brace, 1926

Pulaski MAA: Understanding Piaget. New York, Harper & Row, 1971

Rosenstein J: Perception, cognition and language in deaf children. Except Child 27:5, 276–284, 1961

Schumacher J and Sherman JA: Training generative verb usage by imitation and reinforcement procedures. J Appl Behav Anal 3:273–287, 1970

Sinclair-de-Zwart H: Developmental psycholinguistics. In Elkind D and Flavell FH (eds): Studies in Cognitive Development. New York, Oxford University Press, 1969

Sharp E: Thinking is Child's Play. New York, Dutton, 1969

Skinner BF: The Behavior of Organisms: An Experimental Analysis. New York, Appleton-Century, 1938

Skinner BF: Verbal Behavior. New York, Appleton-Century-Crofts, 1957

Slobin DJ: Cognitive prerequisites for the development of grammar. In Ferguson CA and Slobin SI (eds): Studies for Child Language Development. New York, Holt, Rinehart and Winston, 1973

Smith F: Comprehension and Learning—A Conceptual Framework for Teachers. New York, Holt, Rinehart and Winston, 1975

Templin M: Development of Reasoning in Children with Normal and Defective Hearing, University of Minnesota Institute of Child Welfare Monograph #24. Minneapolis, University of Minnesota Press, 1950

Thorndike EL: Human Learning. New York, Century, 1931

Vernon M: Sociological and psychological factors associated with hearing loss. J Speech Hear Res 12:3, 541–563, 1969

Vorce E: Teaching Speech to Deaf Children. Washington, D.C., Bell Assoc., 1974

# 3
# Establishing and Maintaining Communication

Innate capacity for language learning is a characteristic of every human child. The specific language the child will learn is solely a function of whatever linguistic environment he finds himself in. We will learn in more detail in Chapter 4 that each infant is an active, not a passive learner of rule systems which include language and speech. However, the circumstances through which he learns language depend on the richness and variety of communication interactions between him and his adult caretakers. Studies of environmental influences are being examined as vigorously as the behaviors of the child alone (Farwell, 1975; Landes, 1975).

Evidence is accumulating that caretakers, usually although not always mothers, all over the world talk in special ways to very young children and that these strategies of communication seem best adapted to what children need to hear at any given point in order that communication may be fostered (Snow, 1972; Phillips, 1973; Moerk, 1974). In the following pages, we will examine some aspects of normal mother-child communication patterns and the probable effects of hearing impairment on these processes. Finally, we will try to provide a variety of suggestions that seem to be necessary components to any program which aims to normalize communication between parents and their hearing impaired children.

## NORMAL-CHILD COMMUNICATION PATTERNS

There is an abundance of evidence that from the first months of contact between mother and child, both mother and baby begin to explore the potential of the relationship (Bruner, 1975). Mothers do not merely hold children; they interrelate by feeding, showing, playing, bathing, touching, and talking. Babies are not empty containers but active processors of auditory, visual, tactual, and kinesthetic information which helps to tie linguistic experience to nonlinguistic and cognitive/perceptual experiences. Language could be said to result from the intersection of a linguistic code or set of rules with nonlinguistic experiences, expressed as cognitive understandings. Thus, the first linguistic experiences must be considered as crucial and necessary parts of future language-cognitive development in all children.

When mothers and children interact within a well-structured, familiar environment like that which exists for infants in earliest life, some important events are occurring. First, the mother is directing the child's attention to a specific topic within a familiar environment. That is, by playing with a toy, the mother is in effect saying *Look here because I am going to talk about this toy*. Then, not surprisingly, she does talk about the toy or about an action with the toys that she has selected for joint attention. In this way, language is neatly tied in time and space to a referent or topic of conversation. For the young, nontalking child, such interchanges remind the mother which language she has already presented, so that she knows what she can eventually expect to hear the child talk about. Because so many of the early language attempts of children are articulated poorly and thus seem unconnected to the communication situation, it is not always possible to understand what the child is attempting to say without boundaries and focus. If this is a necessary strategy for mothers of normally speaking children, how much more true must this be for the mother of a hearing impaired child?

## What Children Need to Learn

What is the nature of the linguistic information being derived by hearing children from mother-child interactions? How does this derived information lead to greater linguistic understanding and competence? Mothers tend to use consistent reference in the environment. Through such controlled reference, the child comes to understand that some words refer to objects or events, an understanding which underlies the notion of reference. The learning of reference, however, is not merely attaching a label to an object or an event, but also learning that the word refers to the many features associated with that object or event. Words may mean, in addition to the object itself, the things that an object or person can do, the things that can be done to that object or person, the special functions that the object or person may serve in the child's life. Words can even stand for things that act and things that get acted on. Meaning is attached to semantic categories such as *agents*, entities who do things; *patients*, receivers of action; *instruments*, things that are used to accomplish actions; *beneficiaries*, entities who own either permanently or temporarily other entities or objects; as well as to actions themselves.

For instance, as the mother talks about dogs, she is building in specific reference. The child comes to understand that dogs are four-legged animals that may be dangerous or may be warm furry creatures to play with. At the same time, the child is also coming to recognize that dogs are agents who are capable of performing actions that infringe on the space of objects such as balls or food. It is the categorized reference system especially which allows the child to know where and with what other types of grammatical constructions he can use the word *dog*. To teach any child the *meaning* of a word without also helping that child to learn its potential semantic function within a sentence is to encourage fragmentation of linguistic knowledge. Mothers of normal children seem never to have that shortcoming.

The second important set of linguistic information being established in mother-child interactions is called predication. As a mother comments about activities, she frequently employs statements that include a topic under discussion and a comment or *predication* about that topic. For instance, the mother may be holding a toy dog, the topic, while she says things like *The doggy's head goes up and down*, or *See the doggy's tail wag*. Each of these statements contains the topic, but each also focuses on comments about the dog which are the predicate of each sentence. In this way, the child comes to understand that connected discourse contains both subjects or topics and predicates or comments.

Use of predication may begin at a nonverbal level. If mother says *Look at the doggy* and the child turns to look, he has in effect made a comment on the topic *doggy*; he is paying attention. It would seem reasonable to suppose that children who do not make even this type of comment are not involved in developing basic grammatical understanding, for they are not yet paying attention to one of the critical dimensions of the English language system, the topic-comment relationship in sentence discourse.

As the child does begin to talk, he shows clearly that he has paid attention to mother for he uses topics and comments himself. At first, his utterances may only be comments, common events in the single-word stage. Presumably, he only needs predicates since the topic is almost always present for both mother and child, which makes the child's task easier. He need not use the subject or topic as he takes his communication turn. For instance, the child who knows and uses the word *doggy* may say *bite*, instead, while looking at a picture of a dog biting a bone. The word *bite* is a comment on the obvious topic *dog*. As the child moves into the two-word stage, his utterances expand to include either topic-comment relationships or expanded comment constructions as *dog bite* or *bite hard*. When a child progresses to this stage, he is showing his knowledge of subject–predicate relationships, one of the fundamental characteristics of connected spoken English. It is hard to conceive of any child, including a hearing impaired one, who is able to establish connected language without a rudimentary knowledge of predication and its function in discourse.

Thirdly, while mothers talk in systematic ways to their children, they also communicate with them. They try continually to say something of linguistic or cognitive importance to the child, which accounts for the number of questions, repetitions, and varied intents of the language used by mothers. Through such efforts, the child comes to understand not only the structures but the functions or uses of language as well. This is most important, for the child who does not know when, how, or why to use specific linguistic constructions has missed one of the most important functions of communication. If communication competence is to develop, the child must come to understand that language constructions can be used for a variety of reasons or purposes. For instance, question forms are for asking questions, but they may also be used by a mother as a command as in *Wouldn't you like to close the door?*, which in many standard English contexts is not choice, but an explicit order.

If normally hearing children learn language in environments controlled and focused by their mothers, it seems reasonable that hearing impaired children too could benefit from such systematic linguistic exposure. For reasons that will become clear later in this chapter, mothers of hearing impaired children usually need help in doing what they seem to know how to do well if they are communicating with a normally hearing child. This special help is needed to ensure that each hearing handicapped child has an opportunity to learn about specific and categorized reference, predication, and functions of communication, all facets of spoken language which are basic to future language mastery. These important sets of information are most easily established during the child's earliest life by communication dialogues.

### Characteristics of Mothers' Talk with Children

We have discussed some of the content children need to acquire from mothers. It may now be instructive to focus a bit more on the characteristics of mother talk, particularly the concept of baby register (Ferguson, 1964). *Register* refers to the way language is used by individuals or social groups in communication with one another. Depending on our expectations about the people we are talking to and on the complexity of the topic under discussion, we normally adjust our language so as to communicate in the best way we can to each person. These changes in linguistic style are called changes in register. All over the world, mothers act out their expectations about babies by language style-changes or use of baby registers that are clearly different from registers used with older children and adults. Baby registers have been observed to be used by nursery school teachers and older siblings of infants as well, but not as much by fathers (Granowsky and Krossner, 1970; Berko-Gleason, 1973).

Baby register has the following characteristics: (1) use of a limited set of vocabulary items, specifically kinship terms (mommy, daddy, grandpa), body parts and functions, basic qualities of objects (size, weight, or quantity), animals, and games; (2) emphasis on vocabulary items that are composed of consonant-vowel-consonant and/or consonant-vowel-consonant-vowel combinations such as *big* or *mama*; (3) consistent modification of standard pronunciations to produce baby-like words such as *daddy* or *dada*; (4) use of unusual or highly inflected intonational patterns; (5) use of grammatical constructions that are presumed to be more easily comprehended by the child such as noun constructions in place of pronoun constructions; (6) use of highly redundant output, with repetition of the same construction with the same vocabulary and intonational pattern several times in a single interaction with the child; (7) use of so-called simple sentences containing fewer dysfluencies or hesitation-type pauses, which would be reasonable since so-called simple sentences should be easy to construct and produce; and finally (8) use of variation in communication strategies which are highly dependent on the situation. When mothers talk to their children about real objects or real actions, their language is simpler and more consistent than that used in storytelling involving imagination and pictures. In other words, children are receiving from their mothers a simple but clear language model that is highly redundant, highly intonated, and highly consistent. The sex of the child and his birth order do not seem to be important variables in the selection of baby register by mothers.

Interestingly, a mother's style of baby register is highly dependent on the child's reactions (Moerk, 1975). For example, if the child demonstrates to his mother that his understanding is more sophisticated than she had presumed, the mother will automatically shift to a more complex linguistic form and will often cease to be as redundant or consistent. The ability of mothers to recognize developing comprehension levels in their children is a critical factor in the application of baby register, for it serves as the stimulus to stretch and expand the child's linguistic capabilities. At the same time, mothers seem to be sensitive enough to avoid making linguistic demands that are too difficult for their children. They become excellent judges of a child's language needs.

Unfortunately, these good instincts seem to be impeded, sometimes fatally, by the appearance of a linguistic or sensory handicap such as deafness. One can only speculate as to why such profound communication breakdowns occur. It could result from a lack of feedback from the child, or perhaps from a psychological barrier erected when a diagnosis of deafness is made. Mothers of hearing impaired children need to be assisted in learning to communicate with their children in as normal a mother-child dialogue as possible. Such dialogues are critical if deaf children are to initiate language learning at an early age. Unfortunately, when normalized mother-child interactions fail to occur, siblings may step or be pushed into the void, to establish some system of communication with, or for, the hearing impaired child. Parents begin to depend on their normally hearing children to serve as interpreters, or linguistic babysitters for the deaf child. Such a situation is unfortunate because it blocks parents from learning how to communicate with their child and may even interfere with subsequent attempts to reestablish healthy communication among them.

## Ways Mothers Try to Stimulate Language Usage

In mother-child interactions, it is clear that the mother is not only talking to her child, but is also encouraging her child to talk back to her. It is certainly as important to understand the techniques that mothers of normally developing children use to stimulate the growth of expressive language as it is to understand the type of input they provide to children to encourage linguistic mastery.

Mothers' techniques seem to change over time depending on the child's age and degree of expressive language he demonstrates (Moerk, 1975). In the initial period of establishing meaningful communication, mothers tend to use two major types of techniques for stimulating language, specifically, *prodding* and *expansion*. Prodding techniques are clear indications to the child that he is to repeat what his mother has just said. For instance, mother shows little Harold a ball saying "This is a ball," which is immediately followed by "Harold, honey, this is a ?" with appropriate body gestures and intonational patterns clearly indicating that she expects Harold to complete the sentence.

Expansion consists of repeating the child's exact utterances in an expanded, full grammatical form. As an example, if little Harold did say *ball* when prompted, the mother might next expand his utterance into *Yes, that's a ball*. It is this rotation back and forth between prodding and expansion that best characterizes many of the early mother-child interactions.

Mothers tend to correct very young children's expressive language, but this tendency to correct drops dramatically as the child becomes a more sophisticated language user, probably because he is saying so much that it is impossible to monitor everything. However, it has been found that if mothers do correct an utterance, it is usually to ensure the accuracy of information rather than to rectify misuse of linguistic structures.

As a child matures further, mothers tend to use more question forms to elicit and encourage language growth in their children. Yes/no questions are used with greater frequency with younger children, ages 1½ years, whereas wh- questions beginning with *who*, *what*, and *which* are used with older children. In addition to using questioning in early communication, mothers have also been observed to use modeling. Modeling refers to the process of commenting on a child's utterance, apparently in the hope that the child will produce another utterance in response. For instance, if little Harold had said *bird pretty*, his mother could have said *Yes he is, and he's holding a worm in his mouth, isn't he?*, as a modeled response. This type of interaction, of course, is a useful tool for developing notions fundamental to conversational exchange. In the early stages of modeling, the mother may vary modeling with expansion. She might elicit a response to her comment and then expand the child's utterance to its full sentence form. In this way, the child is stimulated to produce new sentences and is also provided with a fuller model of the sentence he has just attempted.

Teachers of deaf children have reported employing prodding, expansion, modeling, and questioning techniques with good success to encourage and stimulate linguistic usage. Simmons-Martin's (1976) so-called auditory global technique has yielded some particularly impressive results through the aggressive use of expansion and modeling as well as strong auditory emphasis in severely hearing impaired children. In those cases where deafness has interrupted the normal mother-child interactions, one of the most obvious tasks is to help parents in reestablishing normal language stimulation techniques, sometimes in face of long-term sparse responses from the hearing impaired child.

If continued interaction is necessary to the establishment of meaningful dialogue between speaker and listener, it becomes imperative that not only mother-child relations but that teachers for the hearing impaired become conscious of encouraging normalized interactions. If a dialogue attitude is not encouraged, then the communication network dominated by a teacher of the deaf who stops talking just long enough to draw breath will continue as the norm. One-way communication does not allow the child to express the knowledge about language he possesses, nor does it give the teacher opportunity to discover anything about the child's linguistic performance.

## EFFECTS OF HEARING IMPAIRMENT ON
## MOTHER-CHILD COMMUNICATION PATTERNS

It would be very naive to believe that introduction of a handicap such as hearing impairment would not adversely affect family-child communication. Traditionally, emphasis has been on focusing the family's attention on management of the hearing impaired child's liability, his deafness, and on adjustment of the family's life style to compensate for the communication handicaps imposed by hearing impairment. After many years of telling parents about all aspects of deafness, it has become clear to us that when a hearing impairment is detected in a child there are profound human effects which must be dealt with before prosthetic devices or communication modification can or should be discussed with parents. Moses (1977) has pointed out that when presented with the reality of hearing impairment in their child, parents show normal but persuasive psychological reactions to the loss of a normal child, which seriously inhibit their ability to function with their child or even to be concerned about the importance of establishing meaningful communication. Merely providing information on how to develop language or how to use a hearing aid without some attention to how parents feel about their child, about deafness, and about their loss will not in most cases be sufficient to assist parents in establishing language learning environments.

Parental attitudes or adjustment to the deafness itself seems to be a measurable factor in determining overall educational progress. This notion was highlighted in a study (Corson, 1973) which examined educational achievement of hearing impaired children whose parents were themselves deaf and were classified as either orally oriented or manually oriented. Deaf children with normally hearing parents were also included for study. It was found that deaf children of deaf parents regardless of the parents' or children's chief means of communication were linguistically and academically equivalent or superior to children whose parents were normally hearing. Such results seem to suggest that parental attitudes toward deafness and indeed the fact of parents coping with their own hearing impairment may allow a child with a hearing impairment to be accqpted and related to without the grief that comes from a lack of experience with deafness. It would seem that environments where it is all right to be deaf are highly supportive of language and educational growth.

Parents whose experiences have excluded any notion of what deafness means often become frightened and angry upon discovery that they have a hearing impaired child. To them it may seem that a death has occurred, the death of their dream that their child will be a proud extension of themselves. Their feelings and concerns are often shared by other family members— siblings, grandparents, uncles and aunts, and even close friends. Their grief reaction must not be considered abnormal but rather a normal reaction to an unexpected loss. Mourning becomes pathological or destructive only if it is self-contained too long.

According to Kubler-Ross (1975), who has explored the phenomenon of dying in terminally ill patients, grief or mourning stages may vary in length and in order. Three stages—(1) denial, (2) bargaining, and (3) acceptance— can be identified in the reduction of the grief reaction. In some ways parents of handicapped children experience similar types of reactions (Moses, 1977). Initially parents of a deaf child may deny the diagnosis of deafness or refuse to accept it as being permanent even if the diagnosis confirms their suspicions. Some parents go from one physician to another, one audiologist to another, in the hope that the initial diagnosis will be revoked. When this is not so, their grief may be expressed as anger toward others, including the child, or turned inward as a feeling of guilt or depression.

When it becomes evident that a hearing aid will not restore the child's hearing, parents may express anger toward the audiologist who "promised" that the aid would let the child hear. At such times the angry parent may displace his feeling onto the hearing aid and subtly communicate his rage to the child. The aid may be lost, misplaced, or even flushed down the toilet because the child feels free to misuse the instrument.

Unresolved anger may be directed toward the teacher or toward the quality of the educational program. Parents may lash out at transportation difficulties, the lunch program, or playground facilities. Some may threaten to withdraw their child from the program for one reason or another. Reaction to a poor educational program may be legitimate. It is important to recognize a parent's reactions so that they can be dealt with in a realistic manner.

When parents move into the bargaining stage, they seek relief from their burden by attempting to strike an agreement with their advisors. They will agree with the audiologist to have the child wear his hearing aid at home, or with the teacher to talk to the child in sentences instead of burying him with words, but with the subtle and unstated reservation that the child will become normal or at least be able to talk and be graduated from college.

At this point professionals are vulnerable simply because of their desire to help the family solve its problems. No matter what the teacher says, some parents will misinterpret any statement of progress as a promise of normality. In turn, teachers and audiologists must avoid unfortunate statements that cannot be fulfilled such as "All deaf children can learn to talk normally," or "Hearing aids are helpful for all deaf children," or "All deaf children can be graduated from high school."

When parents have arrived at the stage of beginning to accept their child's handicap, they can cope more realistically with it. They can start looking at the child's assets and capitalize on them. When they understand that it is not the handicap itself but their attitude toward the handicap that needs resolution, they are on the way to new and interesting experiences. Unfortunately, all parents are not able to reach this final stage. To say that they are bad parents because they are blocked is to deny the validity of their feelings.

Even parents who may be coping with the presence of deafness find communication with their children difficult. There is some intriguing research

(Wulbert et al., 1975) that suggests that the communication-handicapped child himself is part of the problem, not part of the solution. Characteristically, mothers upon finding that their children have communication problems are less involved with their children than mothers of normally communicating children. Mothers in the handicapped situation generally fail to engage their children in joint activities, show less response to the child's communication attempts, and tend to avoid restricting or disciplining a child for misbehavior. Although these phenomena need to be examined further, they seem to be important evidence that communication-handicapped children and parents may be in a double bind. The children themselves are impaired in language expression and understanding and by the presence of this impairment inhibit communication with the very adults likely to have the largest role in early language growth.

This latter notion is further supported by observations of communication between deaf children who were developing well linguistically and their mothers, as compared to mothers and their less linguistically able deaf children (Greenstein et al., 1976). Exchanges for the mothers of achieving children were characterized by the use of fewer coercive motivational techniques, and by the greater tendency of the mothers to look at, vocalize with, and gesture to their children. They had less tendency to guard their children by touching, moving toward, or staying close. In return, there was a greater tendency of achieving deaf children to move toward or to look at their mothers. This description of the mother-child interaction seems one of a secure and developmentally mature mode. Amount of eye contact was seen as the best indicator of a secure relationship between mother and child. Such contact may be a predictor of linguistic success in deaf children. The mothers of linguistically successful deaf children apparently had made adjustments in communication activities which were compensating for the influence of the child's hearing impairment. Communication style may be as important to progress as the content of the communication itself.

Another factor which plays an important role in establishing communication is the personal hearing aid. The usual expectation is that a hearing aid will somehow make the child hear normally, much in the same way that glasses would make the child see normally. This expectation unfortunately is unwarranted because of the limitations of amplification systems as they interact with an impaired ear. First, one must be careful to make a distinction between the degree of hearing loss or the sensitivity problem the child has and his ability to recognize and sort out speech after it is amplified sufficiently. This latter so-called speech discrimination ability is absolutely crucial to language learning. The essence of speech recognition is the ability to encode the time, intensities, and frequencies of an auditory event simultaneously. With that capacity comes the potential for speech and language learning through the use

of hearing. Fitting a child with glasses to adjust the focus of light will normalize visual acuity so that the ability to detect and sort between visual
experiences is realized. Hearing aids, on the other hand, bring a limited range
of amplified information to the ear, but simple mechanical loudness can not
help improve the distortion caused by the damaged ear. In addition, the
hearing aid also introduces distortion which makes the listening task even
more difficult. The personal hearing aid does make an invaluable contribution
to the habilitation process, but teachers and audiologists must help parents
keep that contribution in perspective. It is a hearing *aid* which may enhance
the child's ability to learn speech and language through the auditory mode, but
the instrument by itself will do neither language teaching nor learning.

On the other hand, it is important to realize that even if a child is deaf, he
may still profit from a personal hearing aid. In other words, consideration
must always be given to use of amplification. It is unfortunately true that
hearing impaired or deaf persons are still too frequently described as persons
in whom the sense of hearing is not functional for language learning. It should
be axiomatic that the number of children who have no usable hearing is
comparatively small. Therefore, the relevant educational question is not *Why
use a hearing aid?* but *Why not use a hearing aid?*

It is evident that even small amounts of residual hearing if properly
amplified and used can be of benefit in providing information about the
pattern and segmentation of oral language. With this auditory experience, the
deaf child possesses some sense of how linguistic units are and should be
grouped together in spoken language. More importantly for many deaf children, a personal head-worn type of hearing aid may provide the vital voice-
to-ear link for self-monitoring of vocalizations and later speech behavior.
Regardless of the exact benefits which may eventually be derived from hearing aid use, the aid must be viewed by parents and professionals as an
ordinary, indeed routine, part of the management of childhood deafness.


## COMPONENTS OF A LANGUAGE DEVELOPMENT
## PROGRAM

In establishing a program that aims to initiate and develop language in
hearing impaired children, administrators must include five basic components: (1) a home-training program, (2) parent education and counseling, (3) a
language development curriculum using normal language development principles, (4) the availability of a variety of educational options, and (5) the use
of amplification for every child in the program.

Most child-parent communication interactions for very young children
occur within the context of joint activities usually initiated by the mother in

the home. The task of the educational program must be to assist parents to overcome communication barriers. This can best be done if the parents are not placed in a teacher role or in a school setting with their young children. Parents who are counseled to perform like teachers, using topics and materials unrelated to the normal home environment, may come to believe that the only language learning they can provide their children is that half-hour a day in a school environment. Parents should be encouraged and reinstructed (not instructed, for it is clear that most parents know how to encourage language development but are inhibited because of the factors previously mentioned) in language stimulation within the context of a home environment like their own. The concept of a visiting teacher or home visitor has been used in Great Britain, Scandinavia, Canada, Japan, and some parts of this country with success (Oyer, 1976). Unfortunately, it is not always feasible to have a visitor go directly to each home because of the cost of transportation, because of a small number of children as in a rural area, or because of parental objections to intrusion on the family. We do not believe that the use of a visiting teacher should be rejected out of hand, however. It has proved most effective in a highly populated area where properly trained and experienced teachers are available.

In lieu of home visitors, establishment of a homelike setting in a school or clinic where parents and children receive instruction together has been found successful (Simmons-Martin, 1976). The setting should be close to reality in terms of furnishings and routine in order to enable the knowledge gained in this setting to be transferred to the parents' own home. Visits by parents and children to the facility may be coupled with an occasional home visit after a firm trust relationship between parent and teacher has developed. This approach has the advantage of conserving professional travel time. Yet not all parents will be able to avail themselves of such a program. Family size and limited resources as well as psychological barriers may restrict its usefulness for some.

For many educational institutions, even the homelike setting is financially unrealistic. Often all that is available to the educational program for use with parents and very young children is a classroom or a therapy room in a school or clinic facility. In these instances, the teacher must create as much of a homelike atmosphere as possible, which includes removing school-oriented materials in favor of homelike furnishings. Parents can be encouraged to bring objects from home that can be used for training sessions. Most importantly, the atmosphere developed by the teacher must emphasize the style and pace of a home rather than the structure and authoritarian approach often characteristic of school.

The best facility available for a parent–child educational program is only as good as the personnel and quality of instruction within that facility. Thus, the second important component in a language developmental program is a well-organized and well-conceived parent education program that will allow (1) for the establishment of a healthy attitude in parents about their hearing impaired children, and (2) for the demonstration of strategies for encouraging language acquisition.

Most teachers have not been trained to deal with the emotional needs of parents. Lacking such training, one approach to counseling might be to employ a staff member, such as a social worker or clinical psychologist, or at the very least to retain such a person on a consultative basis. Such a professional should be able to provide educators with insight into the adjustment and motivation within families, as well as offer specialized services to those parents whose grief reactions are protracted.

Too frequently in the past, if the support of parent-infant programs fell to a school district, administrators did not include a social worker, probably because of the presumed excessive cost of such personnel. And yet these same school districts because of contemporary legislative and societal pressures are now being required to provide educational services for very young children. Administrators must be convinced that high initial costs can be offset by benefits derived from sound educational management in the early stages of a child's school life.

If a professional counselor is not available, the burden of managing complicated family problems falls on the teacher who is typically not prepared for such tasks. If the counseling aspect must be handled by the teacher, she must become a good listener. Many initial sessions may be spent just listening to the parent talk about experiences and feelings. Tears are common from fathers as well as from mothers. Most of us are uncomfortable with such deep feelings, but if we are to help parents, we must be able to identify and deal with feelings, both those of the parents as well as our own. Perhaps the word *empathy* is the best way to describe a productive reaction on the teacher's part. The teacher who deals with parents must also learn to be accepting of the diverse accommodations parents make in their struggle to accept their handicapped child. Parents simply do not do everything they *should*. Within the context of their home and their special family pressures, they may be doing all they can. The teacher must also come to understand her limitations. Many family situations are highly pathological, primarily because the parents had many problems before the discovery of deafness in their child. In those cases, the teacher must be alert to the need for referral to psychological support agencies and knowledgeable about the mechanisms for such referral within the community. More specific suggestions on parent education formats can be found in Northcott (1977).

It is often important that teachers pay attention not only to the parents, but to the complete family including siblings and extended family members such as grandparents. An effective program should provide mechanisms for exploring feelings with these individuals as well as the parents, and also provide additional information so that their efforts will be supportive of parental efforts. Teachers who do not want to deal with families and their feelings should not work in parent-infant programs.

From a counseling point of view, a second important goal is to help parents become the primary decision makers regarding the educational future of their child. This means that parents must be given information about all phases of the educational process, as well as opportunities to observe and then evaluate and discuss their observations. The teacher must accept that parent independence is imperative for any parent counseling program, even if parents make decisions with which the teacher does not agree. Under these circumstances, the teacher should give her best professional opinion about the course to follow while respecting the parents' right to make the final decision about their own child. In the final analysis, of course, it is the child's rights that are to be protected. If the teacher or educational authority believes strongly that the child's best interests are not being served, the professional should be aware of the due process channels available in most states, which are designed to ensure that each handicapped child's educational rights are preserved for him.

Parent instruction should be introduced almost immediately with each parent in conjunction with counseling and in ways that will ensure some success. Individual education, at first, is the most supportive approach. As the parents feel more comfortable, access to group activities should be offered, perhaps on a contract basis (Northcott, 1977). Nothing is a better stimulant to parents than the direct evidence that they can indeed communicate and relate to their deaf child. To achieve this end, they need to have an opportunity to observe others working with their child for modeling purposes. They also need to be observed by someone to obtain the benefit of constructive criticism. Videotaping is particularly useful in the latter aspect of the process if it is available.

Specifically, parents should be encouraged to incorporate normal communication development procedures into their styles: for example, (1) talking in short sentences with consistent vocabulary; (2) initially using prompting and expansion techniques, but as the child begins to talk, shifting to more sophisticated techniques such as questioning and modeling; (3) using highly intonated speech; (4) directing the child's attention to the topic of the conversation, and, having established the topic, shifting to comments about the topic and encouraging the child to use the same approach; (5) compensating for the auditory handicap of the child by positioning so that the child can see and hear the adult.

Let us imagine Mrs. A. sitting on the floor with 18-month-old Roberta, about to begin playing with a large colored ball. Mrs. A. catches Roberta's eye by holding the ball behind her and then suddenly bringing it out, smiling and holding it up, pointing to it, moving it near her mouth and then saying, "Oh, look here; here's the ball!" Her comment has two functions: first, it serves as a vehicle for a bright intonation contour; and second, it is a verbal way to establish the topic. Once having established the topic, Mrs. A. and Roberta can begin to react in the play situation. Mrs. A. says, rolling the ball, "Mother rolled the ball. Roberta roll the ball?" If the ball escapes from Roberta, mother responds with an appropriate utterance, "Roberta get the ball." Should Roberta attempt by gesture or voice to comment on the situation, Mrs. A. will respond by modeling or expanding what Roberta has attempted. This type of communication interplay is what mothers of hearing children do. Conversation or turn-taking is a fundamental aspect of language usage and should also be a part of language acquisition for hearing impaired children.

Many parents are self-conscious of their first attempts to perform under the direction of others. These first awkward moments are unavoidable. To ease the situation, the teacher should make it clear that the parent's best style is acceptable, and the exact emulation of the teacher is not necessary or desirable. When actual communication is initiated, parents often yearn for immediate success, and when it is not forthcoming, may react with comments such as *It's not working*, or *I don't know what to do; you do it*. Parents must be instructed in patience during the early months of work, while learning to be alert to the earliest signs of communication awareness by the child. Many helpful suggestions for this earliest time are available in publications by Simmons-Martin (1976), Northcott (1977), and Mavilya and Mignone (1977).

In regard to the third aspect of an early intervention program for deaf children, it is mandatory that the teacher who works with young deaf children be well instructed about normal language and speech development as the base upon which the content of language acquisition programs for deaf children are built. It is no longer possible to work with any kind of young language impaired child and be unaware or only minimally schooled in the contemporary literature in developmental psycholinguistics.

The fourth aspect of a viable parent-child language development program is the assurance that a variety of instructional options are available to any program. We surely do not believe any longer that deaf children should all be provided with the same educational experiences, or instructed in only one modality. This attitude is totally incompatible with the concept of individualization of instruction outlined in Chapter 1, and at the least it reinforces the methodological animosities which have plagued education of the deaf for far too long. Every preschool program for hearing impaired children should have available to it the possibility of pursuing through different communication modalities—whether aural-oral, total communication, or even sign language alone—the goal of a healthy, literate child.

It is well to clarify our position on total communication, a term that has come to assume a wide variety of meanings. We take the term to mean the aural-oral approach combined with some sort of visual sign system. Visual sign systems can be divided into at least three categories: (1) American Sign Language, the sign system used by deaf people among themselves; (2) the various sign language systems developed by educators of the deaf to reconcile American Sign Language with spoken English; and (3) fingerspelling alone, which utilizes separate hand positions for each letter of the alphabet, as with written language (see Chapter 1).

American Sign Language has only been recently studied by linguists (Wilbur, 1976). These studies indicate that American Sign Language is not a debased form of spoken English, but rather a separate language with its own unique lexical, syntactic, semantic, and pragmatic bases. Many of those studying American Sign Language view the sign language systems used in schools as *pidgin* systems designed to reconcile American Sign Language and spoken English but incompletely representing either language. Pidgin languages, in general, including school-based American Sign Language, tend not to be used for social communication. Consequently, there is a controversy as to which system should be used in total communication. Since American Sign Language does not parallel spoken English, its use in so-called simultaneous instructional settings must be questioned. Such a situation is not unlike hearing French while simultaneously seeing Swahili, a task which may be possible for persons skilled in both languages, but hardly conducive to the learning of either, especially by a young child. On the other hand, use of any pidgin variety of American Sign Language presents a system that is not particularly rich in its own organization and does not actually provide a system equivalent to spoken English. The use of fingerspelling alone as part of total communication has precedence, but may be questioned in the early stages of language development for many children who do not have firm notions about symbolization. In addition, the timing problem in simultaneous presentation of spoken and fingerspelled English seems to lead inevitably to distortion in one or the other system even when presented by the most skilled of communicators.

Because of these limitations, careful consideration should be given to the type of sign system incorporated into total communication instruction. For some children, exclusive use of American Sign Language may be most reasonable to ensure that they gain mastery of any symbol system. The effects of mixing visual and auditorially based systems for instruction and/or for expression are still unclear. The blanket use of total communication should be approached as cautiously as the uncritical application of aural-oral instruction.

Regardless of the communication system employed with a given child, the procedures already discussed for developing language and establishing parent-oriented programs are basic to any language development program.

Consistent use of amplification constitutes the fifth element of any well-organized language initiation program for hearing impaired children. Every program for the hearing impaired should have complete audiological services available to it including informed evaluation of auditory function and potential, facilities for measurement of aided performance, facilities for electroacoustic assessment of each hearing aid, and educational-audiological follow-up. Each child must be evaluated at the earliest possible date by an audiologist familiar with young children to determine his minimum response levels for speech signals and for pure tones, as well as to obtain estimates of speech processing potential particularly in the aided mode. Recommendations regarding the characteristics of wearable hearing aids should be obtained as soon as possible by the cooperative efforts of the audiologist and the parent educator. As important as ensuring the early proper fit of personal hearing aids is the development of routine procedures for monitoring each hearing aid's electroacoustic performance. The rather unfortunate record of hearing aid dysfunction in children's personal aids has been continually documented (Gaeth and Lounsburg, 1966; Zink, 1972; Schell, 1976). One need not be reminded that if the basic component of auditory development is not stabilized, any subsequent auditory program, however consistently applied, will not achieve the desired effects. Routine hearing reevaluation, including impedance measurements, must also be scheduled to ensure that unnoticed changes in hearing levels, middle ear function, or hearing aid suitability do not occur. In some cases, recommendations might be made that air-conduction aids be supplemented with a vibrotactile device with the expectation that tactual cues can be of value in the development of speech and language performance.

The best audiological evaluation and the most informed hearing aid selection process are of no value if parents and teachers do not make aggressive use of amplification. Just ensuring that the child has his hearing aid on in the morning does not constitute effective use of the hearing aid. Any child with a severe hearing loss has to be taught to hear through a hearing aid, to sort speech from noise, to recognize his own voice, and to compare other language and speech models with his own efforts. The rules for aggressive use of a personal hearing aid are the same as for any amplification system. The primary signal must be put directly into the microphone, at a louder level than background noise. This primary signal should be a real speech event, to our way of thinking. To ensure that the speech signal is louder than the background noise, the teacher's or parent's mouth should be no farther than 18 inches from the child's hearing aid microphone. Working consistently at close range, with either a personal hearing aid or a classroom amplifier microphone, will ensure that speech of a conversational loudness will be more intense than most competing signals. It should go without saying that such intimate contact between speaker and child must be actively maintained over a period of months or even years if the benefits of amplification are to be realized. Some other important observations about classroom acoustics and hearing aid performance have been summarized by Ross (1972).

## FAMILIES WITH SPECIAL NEEDS

Three types of families with hearing impaired children pose special management problems. In the first, the parents are themselves deaf and have a deaf child; in the second, the deaf child has been identified only at an older age; and in the third, the deaf child has little or no residual hearing.

Parents who are deaf are no less susceptible to grief reactions about deafness in their offspring than normally hearing parents. The primary difference seems to be that although deaf parents require as much opportunity to express their feelings as any other parent, they may have less difficulty in recognizing the child's potential for life adjustment than persons who have little if any experience with severe hearing impairment. There are, of course, certain cautions in working with many deaf parents which are not of concern when dealing with normally hearing parents. Many deaf adults use American Sign Language for family communication. It is a reasonable expectation that their children will learn and use this language as well. The parent-child educational program will have to deal with this problem, perhaps by asking the parents to change their language style, which is probably the least satisfactory approach, or perhaps by approaching the problem as if it were one of second-language learning, viewing American Sign Language as the primary language with spoken English, pidgin sign, or some combination as the second language. In any case, persons who choose to work in parent-child programs should be conversant with sign language or have access to interpreters if the majority of deaf parents are to be successfully included in parent education programs. Obviously, deaf parents who can speak and wish to have their children exposed to an aural-oral program will also contact professionals. As in every other case, the parents' desires relative to the language system they want their children to learn should be respected.

It must be recognized too that deaf parents or any parent for that matter may have different expectations about education than teachers do. Many deaf parents were sent to residential schools at a young age, and thus see nothing wrong in expecting schools to accept full responsibility for teaching, even raising, their child. Such an attitude may cause parents to be very uninvolved in the instructional strategies discussed in this chapter. Some deaf parents may also be unfavorably disposed toward consistent use of hearing aids. The parents themselves may have tried to use a hearing aid with unsatisfactory results and thus do not value amplification or understand its role.

On the other hand, the child's use of an aid may serve as a way of reintroducing amplification to the parents (Connor, 1976). The intelligibility of the deaf parents' speech may be an issue relative to their serving as oral language models. The possible consequences of such a problem should be discussed openly so that the most satisfactory solution can be arrived at which ensures that the feelings of the deaf parent himself are considered.

The family with a late identified hearing impaired child presents certain problems. Valuable learning time has been lost which may never be recovered if the child is identified after the age of 3 years. The parents of a deaf child who has not developed communication may have unrealistic expectations or attitudes which completely block their ability to relate normally to the child.

It has been argued frequently, although not conclusively, that because of the child's loss of time during the early critical period of language growth the easiest way to ensure linguistic development is to elect non-oral instructional modes, even if the child has a sizeable amount of usable hearing. As with all educational problems, circumstances surrounding the child and his family should be examined before an irrevocable decision about which educational strategies to employ is made.

The child who apparently has little or no residual hearing presents another particularly difficult problem in a parent-child program. First, unless the absence of hearing is clearly established, hearing aid usage should not be disregarded prematurely. Audiograms, although valuable, do not give a complete picture of usable hearing. Minimum response levels with amplification-aided audiograms should be obtained, as well as evidence from a period of instruction with a personal hearing aid before the child is declared a purely visual learner. Conversely, the difficulty of developing comprehensible oral language and speech in a totally deaf child should not be minimized in parent counseling, especially relative to the commitment of time, personal energy, and often monies involved.

In summary, we can say that the ingredients of a successful program for establishing communication in the young hearing impaired child include: (1) an accepting and informed parent, (2) dialogue rather than one-way communication, and (3) encouragement of listening behavior through intelligent use of proper personal amplification, supplemented by whichever communication mode is best suited to the child.

## PARENT-TEACHER COMMUNICATION

As we learned in Chapter 1, PL 94-142 requires participation of parents in the formulation of IEPs, a task which requires relatively frequent communication between parents and school personnel. Children eventually enter educational programs that emphasize child-centered education wherein the child's day is shared with another adult about whom the parent may know very little, and may choose to know little. The teacher also may possess some unfortunate assumptions about parents, even though she may be a parent herself. As the teacher learns about the child and how to communicate with him, one communication barrier is broken down, but another barrier between parent and teacher may be built.

Meaningful communication through creation of a teacher-parent-child communication netword is sometimes difficult to establish as part of the official business of school. If meaningful communication is to occur between parents and teacher, there must be opportunities for mutual interaction apart from the stress usually associated with discussing individual child behavior in schoolrooms. The teacher must not assume that parents who have worked to establish communication in their children do not want a role in the child's education. The parents must continue to view themselves as responsible for their child. The contextual information that both teacher and parent can furnish each other to help in interpretation of the young deaf child's utterances is so vital that communication between home and school must be established early and maintained consistently.

One of the most effective mechanisms for communication is a well-organized parent group. If the school does not have a parent group, one of the first orders of business should be its establishment. A get-together of parents from a single class can be just as effective as one for a whole school. The one aspect to be avoided in establishing parent groups is domination by teachers. Therefore, it is important that parent groups be run *by parents* in cooperation with teachers. The programs or activities of any parent group should be directed toward parent needs and interests, and toward unstressful communication between parent and teacher as well. Parents should be consulted about organizational matters such as how frequently to meet, the types of speakers, and the topics for discussion. It should be recognized, of course, that even under the most ideal circumstances, a 100 percent response from parents will not be possible. Instead, participation by a resspresentative range of parents in the program might be a more reasonable goal with the expectation that attendance will shift depending on the topic, speaker, or mode of communication needed.

Parent organizations are useful, but they do not meet the needs of every parent and teacher. Individual teachers have to learn how to encourage meaningful dialogues with their classroom parents. Such dialogues should not focus on the child's academic progress or lack of it. The teacher might initiate contacts by developing room programs where the children perform some activity for their parents' entertainment. Creating a play, preparing an international luncheon or dinner, or putting on a fashion show might be considered. Discussions with parents should focus on the unit activities or the child's performance on that day, not on difficult behavior that any child shows or how poorly he is doing academically. Meetings with parents should also occur off campus as at picnics, trips to the zoo, or even a party at the teacher's home. Parents should be made to feel free to visit the classroom and be made welcome when they do visit.

There are times, however, when the teacher and parent must meet formally to discuss the child's academic progress. Most schools schedule regular visitations for a full year rather than forcing teachers to call a meeting with the parents only when their child has done something wrong or is doing poorly academically. If such meetings are not established on at least a quarterly or biannual basis, they should be instituted with the schedule posted tentatively at the beginning of the school year. In this way, the family knows that they will have opportunities to meet with the teacher throughout the year.

At these formal parent meetings, it is important that the teacher give as complete a picture of the child in the classroom as possible indicating positive as well as negative aspects of behavior. Dwelling on the management difficulties the child presents, or the lack of intelligibility of his speech, or how far behind he is academically can make this an unwelcome experience for both parents and teachers. The teacher must be willing to listen to parents and their feelings about their child's progress and about his handicap. Feelings about deafness and grief over its appearance do not occur exclusively in parents of preschool children.

One of the major difficulties teachers have in conferences is an inclination to use educational jargon. Often parents do not understand what is being said about their child, but are too embarrassed to say so. It is a good tactic to build into each conference some opportunities for the parents to rephrase or explain what they understand about their child's progress or behavior. Every conference should end with a summary statement about what has been reported and possible follow-up procedures, with both the parents and teacher agreeing to its content. Although formal written acceptance of IEP recommendations is mandated under the due process requirements of PL 94-142, what we are speaking about here is a more informal consensus that would be sent in letter form to the parent and would serve as the basis of discussion in the next conference. With this strategy, parents have a permanent version of the discussion that will allow them to review issues at home without concern about whether they are making a good impression on the teacher. The teacher also has reference material available, so that she does not have to rely on memory alone.

Each parent must assume his proper responsibility in these conferences as well. Nothing is more frustrating to development of a relationship than a parent or teacher who sits and says nothing. The other member of the dialogue cannot know how much information is being received or more importantly what each person's feelings are about the information being imparted. Parents must feel free to ask questions when they don't understand, or at least try to say something in response to the teacher's comments so that levels of understanding can be explored. It is important that both teacher and parent try to come to meetings or conferences without preconceived notions of the outcome. Teachers are not infallible, so some of their information may be incorrect or incomplete, but they are not adversaries ordinarily. By the same token, parents are variable in their understandings of educational problems and in their skill in dealing with the communication problems of their child. If it appears that mutual trust relations are not being built, a third party, such as a social worker or visiting teacher, may be asked to contact the parents for arbitration of misunderstandings. It is important that there be mutual respect for the opinions of each party, but it is unnecessary that there be complete agreement on all educational issues.

One of the outcomes of formal or informal parent-teacher conferences could be some agreement as to how the parent might contribute to the school program. Teachers often need supplementary help. Parents may be especially valuable in special school or class settings where large amounts of individual work are essential. Teachers might outline a series of tasks for the parents, presenting them to all parents during formal school conferences. It would be understood that parents need not be expected to work with their own children, but might assist in another classroom with children the age of their own. Strategies might include using the parents to plot baseline behaviors for a child in preparation for initiation of a behavior management program. In that way the parents learn a technique of observation and recording that they might be able to apply in another way to their home situation. When the full range of activities is listed, parents would have an opportunity to contract for the specific activities or times they could assist. This written contract between parent and teacher could be reviewed periodically to assess the usefulness or reality of the bargain, with renegotiated contracts developed to represent the parent's growth in skill or involvement. It is important, of course, that parents not be forced to follow through with the contract under pain of punishment or threat of discontinuation of a child's program, but rather that such contracts be good faith agreements outlining the commitments the parents really believe they can meet.

Under the best of circumstances, not all parents can be involved. Many children in the urban settings come to school without clearly defined caretakers, because of the absence of parents, extended family situations, or foster home placement. Under such circumstances, it may be necessary to deal with social service personnel, older siblings, or relatives. It is important that every parent or parent surrogate communicate with his child's teachers, whether it be through face-to-face contact, through notes, or by telephone or tape recorder.

In conclusion, establishing and maintaining parent-teacher communication is necessary to ensure the deaf child's rights to appropriate, beneficial educational opportunities.

## REFERENCES

Berko-Gleason J: Code switching in children's language. In Moore T (ed): Cognitive Development and the Acquisition of Language. New York, Academic Press, 1973

Bruner J: The ontogenesis of speech acts. Child Lang 2:1–19, 1975

Connor L: New Directions in Infant Programs for the Deaf. Washington, D.C., A. G. Bell Assoc., 1976

Corson H: Comparing deaf children of oral deaf parents and deaf parents using manual communication, with deaf children of hearing parents on academic, social, and communicative functioning. Unpublished doctoral dissertation, University of Cincinnati, 1973

Farwell C: The language spoken to children. Hum Dev 18:288–309, 1975

Ferguson C: Baby talk in six languages. Am Anthropol 66:103–114, 1964

Gaeth J and Lounsburg E: Hearing aids and children in elementary schools. J Speech Hear Disord 31:238–245, 1966

Granowsky S and Krossner W: Kindergarten teachers as models for children's speech. J Exp Ed 38:23–38, 1970

Greenstein J, Greenstein B, McConville K, and Stellini L: Mother-Infant Communication and Language Acquisition in Deaf Infants. New York, Lexington School for the Deaf, 1976

Kubler-Ross E (ed): Death: The Final Stage of Growth. Englewood Cliffs, N.J., Prentice-Hall, 1975

Landes J: Speech addressed to children: issues and characteristics of parental input. Lang Learn 25:355–379, 1975

Mavilya M and Mignone B: Educational Strategies for the Youngest Hearing Impaired Children. New York, Lexington School for the Deaf, 1977

Moerk E: Changes in verbal child-mother interactions with increasing language skills of the child. J Psycholinguist Res 3:101–116, 1974

Moerk E: Verbal interactions between children and their mothers during the preschool years. Dev Psychol 11:788–794, 1975

Moses K: Mourning theory and parents of hearing impaired children. Presentation, 3rd

Annual Jean W. Rothenberg Symposium on Hearing Impairment, Cincinnati, 1977

Northcott W: Curriculum Guide: Hearing-Impaired Children, Birth to Three Years, and Their Parents (ed 2). Washington, D.C., A. G. Bell Assoc., 1977

Oyer H (ed): Communication for the Hearing Handicapped: An International Perspective. Baltimore, University Park Press, 1976

Phillips J: Syntax and vocabulary of mothers' speech to young children: age and sex comparisons. Child Dev 44:182–185, 1973

Ross M: Classroom acoustics and speech intelligibility. In Katz J (ed): Handbook of Clinical Audiology. Baltimore, Williams & Wilkins Co., 1972

Schell Y: Electro-acoustic evaluation of hearing aids worn by public school children. Audiol Hear Eval 2:9–11, 1976

Simmons-Martin A: Early intervention programs. In Bolton B (ed): Psychology of Deafness for Rehabilitation Counselors. Baltimore, University Park Press, 1976

Snow C: Mothers' speech to children learning language. Child Dev 43:549–565, 1972

Snow C, Arlmann-Rupp A, Hassing Y, et al.: Mothers' speech in three social classes. J Psycholinguist Res 5:1–20, 1975

Wilbur R: The linguistics of manual language and manual systems. In Lloyd L (ed): Communication Assessment and Intervention Strategies. Baltimore, University Park Press, 1976

Wright B: Physical Disability: A Psychological Approach. New York, Harper, 1960

Wulbert M, Inglis S, Kriegsmann E, and Mills B: Language delay and associated mother-child interactions. Dev Psychol 11:61–70, 1975

Zink G: Hearing aids children wear: a longitudinal study of performance. Volta Rev 74:41–46, 1972

# 4
# Language—The Basic Tool

It is commonly known that severe hearing impairment adversely affects language acquisition. The question might be asked as to why this is considered such an important observation. In most societies, language allows people to transmit thoughts to other human beings, to identify their innermost feelings, to aid in solving their problems, to explore the world beyond their reach and the years beyond their time. A deficit in language mastery strikes at the core of successful living in society by creating barriers to adequate interpersonal relationships, to development of healthy self-concepts, and to the ability to acquire knowledge and to understand the world.

Since the language of most societies is heard and spoken, the focus of this chapter will be on spoken English and its acquisition in normally hearing and hearing impaired children. Such an orientation does not mean that a language based on visual transmission is any less a language. Since most educators of the hearing impaired view their main objective to be the acquisition by deaf persons of a symbol system like spoken English it seems reasonable to focus on auditorily based language.

Regardless of the symbol system employed with hearing impaired children certain factors need to be mentioned. First, the role that language serves in the important task of encoding experience and facilitating cognitive growth should be recognized. Acquisition of any language system is never an end in itself, but rather is a means to induct children into full human experiences. Consequently, it makes little sense to compartmentalize language instruction into "language" periods in a school setting. Language must become the means of communicating information contained in the entire curriculum throughout the entire school and nonschool day. No aspect of school or home experience can be exempt from concern about language usage and opportunities for learning.

The second factor to remember is that for normal children, language is learned, not "taught." It has been repeatedly demonstrated that children through the process of continuous exposure, albeit structured, come to learn the language forms being used around them (Bloom, 1970; Menyuk, 1971; Bowerman, 1976). Clearly, parents do not teach their children in the rote learning sense. Instead, they provide suitable models for their children, from which each child extracts the regularities of language in his own way to achieve comprehension and production mastery (Bowerman, 1976). If the normally hearing child is individually responsible for knowing and using language, is the hearing impaired child supposed to be any less responsible, to have any less internal knowledge about language? If anything, the deaf child requires more personal linguistic resources since he may have to actively seek information rather than being able to passively receive it as a normal child does from the myriad of contemporary auditory communication media. Even reading, which should ideally be most helpful to deaf persons, is too frequently closed to the deaf child because of his lack of general linguistic skill. Language to be acquired needs to be tied to experience in a form that is compatible with the child's cognitive growth. Accordingly, the task of the teacher or parent is to provide an environment that will facilitate acquisition and development of language.

We believe that the teacher can best contribute to this process of language acquisition in deaf children by having a rather complete understanding of language as a system of normal language developmental processes.

This chapter will discuss (1) the nature of language, (2) how first language develops in normally hearing children, (3) how hearing impairment seems to disrupt the normal development language process, (4) the effects of sign on language acquisition, and (5) how professionals in education of the hearing impaired have attempted to forestall or correct the effects of hearing impairment on the normal developmental process.

It is important to become familiar with both the nature of a language system as well as how language systems are acquired and develop. By understanding the organization of a language, any teacher may come to understand more completely the problems encountered by deaf children who must master a full range of linguistic rules if they are ever to be classified as language users. A simple knowledge of the adult concept of language rules is not enough, however. Children master language rules in their own fashion. They do not learn language in the adult form immediately, but rather acquire approximations of rules in a developmental fashion. Children may learn one rule before another, if one rule is observed to be more difficult than another or more meaningful than another, or even more useful for expressing the concepts children have in mind. By examining language development data, the teacher will have a guide as to what could be presented first to children learning language, as well as a reasonable idea of what to expect from hearing impaired children as they develop reception and expression of language. This latter information is particularly important for it gives the teacher some guidelines for judging progress in language acquisition rather than insisting upon adultlike performance from deaf children, when it is not expected from normally hearing children at similar stages of language learning.

## LANGUAGE—ITS FORM AND CONTENT

During the 1960s and 1970s, impressive descriptions of the constituents of language have emerged from the field of linguistics, the discipline devoted to understanding and describing parameters of language and its use in communication. These contemporary descriptions have led us to understand that language is a system for encoding meaning. Linguists have formulated four components or parameters for describing language, which, when merged, allow the individual speaker of any language to comprehend and produce linguistic forms acceptable to other members of the same language community. These four basic parameters of language are (1) the morphophonemic or sound component; (2) the syntactic or grammatical component; (3) the semantic or meaning component; and (4) the pragmatic or communicative component (Dale, 1976). A speaker of any language must apply each of these components in a standard way if his communication efforts are to be acceptable to other members of his social group or language community.

Each of the aforementioned components consists of sets of underlying regularities which are consistent across all possible sentences of a language. These regularities are designated as the rules of the language; thus, the child must master the morphophonemic, syntactic, semantic, and pragmatic rules of the language, and must learn how they interface with one another to allow for the production of grammatically complex, communicatively useful sentences. Once he has reasonable mastery of each of these sets of rules and their interrelationships, a child can be designated as a member of a linguistic community, sharing with that community the means for communicating his own feelings, ideas, and discoveries to others.

What is the nature of each of these four components? The morphophonemic component of language refers to those rules that govern the formulation and production of the sound system of any language and how these sounds are joined together to form words (Chomsky and Halle, 1968). These rules allow the speaker to identify and produce the individual sounds of his language, as well as provide the speaker with the ability to arrange these sounds into meaningful vocal relationships. The smallest significant sound units of any language are referred to as phonemes. The study of the recognition and production of these individual speech sounds in English or other languages will not be dealt with here. The reader is referred to contemporary resources on speech development in normal and hearing impaired children if more information on this subject is desired (Menyuk, 1971; Ling, 1976; Stark, 1977).

The smallest meaningful units of the morphophonemic component are called morphemes. In languages, there can be two types of morphemes, free and bound (Thomas and Kintgen, 1974). Free morphemes are those morphemes that can exist alone and still convey meaning. In English, examples of free morphemes are *bird*, *girl*, *pretty*, and *run*. Bound morphemes, on the other hand, have meaning only when affixed to other morphemes. In English, the /-s/ in *birds*, the /-ed/ in *played*, or the /dis-/ in *dislike* are examples of bound morphemes. The combination of free and bound morphemes gives rise to the vocabulary items possible in a spoken language. Thus, the child must learn the rules for forming morphemic units or words by binding or joining significant units, as well as the rules for recognizing the boundaries between one morphemic unit and another.

The ability to arrange sounds and words into meaningful spoken strings, or sentences, comes from knowledge of syntax, the second component of spoken language (Thomas and Kintgen, 1974). Syntax is the ability to organize morphemes into whole utterances that follow an allowable, predictable order. These predictable or allowable word orders are called sentences. Sentences can be further organized into larger units called discourse (Chafe, 1972). Morphophonemic rules of English or of any other language are best learned in the context of or in conjunction with the syntactic rules. This suggests that the fundamental unit of language should be considered minimally to be the sentence. Children seem to decode on a sentence basis; they do not seem to hear words alone, nor do they seem to need to decode on a word-by-word basis (Houston, 1972). As they learn about sentences, they are learning the major components of those sentences, the order in which these components can appear, and the specific words or vocabulary items which constitute these components (Streng, 1972).

What rules do children have to learn about syntax that will aid in the development of connected language or sentences? Two levels of syntax have been postulated, the base structure level and the transformational level (Chomsky, 1957; Chomsky, 1965). For purposes of our discussion, the base structure will refer to the key or basic rules of the language which allow for the comprehension and production of simple sentence patterns. Five basic, simple, or kernel sentence patterns have been identified by Streng (1972) and will be used in this chapter to discuss the various aspects of base structure ordering. These five basic sentence patterns are as follows:

Sentence pattern I: NP + AUX + VI (intransitive verb sentence)
Sentence pattern II: NP + AUX + VT + NP (transitive verb sentence)
Sentence pattern III: NP + BE + NP (predicate nominative sentence)
Sentence pattern IV: NP + BE + ADJ (predicate adjective sentence)
Sentence pattern V: NP + BE + ADV (predicate adverb sentence)

Each pattern is followed by descriptors that characterize the nature of the actual sentences that might be spoken. NP (noun phrase) refers to the constituent Determiner + Noun, whereas AUX (auxiliary) refers to the use of *to be* forms, modals, or forms such as *do* as helping verbs, as well as the application of tense. The reader desiring more detailed information on these grammatical notions can consult Streng (1972), Hargis (1976), and Russell, Quigley, and Power (1976).

All remaining sentences are seen as derivations or operations on these basic sentence patterns (Thomas and Kintgen, 1974). When one applies a transformation to a base sentence, one produces a more complex sentence. Transformations are grammatical operations which result in deleted constituents, added constituents, rearranged constituents, substituted constituents, embedded basic sentence patterns one into another resulting in a single complex sentence, or conjoined sentences resulting again in a more complex pattern. Examples of each of these operations are shown in Table 4-1. By applying various types of transformations, it is possible to generate complex sentences. Before anyone can be classified as a user of language, he must master base structure along with the transformational aspect in order to have the potential to produce all the possible sentences in any language.

The third component of language is the semantic component, which refers to the system that underlies or governs the meanings conveyed by syntax. Each syntactic arrangement conveys meaning quite aside from the dictionary meaning of the words in that arrangement. The choice of which syntactic arrangement to use at a particular time depends on the semantic intent one wishes to convey. In other words, one formulates or selects syntactic structures because one wishes to convey certain meanings to the listener; likewise, the listener decodes syntactic structures in an effort to understand the meaning(s) the speaker is trying to transmit. Semantics or meaning generally takes precedence over syntactic usage since semantic intent determines which language forms are selected for a sentence.

Meaning exists on at least two levels (Bach and Harms, 1968). The first is the lexical meaning level. Lexical meanings refer to the specific meanings that free and bound morphemes carry, the dictionary meanings of individual words. When one is trying to encode or decode sentences, the meaning of

**Table 4-1**
Transformational Operations Possible
in Spoken English

| | |
|---|---|
| Deletion | Contraction: |
| | I didn't want him to go. |
| | I did not want him to go. |
| | Conjunction reduction: |
| | I want to go and see the movie. |
| | I want to go and I want to see the movie. |
| Addition | Negation: |
| | I did not want to go. |
| | I did want to go. |
| | Do- insertion: |
| | I did want to go. |
| | I wanted to go. |
| Rearrangement | Yes-no question: |
| | Is the boy hungry? |
| | The boy is hungry. |
| | Adverb shift: |
| | Last night I went to the movie. |
| | I went to the movie last night. |
| Substitution | Pronoun: |
| | He went to the movie. |
| | The boy went to the movie. |
| | Wh- question: |
| | Who went to the movie? |
| | Somebody went to the movie. |
| Embedding | Relative clause: |
| | The boy who was sick went home. |
| | The boy was sick. |
| | The boy went home. |
| | Nominalization: |
| | Japan's destruction of China was terrible. |
| | Japan destroyed China. |
| | Something was terrible. |
| Conjoining | Coordinating conjunction: |
| | I ate an apple and a pear. |
| | I ate an apple. |
| | I ate a pear. |
| | Subordinate conjunction: |
| | When it rains, I get blue. |
| | It rains. |
| | I get blue. |

each word in the sentence must be congruent with the meaning of all the other words, or the sentence may not be understood. For example, in the sentence *The ball burped.*, the choice of verb was not compatible with features that we ordinarily associate with ball, such as being alive.

The second level of meaning is combinational meaning, which refers to the meaning created when morphemes are joined together into sentences. Combinational meanings as previously suggested are independent of the meanings of the specific lexical items in a sentence.

Combinational meanings are governed in part by the semantic roles which classes of words play within sentences (Chafe, 1970). Certain semantic roles occur frequently in English. For example, in English, there seem to be three types or semantic classifications of verbs. Verbs that represent external activities such as *walking*, *talking*, or *touching* are called action verbs. Process verbs are verbs linked to activities of the mind such as *thinking*, *liking*, *loving*, or *experiencing*. Verbs which describe a state of being or changes in states of being are referred to as stative verbs. Examples of the latter category include *being*, *seem*, *remain*, and *become*.

The sentence's verb(s) determines which semantic role each of the nouns plays within that sentence. The person (noun) who performs action in a sentence is called a *mover* or *actor* (Bloom, Lightbown, and Hood, 1975) indicating that he has performed the action implied by the action verb. If, on the other hand, he performs the action on an object, he becomes an *agent*; the object he performs the action on is called the *patient*. In English, one need not always indicate the agent. For instance, in the sentence, *The vase broke*, *broke* is an action verb, but it is obvious that the vase did not break itself, but that someone broke it. The patient *vase* is indicated; the agent is only implied. The hearing impaired child must come to understand semantic notions such as this early in language development if he is to have mature use of language.

Nouns may play other types of semantic roles such as those mentioned above: *instrument* is the object that someone (the agent) uses to complete the action; *complement* is an object that comes into being as a result of an action; a person who has an internal experience (process verb) is an *experiencer*; the place where something occurs is a *locative*; the time when something occurs becomes a *temporal* noun; an object that simply exists without action being performed on it is an *entity* (Brown, 1973).

How deaf children might easily misunderstand some of these semantic roles can be illustrated. Jay, an 8-year-old deaf boy with limited language, is given a set of watercolors and a piece of paper and is asked to paint a picture. He looks about the room, dabs his paint brush into green, walks over to a magazine cover hanging on the wall, and paints over it. Jay understood ''paint'' only as an action performed on an object, not as an action that could result in the production or creation of an object (complement). In other words, Jay had interpreted the instructions as an agent-action-patient relationship rather than as an agent-action-complement relationship.

Deaf children often confuse the verbs *make* and *arrange*. Make is a complement taking verb, whereas arrange is a patient taking verb. If something is made, it is brought into creation, whereas things that are arranged generally describes changing the form of items that already exist. Often this confusion can be corrected when the child learns that there are two specific types of action verbs, verbs that result in the creation of something and verbs that result in a change in form or appearance.

Children must learn the lexical meaning of individual words in order to have content to talk about, but unless the semantic roles that words can play are also learned, meaning in language will not be mastered. Each of the kernel or basic sentences may convey a variety of semantic relationships. These relationships are summarized in Table 4-2. Teaching syntactic relationships

**Table 4-2**

Possible Semantic Relationships Expressed Through
Sentence Patterns I Through V

| Pattern | Example |
| --- | --- |
| Sentence pattern I | |
| Mover-action | John runs. |
| Experiencer-process | The fish died. |
| Patient-action | The glass broke. |
| Patient-process | The fence rusted. |
| Sentence pattern II | |
| Agent-action-patient | John broke the glass. |
| Agent-action-complement | John painted a masterpiece. |
| Instrument-action-patient | The key unlocked the door. |
| Experiencer-process-patient | John liked the house. |
| Experiencer-process-complement | John thought up the idea. |
| Beneficiary-process-patient | John owns the house. |
| Patient-process-instrument | The plant needs the water. |
| Sentence pattern III | |
| Entity-stative-entity (equivalent) | Mrs. Case was the president. |
| Sentence pattern IV | |
| Entity-stative-attribute | The ball is red. |
| Sentence pattern V | |
| Entity-stative-locative | John is in the park. |
| Entity-stative-temporal | The party is on Friday. |
| Entity-stative-reason | The vaccination is for measles. |
| Entity-stative-beneficiary | The gift is for Mary. |

alone is not sufficient for mastery of language. The appropriate types of semantic relationships must also be specified to keep the linguistic tasks consistent from teaching experience to teaching experience.

The semantic roles described above relate to one aspect of syntax, base relationships. Do transformations carry meaning too? Transformations can be divided into those operations that carry meaning and those that do not. Examples of English transformations that do not carry specific meaning are contraction and the insertion of the grammatical unit *do* in order to perform the negation and question transformations on those base sentences that do not have the AUX position already filled. Almost all the remaining transformations do have semantic functions which are as varied as those for base syntactic relationships shown in Table 4-2.

The multiple semantic intents of a transformational form can be illustrated by considering negation. Negation can be conveyed through the use of the negation transformation, which involves introduction of *not* into the sentence, or through use of negative determiners, pronouns, or adverbs such as *no*, *nobody*, or *never*. Structurally, negative sentences appear to be comparable, but careful examination of the intent of such sentences shows at least three distinct semantic applications, namely, nonexistence, rejection, and denial (Bloom, 1970). Nonexistence refers to the notion that something does not currently exist, or perhaps has never existed. When a child says *no bananas*, he may mean that there are no bananas where he is looking, or that the bananas that are normally there are absent. Rejection refers to the situation in which the child may say *no play* to mean *stop playing* or *I don't want to play*. The third semantic notion conveyed by negation is denial, which refers to the concept expressed by the child who says *no truck, it car* to indicate that he is holding a car, not a truck.

The final component of language to be considered is the pragmatic or communication component. This refers specifically to the truth or logic of sentences and their appropriateness to the situation as they are used by a speaker in dialogue with others. Pragmatics is specifically concerned with propositions, performatives, and presuppositions (Bates, 1976).

Propositions refer to the predicate-subject relationships that are contained within sentences. Each subject of a sentence is considered an argument and each attribute commenting on the subject is a predicate; thus, sentences consist of the juxtaposition of arguments with other arguments and/or attributes. In essence, this is the basic logic that exists within a sentence which, like semantic roles, is usually determined by the verb of the sentence. For instance, *Mary is beautiful.* is considered to consist of an argument (*Mary*) and an attribute (*beautiful*) related to the argument by the verb *is*. Whereas in the sentence *Mary hit John*, both *Mary* and *John* are arguments which are related in a specific way by the verb *hit*. Thus, deaf children must come to understand what the arguments of a sentence are and how they relate with one another and with comments (attributes) on them.

Performatives refer to the rules of linguistic use. Each sentence spoken is intended to have specific effects on the listener, a function which each language learning child must master. For instance, the sentence *Why don't you go outside?* may have two intended effects. One may be to solicit information from the listener; the other may be to command behavior. Hearing impaired children often lack use or understanding of performatives which are frequently cued by intonation patterns with the result that they are often seen as lacking social awareness. This lack of information about performative functions may be described by professionals as concreteness usually defined as literal interpretation of what is being said to them.

Presupposition refers to the amount of information the speaker presupposes the listener to have before he begins a conversation. The speaker's choice of linguistic principles is determined by the kind and variety of information he expects his audience to possess. For example, if the speaker believes the listener to know a lot about the topic, he may use short, simple sentences loaded with pronouns. Whereas if the listener is believed to have limited information, the speaker may tend to employ a considerable number of quantifiers, qualifiers, relative clauses, and perhaps even subordinate clauses to ensure topic clarification.

Thus, it is possible to conceive of a hearing impaired child who may have good syntax and semantic control, but not know how or when to use language. These latter two skills are vital to the hearing impaired child who is to be mainstreamed into classes for normally hearing children. Since communication competence is best obtained through social interaction with others, early mainstreaming opportunities should be provided all hearing impaired children so they can have the chance for developing these pragmatic understandings with the eventual goal being complete integration with supportive assistance from trained personnel.

## NORMAL LANGUAGE DEVELOPMENT WITH
## IMPLICATIONS FOR THE HEARING IMPAIRED

It is now generally accepted that children are born with a predisposition to learn language; that is, human beings at birth have vast cognitive and linguistic potentials to learn and think with language (Lenneberg, 1975). In Chapter 2, it is noted that researchers such as Slobin (1973) have been able to suggest specific ways in which cognitive abilities allow children to pay attention to, to learn, and to hold language information long enough to sort out the rules of language. It has been argued by some (Lenneberg, 1967) that infants are so well programmed for language that there is no need to structure the environment to assist language learning. In Chapter 3, it is clear that mothers do play a role in language learning in that they change their language levels when talking to young children (Farwell, 1975; Landes, 1975). These changes incorporate such important features as consistent vocabulary entries, consistent word orders, and consistent language patterns to assist children in learning language. Children learn language effortlessly and at their own pace, but the environment certainly has a role. Without an adequate, organized language sample, children would probably have a difficult time acquiring a symbol system.

Normal language development can be viewed as being tied to normal cognitive development, at least in the early stages of learning. As the child's cognitive abilities grow, his language abilities grow because he thinks in a more sophisticated way and has greater need for more sophisticated language to express the ideas and understandings he is mastering. What a child says is related to what he knows. What he knows influences the ways in which his language grows. Language develops in stages, which differ in detail from child to child, but which are surprisingly consistent among children even when they are learning different languages (Dale, 1976). It is these stages of language development that we will consider next.

Some people still insist that language development begins with the child's first word. But if we recognize the language potential of any newborn, then language development can be seen to begin with the birth of the child (Kaplan and Kaplan, 1971). From that moment on, the infant is exposed to language, and from that point he seems to be trying to make sense out of what he hears. The early obvious behavior that confirms this idea of the infant seeking out linguistic patterns is his vocalizations (Oller, 1976). Although babies a few weeks old may not be ready to sort out language information, they certainly are paying attention to the speech features of those around them. By the end of the first month of life, normally hearing babies have already mastered voluntary phonation, that is, using their vocal cords when they want to, rather than when their body tells them to. By 6 months of age, most normal babies are practicing what they know about the important timing features of speech, namely, that syllables need to be just the right length to be recognized as speech. The first year of life can be considered the time for paying close attention to the underlying features of this important aspect of communication, speech. At the end of the first year of life, babies begin to shift to consideration of content of what they have been hearing, beginning with the various intonation patterns of the mother, which are recognized by the infant and begin to appear in his vocalizations. The very young child uses the intonation patterns in combination with situational cues to express his comprehension of what is spoken to him, and in turn to communicate with others (Menyuk, 1971).

The suprasegmental aspects of spoken language are full of important meaning which is valuable to the baby in language learning. Intonation, stress, and overall loudness in speech cue the mood of the speaker, a very important consideration if you are a 12 month old who needs to know if Mommy really thinks that breaking that ashtray was not a good idea. Secondly, the suprasegmental aspect of timing gives vital phrasing information, such as what constitutes the most important grammatical units of an utterance. The phrasing information allows the very young child to begin to lump what he hears into meaningful units. For instance, when one says, "The boy's running down the street," that slight pause between the /-s/ and *running* serves to cue the change from one grammatical unit, the subject, to the next, the predicate. Amazingly, although he cannot use it until he matures a bit more, the infant seems perfectly capable of making this auditory distinction by 4 to 6 weeks of age (Eimas, 1974; Morse, 1974). Paying attention to regularity and pattern in what is heard, first through consideration of speech features and then through suprasegmental features of language, is the task of the young child during the first year to 18 months of life.

Auditory training by which we mean learning to use residual hearing is therefore vital to hearing impaired children. There seems to be no infant who can properly be called prelinguistic. Therefore, early proper identification of hearing loss is critical to subsequent acquisition of a symbol system, as well as to development of comprehensible speech if this is a reasonable goal for a particular child. The purpose of a fitting of a hearing aid is to ensure that the auditory features of language are audible, especially features such as pitch change, intonation patterns, and timing of spoken language. Although learning to pay attention to and sort out environmental non-speech sounds is one kind of goal in an auditory development program for severely hearing impaired children, the acquisition of intonational information and the translation of that information into meaningful communication patterns are by far more important for subsequent oral language development.

Normal hearing children focus first on the intonation patterns of what they hear, and next there appears to be actual comprehension of individual words and some syntactic patterns (Kaplan and Kaplan, 1971; Huttenlocher, 1974). Children's comprehension of language in the beginning stages is fragmentary and highly dependent on the situational cues available. This fragmentary understanding of language seems to be true of normal children as old as 18 to 24 months of age. For example, if mother points to the child's stocking feet and says "Get your shoes," it is possible that the child recognizes only the word *shoes* in this sentence, but by virtue of the context, namely, his mother also pointing to his feet, he realizes what he is to do. Since contextual cues usually are present when adults talk to very young children, complete breakdown in communication rarely occurs.

Since it is true that normally hearing children require contextual cueing in the beginning stages of language comprehension development, think how important it must be to the deaf child who is learning language. Language presented in the vacuum of formal lessons where contextual cueing in the form of gestures, pointing, or object arrangement is absent will not be clear to the young deaf child. It is imperative that the deaf language learner have as rich a contextual environment as possible if he is to understand what is being talked about.

As comprehension develops, normally hearing children learn early that the meanings of words take two forms. Some words are recognized to have meanings which refer only to single objects or to persons such as proper nouns; other words begin to have meanings that extend over several objects to form a conceptual class such as animals (Huttenlocher, 1974). Common to both of these meaning categories is the fact that they mean sets of relationships to the child, rather than just the object itself or one way in which the object might be used or acted on (Clark, 1974; Nelson, 1974). To ensure normal growth of comprehension, then, language associated with real experiences and relationships must be provided the young deaf child to permit him to understand how objects relate to each other, both verbally and nonverbally.

Unfortunately, children often lack sufficient production capacity to express all they know, so they often have to make those aspects they can produce do extra work (Huttenlocker, 1974). A child may recognize, for example, that cats are different from dogs, but because he lacks enough spoken vocabulary, he often calls a cat a *doggie*. How does a child decide what to call something if he lacks the real word to designate it? Children seem to make decisions of this sort by paying attention to dimensions such as size, shape, movement, taste, and texture (Clark, 1973). This tendency to overgeneralize by using one word for any member of a given category is extremely common in normal language acquisition. Extreme restriction of the meaning of a word, that is, using a label of only one instance of a category, is also quite common (Bowerman, 1976). For instance, *Doggie* can be used to only mean the family pet and is never applied to Fido who lives next door.

This tendency to overextend and underextend words is a phenomenon often seen in the language of deaf children. Their ability to acquire language is very slow, so they have to use the few words they may have in very creative ways. Thus, they may give objects names that are not correct according to adult standards. We might consider this strange or deviant language behavior. In fact, it is a normal occurrence in the early stages of language development.

As a child begins to develop cognitively and to see important differences between objects in his environment, he begins the process of increasing his vocabulary. This process involves noticing differences called features, which are characteristics that identify or make special a set of objects (Clark, 1973). As children develop appreciation of features, they begin the process of dividing their cognitive fields, which results in finer or smaller categories. As a child separates out a new concept, he requires a new word, which is how he increases his vocabulary in the beginning stages. Thus, it would seem important to plan conceptual-type games with young hearing impaired children with the emphasis of these games on discriminating the features that make one object different from another. For instance, horses go with cows because they are animals, but differ because cows give milk, have udders, and walk more slowly. As this sorting is being done, the labels for cows and horses can be presented. Just labeling these animals without some discussion of how they are the same and how they differ does not serve the process of conceptual differentiation, a shortcoming which can slow vocabulary acquisition. Such differentiation could be done easily even with more sophisticated notions such as distinguishing among styles of talking, as *discussion*, *argument*, *conversation*, *lecture*, and *debate*. It is important that deaf children be asked to contrast concepts in order for them to practice how to differentiate and categorize relevant features of vocabulary items.

According to Piaget, as presented in Chapter 2, when children begin to develop language, they relate this language to what they know about the world—usually elementary notions of object constancy, coordinated space, causality, and temporality, and to what they know about communication. Thus far we have considered mostly the process of comprehension. The first language expression or the single-word stage seems to be the time when the child's cognitive understandings are being tied to his linguistic system, not only in terms of the meaning of specific words, but also in terms of general semantic categories of agent-action-patient or instrument. Some researchers contend that this process is quite orderly. For instance, children in the two-word stage speak only those general semantic notions that they have developed at the single-word stage (Bloom, 1973; Bowerman, 1976). If this is so, the more cognitive understandings developed at the one-word stage, the more material would be available for future language growth.

Semantic categories that form the basis for the single-word stage in normal hearing children can be placed into two categories (Bloom, 1973). One category is usually labeled functional words, that is, words that represent nonexistence, recurrence, and existence. Words such as *no*, *more*, *that*, or *this* indicate functional notions. This category of single-word utterances appears in the earliest stage of language acquisition and is the most stable of the child's lexicon. Appearance of functional expressions is consistent with Piaget's developmental theory, which stresses the early development of schemas and the notion of object constancy. As you will recall from Chapter 2, object constancy involves the understanding that an object exists, that it can cease to exist, and that when it disappears it can recur.

The second semantic basis for single-word utterances is labeled the referential category. Referential words encode the ideas of actor, action, patient, location, or instrument. Unlike functional words, referential words tend to be quite unstable in that they appear quickly in speech, remain for a few weeks, and then disappear, almost as if the word has been placed in the child's memory bank and is no longer of interest for the time being. In normal hearing children, this appearance and disappearance of referential words is an ordinary event in language development, but with young hearing impaired children such movement of referential words is often quite disturbing to the teacher as she may equate it with some serious language learning or memory problem. What must be remembered is that rapid evolvement of referential words at the earliest stages of language development even in older deaf children who are just learning language has its parallel in normal language learning. As the deaf child progresses toward linguistic maturity, he should be afforded the opportunity to express his mastery of language as normal hearing children do. The less information the teacher has about normal language acquisition, the more likely she is to label normal processes as deviant. And if she seeks to intervene before the child can express these developmental processes, she may be contributing to deviancy of language acquisition in her hearing impaired students.

Even as the normal child uses single words, he is trying to string his words into longer utterances. These strings or successive utterances should be differentiated from true two-word combinations (Bloom, 1973). Successive utterances are single words strung together with a downward pitch contour on each word. In contrast, two-word combinations are joined together so that the timing and intonational contour of the whole utterance show the words to be related. The downward pitch contour after the second word indicates that the two words are to be interpreted as a complete semantic unit.

To illustrate the successive utterance stage, Bobby is encoding various aspects of his actions, but is not able to connect them to form a "sentence" relationship. As he observes his brother bouncing a basketball, he might say *ball*, *boy*, *bounce*, to encode his observations of patient, agent, and action. He has not joined them into an agent-action-patient relationship, but rather is stringing these notions which he must do developmentally before he is able to express his notion in a more mature syntactic relationship.

In successive utterances, the aspect the child encodes first seems related to the type of information that needs to be transmitted in the communication situation (Greenfield and Smith, 1976). The child generally encodes only those aspects of an event that are open to interpretation or confusion. For instance, if Bobby broke his toy and went to report this fact to his mother; in all likelihood, he would say something like *broke, truck*. His role is obvious from the context; on the other hand, his mother does not know what action has occurred until he says *broke*. The addition of *truck* is useful to clarify for mother which object was broken. This notion of information giving in communication which normal children acquire quite early is an important concept for teachers of the hearing impaired. Too often in communication situations, we ask deaf children to indicate the obvious when stress should be on communication of less obvious aspects of the situation. Likewise, too many language teaching situations are created having little or no communication value. Children must learn that language has an important communication function. Language development sessions whether for the preschooler or the high school student must be geared for maximum communication exchange rather than simply repetition which may offer practice in forms but does not consider the function of language.

As the child begins to merge information on semantic categories with some notion of word order, two-word combinations emerge (Bowerman, 1976). Normal children who enter this stage do not adhere to rigid word orders, but seem to move toward English syntax during this developmental period (Bloom, 1973). This observation is quite important for early development of language in hearing impaired children. As do normally hearing children, deaf children should be allowed to develop semantic categories first and then adherence to mature word order.

Researchers (Bloom, 1970; Brown, 1973) have found that, as with the single-word stage, there are functional relationships and grammatical relationships in two-word utterances. Functional relationships generally reflect statements of existence (that ball), nonexistence (no ball), and recurrence (more ball). Grammatical relationships are expressions of the agent-action-patient-locative components in utterances such as mover-action (me run); agent-action (me hit); action-patient (hit ball); and agent-patient (me ball, implying "I hit the ball"). A given child's utterances may be characterized by mostly grammatical-like or functional-like relationships. It appears, however, that children's two-word utterances must eventually reflect an expansion to include both types of linguistic encoding before they progress to more complex language development (Bloom, Lightbown, and Hood, 1975). Some children may fail to make a natural transition to this combined form of linguistic encoding and may thus earn the designation of language delayed (Morehead and Ingram, 1973).

If this can occur with normally hearing children, it is just as likely that there may be deaf children who also do not make a transition from functional relationships to grammatical realtionships and thus fail to progress linguistically beyond the two-word stage.

The functions of children's language also seem to have developmental stages (Halliday, 1975). At first children seem to use language at any one time for simpler communication purposes, namely, instrumental needs, the satisfaction of one's own needs; regulatory needs, the control of the behavior of others; and personal needs, the expression of individuality and self-awareness. Eventually, these functions are joined by a heuristic need, the urge to discover or seek information, and an imaginative need, the development of a fantasy life. These primitive functions eventually merge into two constellations of need: the so-called mathetic, which is the personal or finding information function, and pragmatic, which is the socially oriented or control function. This merging of communication functions serves as another impetus for the development of syntax. The best way to express multiple needs is through the juncture of intonation, vocabulary, and syntax. We can see that there are communicative reasons as well as linguistic-cognitive ones as to why two-word combinations, indeed, all subsequent grammatical growth, occurs.

Recognition and appreciation of the communication functions of language are critical for teachers of the hearing impaired. Too often language learning in the classroom focuses just on finding out information, whereas the normal communication pattern involves multiple communication purposes. For example, the teacher who asks *Wouldn't you like to get a book?* may be identifying a child's need for activity, as well as establishing that she would like more quiet and organization in the room. Simply saying or gesturing *book* would hardly have conveyed the full social impact of this question-command. Understanding of multiple purposes in communication is often lacking in hearing impaired children's linguistic attempts or mastery, a fact that may be directly related to teaching strategies which imply that language has only one communication purpose at a time.

With the appearance of two-word combinations in the child's expressive repertoire, he next works on three-word combinations and the establishment of the finer details of language usage. Specific linguistic details or modulations which appear at this stage include word endings, articles, prepositions, and auxiliary positions (Brown, 1973). While developing modulations, children tend to focus first on those modulations that convey useful semantic information to the sentence. In addition, children tend to focus on those modulations that are grammatically the most consistent in their application in sentences. These are important observations, for there may be situations in which drilling deaf children on certain forms or word endings may be useless unless the child has developed appreciation of how such modulations contribute meaning to sentences and the fact that some modulations must be learned in a rote fashion as was suggested in Chapter 2.

For instance, it is a convention in English to include a verb in all sentences, so we insert *to be* (a copula) in sentences such as *He is big*. One can say *He big*, which is easily understood, but generally not standard grammatical usage. The sentence is understandable of course because the copula carries little semantic information. Consequently, copula development is rather late in the overall development pattern of modulations. Thus, it might be more profitable for a teacher of the hearing impaired to work on more meaningful modulations than to spend hours drilling deaf children to insert the copula properly in Sentence Patterns III, IV, and V. Once the child has mastered these more meaningful modulations, the teacher could then turn to copula mastery, but approach it as a rote memory task. By this time, hopefully, the deaf child will have enough language skill to be able to complete this latter task with relative ease.

As children are developing modulations, they are also developing understanding and use of simple transformational sentences or modalities. Research on various modality development indicates that there is a predictable sequence to children's acquisition (Ervin-Tripp, 1970; Menyuk, 1971). For example, when a child begins to develop the modality of negation, he concentrates on one negation word, in most cases *no*, and affixes it to either the front of back of his two word combinations. Children do this because they seem reluctant to disturb the word order they have built up in their two-word combinations, so they merely attach new information (negation) onto the two-word combination. Eventually, the child embeds the negation element into the two-word combination. From this point on, the child refines his usage until he arrives at the adult form which contains the inclusion of a modal and the use of a variety of negation words such as *no*, *not*, and *never*.

This type of information is important to teachers of the hearing impaired for two reasons: it provides some guidelines as to what one can expect in the development of this and similar types of transformations, and it stresses the fact that linguistic rules, even in older children, are not automatically acquired in their mature, completed form. This latter point becomes even more important when it is recognized that even adults who are learning English through a total immersion approach to language instruction never attain a mature rule without first approximating stages very like those documented for children who are learning the same rule (Bailey et al., 1974). Language growth in hearing impaired children must be judged not against mature linguistic performance, but against normal child developmental patterns.

After the child is well into understanding and possibly producing modulations and modalities, he begins to turn his attention to the development of complex sentences resulting from the conjoining of sentences to one another and embedding of one sentence into another. Research (Donaldson and Balfour, 1968; Clark, 1973; Limber, 1973) indicates that the acquisition of these forms as with those discussed previously is governed by cognitive, as well as by psychological and perceptual constraints.

One complex operation of interest is conjoining, which involves the joining of two or more sentences with a conjunction. The conjunction may be a coordinating conjunction such as *and*, *but*, *or*, or a subordinate conjunction such as *after*, *before*, *therefore*. Research (Ingram, 1975) on the use of complex transformations by children indicates that coordinating conjunctions are acquired before subordinate conjunctions. Within each class, of course, semantic constraints dictate the order of development. For coordinating conjunctions, *and* as an indication of equality, as in *I ate an apple and an orange*, appears first. Exception and choice as signaled by *but* or *or*, respectively, appear next. Finally, *and* as a temporal (time) coordinator is mastered as in *I went to the store and then I went to the movie*.

The development of subordinate conjunctions has also been studied (Donaldson and Balfour, 1968; Clark, 1973). Those units which reflect temporality have received particular attention. Children tend to encode temporal sequences on a time line basis, that is, things that happen first come first in the sentence. Time is first encoded by the use of *and*, or *and then*. Later, young children begin to use *after* and *before*. At first, those latter conjunctions are defined simply in terms of what comes first and what comes second. As a child discovers that events do not always follow rigid time lines in sentences, he begins to redefine *before* and *after*, so that both words refer to the same concept, namely, *before*. Eventually, the child conceptualizes that *after* means the opposite of *before*. When these language concepts finally appear in his comprehension and usage, the concept has been truly mastered.

The process just described seems to be a common trend in the learning of complex sentence notions such as those encoded by subordinate conjunctions. Easy concepts which may or may not reflect adult use of a word appear early. Eventually, the semantic issues are sorted out by the child so that a term communicates meaningful information to others. Again, it should be stressed that teachers of deaf children should not automatically assume that language usage which is not adultlike is wrong. Within the context of the language acquisition process, a deaf child may be understanding or using a language form in a very productive way. An example can be shown in the use of the word *because*. Many normal children use *because* developmentally to answer *how* and *when* questions (Ervin-Tripp, 1970). Deaf children too often are observed to overuse *because* types of constructions, but when such use is considered in terms of the types of questions to be answered, *because* occurs frequently in response to *how* or *when* questions. Such responses are more likely to be viewed as abnormal for deaf children because they are used by 12 or 13 year olds. If deaf children are still developing language, this behavior, even if it occurs in older children, should be considered developmental, not deviant. A true developmental viewpoint of course requires that the teacher have clear expectations about stages of acquisition, so that she can sort language behaviors that are developmental from those that are not. And having identified developmental responses, she can prepare a child to acquire the next level of sophistication in a particular language form.

Another complex form, embedding, begins as a verb complement confined to a subset of words such as *got*, *have*, and *want* (Limber, 1973). This results in child sentences such as *I have go to store*. It is hypothesized that young children memorize forms like *I have* or *I want*, and attach sentences to these memorized forms. For most children, sentences that share the same subject tend to appear first, but they learn to drop the second subject resulting in sentences such as *I like go to store*; later they add sentences that have different subjects as in *I want Mary go to store*. Eventually, these forms appear in mature style with the appearance of embedded constructions in positions other than the object position, or the expansion of the verb class to include other verbs.

Other complex constructions such as relative clauses also appear in children's language in object position first, a practice which may be related to short-term memory, as discussed in Chapter 2. That is, it may be easier for a child if such complex forms are produced and heard at the end of a sentence rather than at the beginning, simply because the forms are easier to retain in short-term memory.

The semantics of embedding may be as important as the grammatical operations to a child (Chomsky, 1969). When asked to perform the meaning of sentences involving *tell*, *ask*, and *promise*, children interpreted the embedded sentence as conforming to the word order of the main sentence, even when the subjects did not correspond. For example, a child instructed to *Ask Mary about the story*, interpreted this sentence as if the person spoken of was the object of the embedded question. The child then told the story to Mary instead of asking her about it.

From the preceding examples, it should be clear that teachers must focus on more than the surface structure or the form of language. Consideration must be given to the semantics of the forms that are to be acquired. The meanings that are encoded into complex language forms often determine the rate and type of acquisitions seen in children. Language forms must be tied to the meanings being conveyed. The meanings a particular child acquires, however, are determined by *his* understanding of the language rule, not the teacher's.

Although this discussion on normal language development covers only a few aspects, it is hoped that we have made three points clear: (1) normal language development is very complex, and it is not less complex for deaf children; (2) language development is highly dependent on cognitive maturation and understanding of meaning; and (3) language development is highly predictable even in its complexity, but it must be studied thoroughly by anyone who proposes to teach deaf children.

## THE EFFECT OF HEARING IMPAIRMENT ON
## LANGUAGE ACQUISITION

It has been repeatedly demonstrated by researchers that language abilities of many hearing impaired children are quite delayed (Reamer, 1921; Thompson, 1936; Heider and Heider, 1941; Pugh, 1946; Goda, 1959; Myklebust, 1960). What has been lacking in many of these research efforts, however, are detailed descriptions of particular aspects of language that are affected. It is still not clear whether deaf children generally learn language like normal hearing children, albeit at a slower rate, or whether they are different or even deviant in their developmental patterns. This lack of precision has in part been due to the absence of precise techniques for language acquisition which have finally become available from linguistics (Cooper and Rosenstein, 1966). Few models have been used to describe rule acquisition in deaf children, but their number is growing. We will attempt to summarize these studies, and then indicate how such information may be useful in language teaching.

Research on the language comprehension and production of deaf children can be divided into three basic areas, specifically, those studies that examined phrase structure rule acquisition, those studies that have examined transformational rule acquisition, and those studies that have emphasized pragmatic rule acquisition.

Research into phrase structure rules of spoken English indicates that deaf children do acquire many of the phrase structure rules of English much in the same way as do normally hearing children, but in a delayed fashion with some exceptions of deviant rule acquisition (Hess, 1972; Pressnell, 1973; West and Weber, 1974; Wilcox and Tobin, 1974). In some cases the delay was so extreme that it apparently penalized hearing impaired children's performance on comprehension and memory tasks (Odom and Blanton, 1967; Sarachan-Deily and Love, 1974). For instance, the growth patterns of normally hearing and hearing impaired children of comparable language ages have been studied showing the groups to be similar particularly in the sequence of their development (Hess, 1972; Wilcox and Tobin, 1974). However, when such groups of children were given a sentence repetition task, the hearing impaired subjects frequently violated the syntactic integrity of the sentence, whereas the normally hearing subjects did not (Sarachan-Deily and Love, 1974). In such a test situation, normally hearing children tended to use synonyms for test lexical items, substitutes that preserved the original semantic intent of the sentence. In contrast, hearing impaired children produced agrammatical sentences or inserted words that seriously distorted the semantic intent of the sentence. Likewise, in another study when deaf children were presented with a series of English strings that varied in their grammatical correctness from completely correct to totally agrammatical, grammaticality did not assist them in remembering these strings, which was not true of normally hearing subjects' performance, particularly with strings that approached complete grammatical correctness (Odom and Blanton, 1967). Some interaction between a lack of coding in short-term memory and insufficient competence in the base rule system of English may have affected performance. We feel this is evidence of a lack of depth in language acquisition, not evidence of deviance. The problems of bilingual children who are tested in their nondominant language offer a reasonable analogy to the performance problems of many hearing impaired children on tasks involving spoken English.

Studies of phrase structure knowledge by use of the written language of deaf children show a somewhat more confusing picture. Some research could be interpreted as indicating that the base structure of hearing impaired children is deviant from that of normally hearing writers (Ivimey, 1976; Kretschmer, *in progress*). For instance, one research project (Ivimey, 1976) indicated that a deaf child consistently omitted tense in favor of cueing time through the use of temporal adverbs, for example, *now* and *yesterday*. This rule resulted in sentences such as *Now Bob write on blackboard* and *Yesterday I write letter home*. Another study (Kretschmer, *in progress*) seems to indicate that deaf children irrespective of teaching modality tend to focus on the agent-action-patient-location type of sentence with reduced use of process, stative, or process-stative verbs. It cannot be questioned that many deaf children do poorly in tests of oral and written language. Even the written language studies with deaf adolescents show sizeable deficiencies in the mastery of English at the phrase structure level (Kretschmer, 1972). We still contend that the problems revealed are merely a reflection of the lack of mastery of the particular language system being tested, and do not describe a language acquisition deviance in any different sense than tests of English show a Spanish-dominant child to have language problems. The single unfortunate difference may be that unlike the Spanish-dominant child, too many deaf children are not dominant in any language system.

Transformational growth in deaf children also seems to parallel that of normally hearing children, with some exceptions noted (Jarvella and Lubinsky, 1975; Quigley et al., 1976). For instance, deaf children have been observed to encode temporal sequences in precisely the same way that younger hearing children do, namely, by using *and* to conjoin descriptive sentences in a linear time frame (Jarvella and Lubinsky, 1975). In contrast, however, when using *and* in conjunction reduction sentences such as *He ate the hamburger and then the pickle*, deaf children, unlike normally hearing children, eliminated any item in the second sentence that appeared in the first sentence, resulting in incorrect sentences such as *The dog chased the cat and ran away*, instead of *The dog chased the cat, and the cat ran away* (Quigley et al., 1976). A deaf child who produces the former sentence has over-generalized the reduction rule, which could be the result of the way the rule is taught. If reduction is taught by writing out the two sentences to be joined, then joining them by inserting the word *and* and crossing out the redundant item(s) in the second sentence without explanation that the reduction rule applies only to subject and verb deletion, the deaf child might easily conclude that the process involves the elimination of all redundant items from the first sentence to the second, a conclusion that is entirely incorrect and can only result in the production of ambiguous sentences like the first one above.

Another good example of how deaf children parallel, but at the same time diverge, from normal usage is reflected by a study on relative clauses (Quigley et al., 1976). Both deaf and normally hearing children found relative clauses embedded after the subject to be the most difficult to comprehend and produce. However, because of deaf children's overcommitment to the subject-verb-object (S-V-O) order in sentences, they tended to treat the object of the subject-embedded relative clause as the subject of the main verb. Thus, in the sentence *The woman who kissed the man left*, a deaf subject would assume that the *man*, not the *woman*, had left. These latter trends were not noted among the normally hearing subjects.

Similar trends for deaf and normally hearing subjects have been observed in tests on passives, question forms, negation, pronominalizations, verb forms, and subordinate conjunctions (Tervoort, 1970; Quigley et al., 1976).

Studies of pragmatic growth in deaf children as compared with normally hearing children have been limited (Gorrell, 1971; Hoemann, 1972). Preliminary findings, however, are of interest. When deaf children were asked to communicate specific information about a task to other deaf children, it was found that the listener received minimal information (Hoemann, 1972). Even when the sender deduced that this was true, he was unable to modify or add any information that was more helpful to the receiver in completing a task. The deaf sender tended to keep repeating himself with the expectation that simple repetition would make the information understandable. In other words, deaf children often lack an understanding of how to communicate information to others, an observation that is not surprising if one considers the ordinary communication situation in many classes for the deaf. The teacher frequently does too much talking and too little communicating. The child's primary communication partner is the teacher.

In another study (Gorrell, 1971), triads of hearing impaired children were observed interacting with one another, and their behaviors were compared to those of triads of normally hearing children interacting in the same setting but at different times. The amount of interchange among deaf children was much less than for normally hearing children, and these interchanges tended to be more directive or physical. Hearing children tended to use more modeling techniques, that is, they demonstrated something to another child in the hope that he would "follow the leader." Hearing children also tended to use more direct verbal commands. The deaf children in this study were less comfortable in social interchanges and lacked basic communication or social interaction skills with which to establish relationships with others. When interaction was established, it tended to be on a physical basis rather than relying on more socially approved methods of demonstration and verbalization. Again, such observations are not surprising in light of the necessity of stressing adult-child interactions for young deaf children, who are in the critical early stages of language learning. Interactions to develop language do not necessarily develop communication competence.

## SIGN LANGUAGE AND THE ACQUISITION OF ENGLISH

Our focus thus far has been on the acquisition of various forms of spoken or written English. It must be recognized that most deaf adults do not use oral English in their social communication; instead, they use American Sign Language (ASL). The question of the relation between ASL and English has prompted considerable interest in the language learning implications of deaf children's use of sign or natural gesture language systems. Consequently, we wish to consider briefly the linguistic nature of ASL and its use by hearing impaired persons.

ASL is the language system that deaf persons use among themselves or with hearing persons who have been incorporated into deaf society, either by virtue of their having been brought up by deaf parents or relatives, or by virtue of voluntary efforts to learn sign. ASL must be differentiated from some of the sign languages used in educational programs for the deaf, from the highly stylized language used in presentations by the American Theatre of the Deaf, from the sign language usually taught in colleges or universities, and from the sign language necessary to pass the manual interpreter's certification examination. These latter sign languages must be viewed as attempts to regularize ASL into a system that conforms with the syntactic and semantic patterns of standard spoken English. Adjustments are usually accomplished by incorporating special morphological indicators for features such as plurality, past tense, or progressive aspect; by teaching a sign system that conforms to the word order of spoken English; by inventing new word signs that correspond to the diversity of lexical items in spoken English; or by eliminating other special characteristics of ASL that make it a successful visual symbol system. These modifications have been offered in order to make ASL enough like spoken English to make it acceptable for use in schools or with the hearing population. It can and has been argued, however, that these attempts, although well intentioned, have not really resulted in creating a "new" sign language, but rather have resulted in the establishment of pidgin sign-language varieties that

are school based, but not used by the majority of deaf society (Wilbur, 1976).
Linguistically speaking, pidgin languages tend not to become the mother
tongue of any linguistic group, but rather are attempts to bridge the gap
between two languages for purposes of trade or social interaction. Pidgin
languages tend to amalgamate features from the two native languages into a
single coding system, but this process often results in the loss of important
syntactic or semantic subtleties present in both of the original languages.
Linguistic specifics are deliberately sacrificed to achieve the goal of practical
communication. This collapsing process seems to have occurred with respect
to ASL as used in schools for the deaf. Attempts to make ASL conform to
spoken English do not seem to have enhanced ASL and have frequently
resulted in the loss of many useful syntactic and semantic ASL coding devices
without a concomitant gain for many deaf persons of the equally subtle syntactic and semantic features of spoken English.

~ The distinguishing characteristics of ASL have been the center of recent
linguistic research. The cataloging of such characteristics has confirmed the
symbolic status of this visual communication system. One such interesting
characteristic is indexing, which refers to the process of establishing space,
time, and person reference in ASL conversation (Friedman, 1975). This process consists simply of using the index finger to set the stage within space for
the *where*, *when*, and *who* of the topic under discussion. To be more specific,
person reference is indexed so that each potential participant in the discourse
(or sentence) is located within the space that exists between the user of ASL
and the watcher. First-person reference is usually indicated by the signer
pointing to himself with his own index finger. Second-person reference is
achieved by the signer pointing to the watcher. Third-person reference is
located either to the right or left of the speaker so that it can be pointed to
whenever the third person's name appears in the conversation. To clarify
person indexing further, which may seem confused but rarely is, whenever
person reference occurs within discourse, person designation is marked by
making a gesture toward the space designated for that person. For instance, if
Bob's spatial position is to the right of the signer and Bill's is to the left, the
sentence *Bob hit Bill* would be managed by signing the word *hit*, but moving
the sign from the right (Bob) to the left (Bill). Pronouns and proper names are
rarely used after their introduction in ASL, instead, indexing is used to convey
these notions.

Another feature of ASL is reduplication. Within ASL, verbs can be
divided into stative verbs such as ''looks like'' and nonstative or action verbs
(Fischer and Gough as quoted in Wilbur, 1976). The action verb category can
be subdivided into durative (*sleep, talk*) and nondurative (*kill, win*) verbs. All
these verbs can be reduplicated in ASL, that is, the same sign can be produced
over and over in a sentence. Stative verbs are reduplicated quickly, whereas
nonstative verbs can be reduplicated either slowly or quickly. Slow reduplica-

tion of nondurative verbs is interpreted as interaction or repetition, whereas slow reduplication of durative verbs signifies continuation of an action or a long duration. If body rocking accompanies slow reduplication, this is meant to convey the notion of *too much*. Fast reduplication means plurality if two subjects are involved, or habitual if only one is involved.

Linguistic contributions made by body and facial gestures are very important in ASL (Wilbur, 1976). Researchers (Bellugi and Fischer, 1972) have determined that the space used for signing consists of a bubble that extends from the top of the head to the waist of the speaker. This bubble is usually extended only in such situations as communicating to a crowd or for the sake of emphasis. Within this personal space, the signer moves hands and arms, while using facial and body gestures, all as part of the linguistic code. For instance, differentiation among statements, questions, and/or exclamations is usually made on the basis not of the signs themselves, for in each case the set of signs is exactly the same, but rather of where the hands are positioned upon completion of the signed utterance, where the body is in relation to the hands, or what position the eyebrows assume. With statements, the face assumes a natural pose and the hands are dropped slightly, whereas for questions, the hand stays in the position of the last sign, the body moves forward slightly, and the eyebrows assume the "quizzical" position. For exclamations, the hand stays in the same position as the last sign, the body straightens or moves slightly forward, and the eyebrows assume the "surprised" position. The question or exclamation punctuation signs noted in some educational sign systems are not employed in ASL. In those systems employing a sign to indicate a question or exclamation, positioning and facial gesturing tend not to be used.

Body gesture can also be used to establish, maintain, or inhibit communication in ASL (Wilbur, 1976). For instance, as a person signs, his hand position upon completion of each ASL utterance is a communication signal to the watcher whether interruption will or will not be tolerated. Unless the signer drops his hands completely, interruption is not to occur. If the watcher wishes to interrupt over the protest of the signer, he must physically touch the signer, preferably on the shoulder or arm to indicate that he now wishes a turn to "speak."

This discussion on ASL is intended to support the notion that ASL is a language with its own set of syntactic, semantic, and pragmatic rules. It must also be recognized that these rules often include aspects of processing that have no analogy in spoken English and do not conform in many cases with rules of spoken English.

What does this discussion mean for education? The use of ASL raises some basic problems depending on what the goal of the educational program is. If the goal of the program is to impart a form of standard English through speech, writing, or a formal sign system, then the use of ASL should be avoided, for its introduction will create predictable interferences with the acquisition of spoken or standard English forms. The analogy to normally hearing children from bilingual environments is a reasonable one. The very young child who is being raised in bilingual environments shows predictable, and at most stages of acquisition, sizeable amounts of interference with development of both language systems. The tragic circumstances of the recent past for Spanish-dominant children in many schools in this country highlight this example. The Spanish-dominant child when tested in English performs dismally. Unless some separation between the languages is established for him, he may also fail to properly acquire his native Spanish, especially with regard to reading and writing. The deaf child's problem is no smaller in this regard. He must have mastery of some language system before he can be expected to read and write. Thus, instruction in ASL and any other simultaneously taught language system must be clearly separated for him if he is to master both. If reading and writing in standard English are also educational goals, then familiarity of a spoken (or signed) standard English system must precede development of reading and writing.

If, on the other hand, the primary goal of the educational program is to establish some communication system in a deaf child, it seems reasonable to use ASL, which accommodates to visual processing and will probably be used the most in his society. If ASL is the child's native language, then spoken or signed English must be considered as a second language. Teaching signed English, although difficult, would probably be easier than transfer to an auditorily based system such as spoken English.

The matter of whether to establish a visual communication system or to encourage comprehension and use of spoken English should properly be decided individually by educators and parents in view of a particular deaf child's needs and capabilities. We believe that each deaf child should have an early opportunity to be exposed to and if possible to develop spoken and written forms of English. This exposure could ensure that, as with the truly bilingual normally hearing child, the deaf child's social and vocational choices will be varied. The focus of the following chapters therefore will be on ways to guide deaf children into becoming competent users of language, with special attention to the spoken and written forms of standard English.

## REFERENCES

Bach E and Harms R (eds): Universals in Linguistic Theory. New York, Holt, Rinehart and Winston, 1968

Bailey N, Madden C, and Krashen S: Is there a "natural sequence" in adult second language learning? Lang Learn 24:235–243, 1974

Bates E: Language and Context: The Acquisition of Pragmatics. New York, Academic Press, 1976

Bellugi U and Fischer S: A comparison of sign language and spoken language. Cognition 1:173–202, 1972

Bloom L: Language Development: Form and Function in Emerging Grammars. Cambridge, Mass., MIT Press, 1970

Bloom L: One Word at a Time. The Hague, Mouton, 1973

Bloom L, Lightbown P, and Hood L: Structure and variation in child language. Monographs of the Society for Research in Child Development, 40 (Serial No. 160), 1975

Bowerman M: Semantic factors in the acquisition of rules for word use and sentence construction. In Morehead D and Morehead A (eds): Normal and Deficient Child Language. Baltimore, University Park Press, 1976

Brown R: A First Language: The Early Stages. Cambridge, Mass., Harvard University Press, 1973

Chafe W: Meaning and the Structure of Language. Chicago, University of Chicago Press, 1970

Chafe W: Discourse structure and human knowledge. In Freedle R and Carroll J (eds): Language Comprehension and the Acquisition of Knowledge. New York, V. H. Halstead, 1972

Chomsky C: The Acquisition of Syntax in Children from 5 to 10. Cambridge, Mass., MIT Press, 1969

Chomsky N: Syntactic Structures. The Hague, Mouton, 1957

Chomsky N: Aspects of the Theory of Syntax. Cambridge, Mass., MIT Press, 1965

Chomsky N and Halle M: The Sound Pattern of English. New York, Harper, 1968

Clark E: What's in a word? On the child's acquisition of semantics in his first language. In Moore T (ed): Cognitive Development and the Acquisition of Language. New York, Academic Press, 1973

Clark E: Some aspects of the conceptual basis for first language acquisition. In Schiefelbusch R and Lloyd L (eds): Language Perspectives: Acquisition, Retardation, and Intervention. Baltimore, University Park Press, 1974

Cooper R and Rosenstein J: Language acquisition of deaf children. Volta Rev 68:58–67, 1966

Dale P: Language Development: Structure and Function (ed 2). New York, Holt, Rinehart & Winston, 1976

Donaldson M and Balfour G: Less is more: a study of language comprehension in children. Br J Psychol 4:461–471, 1968

Eimas P: Linguistic processing of speech by young children. In Schiefelbusch R and Lloyd L (eds): Language Perspectives: Acquisition, Retardation, and Intervention. Baltimore, University Park Press, 1974

Ervin-Tripp S: Discourse agreement: how children answer questions. In Hayes J (ed): Cognition and the Development of Language. New York, John Wiley, 1970

Farwell C: The language spoken to children. Hum Dev 18:288–309, 1975

Friedman L: Space, time, and person reference in American sign language. Language 51:940–961, 1975

Goda S: Language skills of profoundly deaf adolescent children. J Speech Hear Res 2:369–376, 1959

Gorrell S: An investigation of the social interactions occurring in comparable triads of normal-hearing and hearing-impaired children, using an interaction scale. Unpublished masters thesis, University of Cincinnati, 1971

Greenfield P and Smith J: The Structure of Communication in Early Language Development. New York, Academic Press, 1976

Halliday M: Learning how to mean. In Lenneberg E and Lenneberg E (eds): Foundations of Language Development: A Multidisciplinary Approach. New York, Academic Press, 1975

Hargis C: English Syntax. Springfield, Ill., Charles C. Thomas, 1976

Heider F and Heider G: Studies in the psychology of the deaf. Psychol Monogr 242, 1941

Hess L: A longitudinal transformational generative comparison of the emerging syntactic structures in a deaf child and a normally hearing child. Unpublished masters thesis, University of Cincinnati, 1972

Hoemann H: The development of communication skills in deaf and hearing children. Child Dev 43:990–1003, 1972

Houston S: A Survey of Psycholinguistics. The Hague, Mouton, 1972

Huttenlocher J: The origins of language comprehension. In Solso R (ed): Theories in Cognitive Psychology. New York, John Wiley, 1974

Ingram D: If and when transformations are acquired by children. In Dato D (ed): Developmental Psycholinguistics. Washington, D.C., Georgetown University Press, 1975

Ivimey G: The written syntax of an English deaf child: an exploration in method. Br J Dis Commun 11:103–120, 1976

Jarvella R and Lubinsky J: Deaf and hearing children's use of language describing temporal order among events. J Speech Hear Res 18:58–73, 1975

Kaplan E and Kaplan G: The prelinguistic child. In Eliot J (ed): Human Development and Cognitive Processes. New York, Holt, Rinehart and Winston, 1971

Kretschmer R: Transformational linguistic analysis of the written language of hearing impaired and normal hearing students. Unpublished doctoral dissertation, Teachers College, Columbia University, 1972

Kretschmer R: Development of Written Language in Hearing Impaired Children (in progress)

Landes J: Speech adressed to children: issues and characteristics of parental input. Lang Learn 25:355–379, 1975

Lenneberg E: Biological Foundations of Language. New York, John Wiley, 1967

Lenneberg E: The concept of language differentiation. In Lenneberg E and Lenneberg E (eds): Foundations of Language Development: A Multidisciplinary Approach. New York, Academic Press, 1975

Limber J: The genesis of complex sentences. In Moore T (ed): Cognitive Development and the Acquisition of Language. New York, Academic Press, 1973

Ling D: Speech in the Hearing Impaired Child. Washington, D.C., A. G. Bell Assoc., 1976

Menyuk P: The Acquisition and Development of Language. Englewood Cliffs, N.J., Prentice Hall, 1971

Morehead D and Ingram D: A development of base syntax in normal and linguistically deviant children. J Speech Hear Res 16:330–352, 1973

Morse P: Infant speech perception: a preliminary model and review of the literature. In Schiefelbusch R and Lloyd L (eds): Language Perspectives: Acquisition, Retardation, and Intervention. Baltimore, University Park Press, 1974

Myklebust H: The Psychology of Deafness. New York, Grune & Stratton, 1960

Nelson K: Concept, word, and sentence: interrelations in acquisition and development. Psychol Rev 81:267–285, 1974

Odom P and Blanton R: Phrase-learning in deaf and hearing subjects. J Speech Hear Res 10:600–605, 1967

Oller D: Analysis of infant vocalizations: a linguistic and speech scientific perspective. Mini-seminar, American Speech and Hearing Convention, Houston, 1976

Pressnell L: Hearing-impaired children's comprehension and production of syntax in oral language. J Speech Hear Res 16:12–21, 1973

Pugh G: Appraisal of the silent reading abilities of acoustically handicapped children. Am Ann Deaf 91:331–335, 1946

Quigley S, Wilbur R, Power D, et al.: Syntactic Structures in the Language of Deaf Children. Champaign, Ill., Institute for Child Behavior and Development, 1976

Reamer J: Mental and educational measurements of the deaf. Psychol Monogr 29, 1921

Russell K, Quigley S, and Power D: Linguistics and Deaf Children: Transformational Syntax and its Applications. Washington, D.C., A. G. Bell Assoc., 1976

Sarachan-Deily A and Love R: Underlying grammatical rule structure of the deaf. J Speech Hear Res 17:689–698, 1974

Slobin D: Cognitive prerequisites for the development of grammar. In Ferguson C and Slobin D (eds): Studies of Child Language Development. New York, Holt, Rinehart and Winston, 1973

Stark R: Speech acquisition in deaf children. Volta Rev 79:98–109, 1977

Streng A: Syntax, Speech, and Hearing. New York, Grune & Stratton, 1972

Tervoort B: The understanding of passive sentences by deaf children. In D'Arcais F and Levelt W (eds): Advances in Psycholinguistics. Amsterdam, North Holland, 1970

Thomas O and Kintgen E: Transformational Grammar and the Teacher of English (ed 2). New York, Holt, Rinehart and Winston, 1974

Thompson W: An analysis of errors in written composition by deaf children. Am Ann Deaf 81:95–98, 1936

West J and Weber J: A linguistic analysis of the morphemic and syntactic structures of a hard-of-hearing child. Lang Speech 17:68–79, 1974

Wilbur R: The linguistics of manual language and manual systems. In Lloyd L (ed): Communication Assessment and Intervention Strategies. Baltimore, University Park Press, 1976

Wilcox J and Tobin H: Linguistic performance of hard-of-hearing and normal-hearing children. J Speech Hear Res 17:286–293, 1974

# 5

# The Learning Environment in the Classroom Setting

Learning is so complex that one theory cannot account for all that goes on in the mind of a child as he grows and develops into a thinking adult. Stimulus-response psychologists talk about positive reinforcement as an effective motivator in learning. Repetition forms the bulwark of their theory. Piaget urges active participation in learning and, with perceptual psychologists, emphasizes the individual's search for meaning through refinement of perceptions. To them processing and integrating of new information with what is already known is the keystone to learning. Those psychologists interested in the development of attitudes and values point out how important a sense of emotional freedom is if cognitive and social learning are to take place. There is no use in trying to teach a child the theory of fractions if he feels he has to expend all of his energy and thought in proving to himself and everybody else that he is or is not a worthwhile person.

Although learning theory has not particularly been directed toward supporting education, teachers have been looking to theory in the hope of finding answers to some vexing educational questions. Consequently, current classroom practices reflect a composite of many theories just because no unified theory has ever been developed. Until that occurs, teachers will be searching for and selecting aspects that have practical application to their problems. Those who have a broad knowledge about learning and learners should have an advantage in being better able to select suitable learning experiences for their pupils and to provide a good climate for learning. This chapter reflects a personal philosophy, a synthesis of what I have come to believe in over half a century of contacts with hearing impaired children.

## PROVIDING A GOOD CLIMATE FOR LEARNING

Teachers have always played a crucial role in education, for they are the final arbitors of what goes on in the classroom from hour to hour and day to day, despite what the curriculum suggests. What they know, what they do, how they treat their pupils, how rich an experience they provide, how they organize opportunities for learning, and how they cooperate with the home all determine the kind of education that prevails in their classrooms.

Most teachers are truly committed to providing a classroom climate that is right for optimal learning. An important requisite for the child is freedom from fear and freedom to make mistakes without punishment or threat of punishment. Anxiety is not an uncommon accompaniment of attendance in school. A child who is afraid to make a mistake has to take more time to defend his existing knowledge. He needs more access to information than one who is willing to take chances. Anxiety raises the activity level, and at the same time interferes with comprehension and memory (Smith, 1975).

Teachers of deaf children find themselves continually in the position of having to point out errors of commission and omission in the language and the speech of their pupils. It is very important that correction take place but just as important that it does not become threatening. When a teacher is attuned to a child's mistakes she can unconsciously communicate to him by facial expression or by words that he has made a mistake, that he is wrong, that he has failed again. The chances are that the child is wrong, has made the same mistake over and over, and in doing so has frustrated his teacher, who wants him to be right for a change. In order not to create anxiety over errors but yet to indicate that there are corrections to be made, the teacher could choose to make them in an informal, nonthreatening manner rather than with a frown on her face and a peremptory, "No, that's not right. How many times do I have to tell you?" Perhaps the person she is really displeased with is herself because she has not been clever enough to eliminate all mistakes instantaneously. She must conceive of her task as guiding children to find alternate ways of behaving, of solving problems or making decisions all day long and not as being the ogre ready to pounce on the guilty.

Children learn best from being successful. Success engenders success. A child is not strengthened by continuous failure. Although he must acquire a certain amount of tolerance for frustration and failure, which he is bound to experience even in the most protective of environments, he will thrive and learn best when he tastes success. In order to judge what a child has or has not comprehended, or what he can or cannot assimilate, a teacher must be a close observer of the child's responses. She must be attuned to the types of errors a child can make. Some of them can be ascribed to developmental stages common to both the hearing and hearing impaired child. For instance, singular pronouns are easier to acquire than plural ones. It is easier for little children to understand and use the first person "I" than the third person. The masculine *he* is easier to acquire than the feminine *she*. Although deaf children are greatly retarded in acquiring pronouns, their misuse does not necessarily result in deviant structures (Russell, Quigley, and Power, 1976). Errors that result from generation of nonstandard transformation rules as in *A girl saw a cat and caught the mouse* are much more critical. They should receive high priority in correction so as to avert future errors resulting from the misconceived grammatical rule. However, if a child is expected to learn language beyond his stage of cognitive development, he may be so overwhelmed or confused that he cannot learn at all. What looks like laziness may be a coverup for what a child considers an impossible task. What looks like stubborn refusal to participate in a lesson may be a lack of comprehension of the task at hand. Only constant evaluation and reevaluation will shed light on why the child responds as he does.

It is very tempting to a teacher to try to correct instantly a host of errors every time a child opens his mouth to speak. The teacher must remember that a child can best process one error at a time, especially if rehearsal is required to get the item from short-term memory into long-term memory. It is best to start correction with the language structure and then superimpose the correct speech on the correct language. Suppose a profoundly deaf 5 year old comes to school late one wintry morning and says, not very intelligibly, "No bus. I cold. Mother car to school." There are enough differences here from normal sentence patterns for several comprehensive language and speech lessons, but the wise teacher will rephrase the child's message in correct structures in a conversational approach. Then she can comment on the situation with, "I'm glad you're here. Are you cold now?" She feels his hand to determine if he is still cold. "You were cold while you were waiting for the bus, weren't you? Can you say, 'I was cold?'" The teacher is quite sure that he can, for he had been exposed to the sentence form in the past but has obviously not generalized its use to this instance. If the child is successful in repeating the correct sentence, the teacher may say, "Now your sentence is good. I'll help you with your speech later." The child was corrected in a relaxed atmosphere with sufficient knowledge about the meaning and the form of the language, yet he was not frustrated by having to remember three correct sentences and six misarticulated phonemes all at once. The teacher has to make mental notes of the deferred corrections, but keeps in mind that the child will need rehearsal of the one she has focused on. After the children come in later that morning from recess, she might ask all of them, "Were you cold outside?," expecting answers such as "No," "Yes," "No, I wasn't," "Yes, I was." Then she might ask each child to tell her about one other child in the class, as "Mark was cold," or "Sue wasn't cold." If errors occurred, she would take time right then to clarify them and go over the responses again. During the individual speech lessons, she would zero in on the errors of each child and then hold him responsible for both correct structure and speech. Following the noon lunch period and after the next recess period she would go through the same procedure again asking the same questions hoping to stimulate a conversation in which the children volunteered sentences about how they felt. After these rehearsals that day, she might hope that the children had generalized to the sentence pattern and its negative transformation. If a teacher keeps the level of instruction at the level of comprehension, there is a good chance that the success a child feels will be the only reward he needs to take the next step.

Even teachers like to feel successful. They take heart from their ''good'' days and learn to tolerate their ''bad'' ones. Every day teachers are bound to make dozens of mistakes involving judgments about children, the best ways to control a difficult situation, and techniques of teaching. Some learn from their mistakes but others do not. If one is not conscious of errors, he cannot correct them. Watching oneself perform on video tape is perhaps the most illuminating experience a teacher can have. More accurate perception of one's performance permits more decisive action. An open mind provides a person with more data, and with more data behavior can be more effective. A willingness to profit from experience and from supervisory guidance could ensure that the same mistakes that occurred during the first year of teaching would not be repeated during the next 10. Teachers who are secure persons, who wish to grow professionally, and who are open to self-evaluation and guidance should be able to change their performance in order to improve it, yet still be comfortable in doing so.


## STIMULATING LEARNING IN THE CLASSROOM

Learning comes from doing something purposeful and worthwhile. A person cannot absorb everything he sees or hears, so he selects what makes sense to him. If a child sees no purpose in learning something, he simply rejects it. Often schools expect children to learn what seems like nonsense to them. In order to find out what does make sense to a child, a teacher should allow him to have freedom to explore, to have time to interact with the environment, to make mistakes, and to assimilate what has meaning for him. He cannot do this in a barren classroom. It must contain interesting materials appropriate to a child's stage of intellectual development. In effect, the teacher must arrange the environment to exploit the child's interests and natural curiosity. That in turn should direct his learning. Little deaf children do take advantage of their environments and explore as hearing children do, although they may not manifest their curiosity in the same way. Hearing children ask hundreds of questions, whereas deaf children cannot do so. It is much easier for a teacher to say to a deaf child, "See this," "Do that," or "This is a fish" than to try to ferret out what he is focusing on to learn. Persistent observation should make it possible to identify the knowledge a child is seeking.

One of the most useful early questions for a deaf child to learn in his search for information is *What's that?* When Helen Keller, as a deaf-blind child, discovered that things had names, she wanted to know the name of everything she touched. Little deaf children are often unaware that people or things have names. In fact, many are quite content not to know the names of things if a gesture or pointing gets them what they desire or need. When a deaf child really learns the power of the question *What's that?*, he is well on the way to gaining a useful vocabulary which he can use to gather further information. Learning thousands of words during his lifetime will occupy much of his efforts. If he learns to use the words to meet his needs, he will find satisfaction in discovering how they can work to his benefit.

The one question that young hearing children use often to satisfy their curiosity is *Why____?*, a question much more difficult than *What's that?* to teach deaf children to use. If a teacher notices any manifestation of a child's interest or curosity in his manipulation of things or in his relations to people or events, the child should be equipped as soon as possible with the form of the question that satisfies his curiosity. The question form may be a primitive one such as *Why?* or *Where?* until he has gained control over the structure of the complete question. When a child discovers that he can find out more than meets the eye by asking questions, he has a symbolic tool to increase his level of knowledge. Learning to ask questions should receive high priority in the language acquisition of hearing impaired children.

During adolescence deaf children, like all children, continue to search for what has meaning for them and what suits their purposes. As teenagers, they are usually more interested in each other than in the Greek and Roman Wars, and find learning of facts about these wars quite a bore. Perhaps this is why secondary schools now offer courses in personal relations as well as ancient history. But when and if a subject interests a child, he will pursue it relentlessly, read about it, talk about it, and assimilate it. Deaf children should be given choices about what they wish to learn yet be encouraged to widen the scope of their interests. A flexible curriculum and good teaching can accomplish this.

A school in which deaf children are expected to sit and look at and listen to the teacher offers minimal opportunity for learning. Teachers can get excellent clues as to what their pupils' interests and concerns are simply by watching and listening to them. It is very difficult to do this since most teachers are programmed to do the talking and to think of teaching as telling. Except for a few secondary school courses such as the sciences, home economics, shop, and vocational education, the accepted mode of instruction is verbal. For children who have not mastered language, lecturing to them is less than satisfactory as they try to cope with everyday problems, to solve social relationships, and to understand the forces impinging on them from home and school. To get a sense of what is happening to them, and to feel successful, they must continue to have an experiential base to undergird their cognitive and personal growth. They must also continue to refine their comprehension and production of language as it relates to their new knowledge.

## MEDIA, THE TEACHER'S FIRST AID

Today's teachers have access to a great amount of visual and auditory instructional material to supplement children's experiences or to substitute for those a child will likely never have. Perhaps in the future, going to the moon will be a common experience for man, but until then most of us will have to be content to go there vicariously through picture and words. However, we must guard against substituting visuals in the education of hearing impaired children when actual live experiences are readily available. More learning takes place when the learner is actively involved with all his senses than when he sits back passively and just looks at pictures, film strips, slides, movies, or a TV cartoon.

Each viewer sees in a picture only what he is prepared to see. His background knowledge and his perceptual set determine how he will interpret the visual material. On viewing a TV film that shows how genetic material is transferred from one generation to another, a scientist might dismiss it as grossly oversimplified. An interested but untutored lay person might see the model of a double helix as a welter of colored rectanges or think of it as a decorative mobile. He might recall in his mind's eye how all the little rectangles scurried to their opposite numbers on the ladder during the animated presentation, but he cannot state the concepts that the film was trying to present because he lacked sufficient knowledge to interpret what he saw.

In most pictures there is a good deal to ignore. The more complex a picture is, the more "noise" there is in it (Smith, 1975). When a person is inundated with information he cannot use, he may be confused in what to look for. The more irrelevant data there are in a picture, the more ways it can be interpreted. When a teacher chooses the picture of a cute little baby holding a teddy bear to associate with the word *baby*, she takes the chance of confusing the child if she does not remove the "noise" from the picture. Words and pictures are not readily interchangeable.

It takes a certain amount of perceptual maturation and cognitive development to read pictures. Piaget has demonstrated that the egocentric view of children makes it difficult to imagine what a scene looks like from a different vantage point. It takes time for children to comprehend that what is

*in front of* one person may be *in back of* another or what is to one's right may
be to the left of a person on the opposite side of the table. Young children
might interpret a picture of a man standing on a railroad track in the distance
as being a tiny man while one in the foreground looks like a tall man to them.
Only when they have gained ability to see the world from other viewpoints
than their own can they interpret pictures that require mature concepts of
space.

Some children find it difficult to distinguish foreground from background
in pictures. In the classic example of the "vase vs. face" illustration found in
old psychology texts, the viewer's focus may fluctuate from seeing two identical profiles facing each other from across a central space, or from seeing the
space between them as a vase. He is able to switch foreground and background at will. Children who have a problem in separating foreground from
background may be unable to interpret pictures as expected. When they look
at printed matter, they may see the white spaces between the letters rather than
the words. This could lead to problems in learning to read unless steps were
taken to help them in foreground-background confusion. It is most important
when using any visuals, even the simplest of pictures cut from magazines, that
the viewer have the relevant information and skills necessary to interpret what
he is looking at.

## PROGRAMMED INSTRUCTION

Very few concepts embodied in learning theory have found application in
the classroom, but one of them, programmed instruction (PI), has. Based on
S-R theory, it gained popularity in the 1960s and 1970s. The subject matter to
be taught is called the *program*. It takes various forms as in specially designed
books, tapes, filmstrips or slides. The program is composed of many small
steps or *frames* that require a response from the student. The information
needed to respond to each frame in a linear or step-by-step program appears in
prior items so that success is almost assured. Programmers believe that early
failure in a task could begin an extinction process while success serves as a
reinforcer (Green, 1962). Each student paces himself as he uses the program
individually and feels no threat of punishment if he makes mistakes. When a
machine is used to dispense the program, it does not chastise him. It merely
refuses to advance to the next frame. At times it may even break down and
refuse to move at all!

A project to teach language through print and pictures to deaf children,
ages 4 to 8+, by PI was undertaken in the 1960s by the National Education
Association under a special grant from Media and Captioned Films, Bureau of
Education for the Handicapped, United States Office of Education, and is still
available from a commercial source (General Electric/Project LIFE Program,

1971). A specially designed electronic machine is used to present 20-minute filmstrips that make up the program. Each filmstrip is accompanied by a teacher's guide that lists behavioral objectives. These objectives state the entering behavior or the language that a child needs to know before attempting the language learning task; they outline the specific objectives of the filmstrip and list the expected outcomes. At about the same time that the Project LIFE films were being developed, Stanford University prepared several programs to teach computational skills, language, and reading to deaf children through computers. Computer-assisted instruction is more flexible and sophisticated than the linear type of program used in Project LIFE, but the expense of installing computers limited its use to those few schools with computer connections (Friend, 1970).

Programmed instruction was not conceived of as a substitute for the earliest stages of language acquisition. Neither is it a substitute for later language learning. PI is designed to help a child comprehend rather than produce language independently. Although it aims to teach hearing impaired children new vocabulary and new syntactic structures, its value actually lies in reinforcing the written form of the language that the children should have been learning through sensory-motor experiences in the oral or signed form. Even the best of programs cannot meet criteria that are universally applicable to all children. If learning is the seeking of inner meaning, it is obvious that learning is an individual matter, especially the learning of language. However, teachers can look at the construction of the various programs for hearing impaired children, note their applicability, judge their effectiveness, and even use some of the ideas in their own planning for language growth in their pupils. The idea of individualizing instruction is so meritorious that Chapter 8 will be devoted to the analysis and evaluation of children's language production. The difference between success and failure often lies in the teacher's ability to spot a child's confusion in producing a particular structure, in clarifying its usage, in defining its limits, and in providing opportunities to practice it in meaningful situations. A teacher who knows what a child knows can program his language growth better than any commercial program can. To do this a teacher must have a strong background in English if that is the language she expects to teach.

## LIVING TOGETHER IN THE CLASSROOM

In order that the classroom can be a comfortable and enjoyable place to live and learn, children need rules for living together. The classroom is a place for social interaction as well as a place to learn to read and write. Some teachers choose to be authoritarian, imposing strict rules for behavior with no deviations tolerated, whereas others are permissive, accepting any sort of erratic behavior. Still others vacillate between being authoritarian and permissive, thus adding confusion to the children's understanding of how they are expected to conduct themselves. Some teachers have older pupils formulate their own rules and set their own standards for behavior in conjunction with teacher guidance and input. When children participate in such procedures, they are more likely to understand the rules and respect them.

If a child is constantly out of step, his behavior gets in the way of his concentration and intellectual functioning. In order to be free to learn, he must be able to conduct himself within accepted behavioral standards. Undoubtedly, the best kind of discipline occurs when behavior is self-directed without control of outside authority. Self-discipline is the outgrowth of perceiving better ways of doing things or relating to persons (Combs, 1967). It occurs through interaction, not through superficially imposed rules that make no sense to the child. Whether a teacher uses behavior modification techniques or not to gain control of a particular child or a group will depend on her view of how the children in the class can best learn to function together. Ability to act in accordance with expected standards is the basis for good interpersonal relations. It permits children to form friendships, to work together, and to settle down comfortably to the tasks at hand.

A well-prepared teacher who provides an environment in which children are free to interact with each other within acceptable boundaries of self-control, are free to explore and to gain knowledge that is supported by meaningful language learning, and are free to make mistakes without fear of chastisement or embarrassment should have no difficulty in convincing her pupils that school is a place where they can profitably spend their time. Under these optimum conditions, the teacher will find that she, too, has gained freedom to observe her pupils, to assess their capabilities, and to plan for them accordingly. A sound philosophy, buttressed by thoughtful goals and tried techniques, should guarantee that each school day can truly become an investment in learning.

## REFERENCES

Combs AW: A perceptual view of the adequate personality. In Perceiving, Behaving, Becoming. Yearbook of the Association for Supervision and Curriculum Development. Washington, D.C., National Education Association, 1967

Friend JE: Computer Assisted Instruction for the Deaf at Stanford University. Stanford, Ca., Institute for Mathematical Studies in the Social Sciences, Stanford University, 1970

General Electric Project LIFE Program. Schnectady, N.Y., Education Support Project, Corporate Research and Development, General Electric Company, 1971

Green EJ: The Learning Process and Programmed Instruction. New York, Holt, Rinehart and Winston, 1962

Russell WK, Quigley SP, and Power DJ: Linguistics and Deaf Children— Transformational Syntax and its Applications. Washington, D.C., A. G. Bell Assoc., 1976

Smith F: Comprehension and Learning—A Conceptual Framework for Teachers. New York, Holt, Rinehart and Winston, 1975

# 6

# Developing and Stabilizing Language Through an Experience-Based Integrated Language Arts Program

During the first four years of his life a hearing child accomplishes a most remarkable intellectual feat. He learns language. If a deaf child learned language independently or intuitively as hearing children do, there would be no need for language teachers or language programs for him. But he doesn't, so the role of the teacher becomes critical. She must be prepared to help each child unlock the door closed to him because of his hearing deficit. But first she must have the key that opens this special door. It consists of a great deal of knowledge about children and about language.

In this chapter we will concentrate on ways to help those children whose hearing losses stemmed from birth or before their language was established. A teacher who understands procedures for guiding these children should at the same time be equipped to meet the needs of children with partial hearing who have acquired partial language through their ears, those who became deaf after the age of 3 or 4 whose language is fairly well established, and those who entered school at a later age without prior language stimulation. In Chapter 9 we will have something to say about language help for children who have been deprived of adequate early instruction and those with multiple handicaps, as the mentally retarded, the emotionally disturbed, and those with so-called learning disabilities.

We will assume that the children under consideration here will have the best possible hearing aids, that they are intact neurologically, and that they are emotionally stable. Moreover, we will assume that their parents have been highly involved in their education, and that the children have had access to stimulating and rewarding preschool experiences. You may smile to think that anyone would conjure up such seemingly idealistic conditions for the basis of a discussion about what may not exist in reality. But such conditions do exist, and unless they do we are putting barriers in the way of having our deaf children learn language. Only when we try to simulate the language learning conditions that are the birthright of hearing children can we expect our children to succeed in what for them is a tremendous challenge—the learning of language.

## MODEL FOR THE YOUNG DEAF CHILD'S EARLY LANGUAGE LEARNING

The deaf child's first words will be serviceable words that he can eventually use in his daily communication. His first sentences will be one-word sentences; then he will form two-word sentences and finally he will use simple sentences: a human actor will perform an action on an object, or a sentence may state a simple fact. Conditions may require negative statements, requests, or simple questions. Teachers and parents will use these simple transformations when they talk to the child. He will see and hear the same words and the same sentence structures every day in meaningful situations just because his daily routines are going to be rather repetitious at ages three and four. But he will also have many new experiences and encounters every day and every week. These will require new vocabulary but the sentence structures will remain constant for a long time. He will see and hear new vocabulary in familiar structures. His caretakers will encourage him when he tries to communicate. They will respond to every attempt that he makes. They will reinforce him liberally!

## GRAMMAR I—A MINIMAL GRAMMAR FOR DEAF CHILDREN

You can see how the procedure for stimulating language in the young hearing impaired child is analogous to that which a hearing child encounters when he first learns language. He hears language simply stated by his parents, concretely based, useful for his communication purposes, and repeated in his routinized schedules. But here is where we will have to make adjustments in planning for language acquisition by the deaf child. Although the hearing child chooses the rules he is able to induce from a welter of constructions, we are not going to expose a deaf child to as wide a variety of structures as the hearing child. So as to keep the initial language learning within the boundaries of probability for success, a simple minimal grammar, designated Grammar I, is recommended as the target for all deaf children (Streng, 1972; see Appendix A). The paragraph immediately above was written within the confines of this grammar. If you reread that paragraph, you will notice that the writing is rather stilted, most of the sentences are quite short, and the transformations relatively few in number. Although the structural boundaries of the grammar are limited, the semantic aspects need not be. Vocabulary and concepts may be quite abstract and the structures themselves may take on many meanings. For instance, prepositional phrases such as *at home*, *at noon*, *at once*, and *at bat* have similar surface structure but the meaning of the preposition differs in each one. A simple grammar does not restrict the development of mature concepts. In fact, it allows for and can promote expansion of the semantic aspects of language without confusing the child by having to learn both structure and meanings at the same time. Moreover, there is no reason why other grammatical structures not listed in Grammar I cannot be introduced to any child at any time when necessary and appropriate. Comprehension of more complex structures is essential for purposes of reading, and any child who is capable of using more complex language should be encouraged to do so. Grammar II (Streng, 1972) may serve as a guide to expanding a child's syntax. It contains complicated phrase structure rules for nouns and verbs, has more transformations, and suggests multiple embeddings. Grammar I is a minimal grammar to be mastered for expressive purposes, both oral and written.

Table 6-1 allocates various aspects of Grammar I to age levels that correspond roughly to Piaget's periods of cognitive development, namely, the sensory-motor, ages 1 to 2½; the preoperational-preconceptual, ages 2½ to 4; the preoperational-perceptual, ages 4 to 7; the concrete operational, ages 7 to 11; and the formal operationa, ages 12 to adulthood. The factors that influence the distribution are (1) the child's physical, social, and cognitive development, which more or less prescribes the content of his language, and (2) the complexity of the syntactic items themselves. By reading across the chart, it is possible to follow the progression from simple structures to more complex ones, and by reading down each column, it is possible to get the sense of what each period includes. The allocation of items is merely suggestive and should not be considered inviolable.

Starting with the sentence as the basic unit of thought, the chart shows the development of the five basic sentence patterns through (1) the addition of optional adverbs, first as words, then as phrases and lastly as clauses; (2) the development of noun and verb phrases from single words to structures that require ordered sequences as well as morphemic changes; and (3) the use of transformations that first involve only rearrangements, additions, or deletions of words within the basic patterns such as negatives, requests, and questions, and later more complex ones involving several sentences and embeddings.

No attempt is made to suggest a complete vocabulary of nouns or verbs to be used in the syntactic structures. Years ago most language outlines used in schools for the deaf contained lists of nouns, verbs, and adjectives to be taught during the school year. The criterion for selection of the words was usually the child's ability to produce them in speech. Consequently, a teacher could find herself teaching words such as *bee*, *fan*, and *muff* to preschoolers, but since there were no bees, fans, or muffs within miles, the child had no use for these words. Word lists are stultifying and limiting to teacher and child alike. They inhibit creativity and inhibit a child's notions of what words are for. The earliest words a child learns should make sense to him and serve him in his communication. Vocabulary and syntax must be coordinated with experiences which in turn are based on the child's interests and his cognitive development.

## BUILDING LANGUAGE FOR THINKING

Although Piaget's tasks can be illuminating for pegging a child's cognitive development, the child must first acquire language specific to the task and understand the directions for carrying it out before he can be expected to react to it. In performing a task a child was always asked by Piaget why he thought as he did, but one who does not have adequate language can hardly be expected to tell what he is thinking. Consequently, it seems logical that in classes for deaf children, the teacher must anticipate the language of the tasks and teach it before a child is confronted with having to respond either to directions or to justify his conclusions. For instance, in the conservation task of quantity of liquids, the teacher can introduce the language at lunch time by asking each child to choose his own juice glass from two 4-ounce glasses of differenc size and shape. A 5 year old would undoubtedly pick a tall thin glass in preference to a short fat one. The teacher would call attention to the fact that her glass was short and fat. After the child had learned the vocabulary and the structure: *My glass is thin*, *My glass is tall*, or *My glass is short*, *It is fat*, he could be ready to talk about the glasses in conjunction with the conservation task. A subsequent conversation would go something like this:

T: My glass is short. Your glass is tall. (Teacher points to both glasses.) Do you have more juice? Do I have more juice? Who has more juice?
C: I have more.
T: Let's see. (She pours juice from another identical short glass into an identical tall one and back again, reversing the operation.) The juice is the same! Are you surprised?

The next day she may go through the same procedure, first reviewing the language.

T: Which glass do you want?
C: The tall glass.
T: Why do you want the tall glass?
C: I like it.
T: Why do you like it?
C: It is more juice.
T: Can you say, "It has more juice?" (Writes sentence for child).
C: It has more juice.

Again the teacher pours juice from a tall to a short glass to let the child observe that the glasses hold the same amount. Obviously the child has not understood the concept and the teacher will wait for time to pass before she resumes questioning the child. In the meantime she will let the child do the pouring, and eventually the child will have gained understanding of this conservation task. The teacher will continue to use the language appropriate to the task and for its justification by the child. Much of the language of arithmetic must be developed in like manner before children can be expected to understand concepts underlying time, space, distance, and rate.

Thinking can be promoted in many ways. Exercises such as the following can stimulate vocabulary growth as well as thinking. Material can be prepared in advance or produced spontaneously for use on an overhead projector. Following are some examples:

Figure 6-1.

(1)  T: (pointing to empty box in Figure 6-1) Tell me what goes here.
     C: Meat.
     T: Why do you say meat?
     C: To cut with a knife.

Another child may say *fork*, *cup*, *saucer*, *knife*.

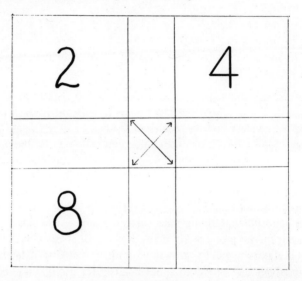

Figure 6-2.

(2)  T: What goes here? (pointing to the empty box in Figure 6-2)
     $C_1$: Six, because I counted 2—4—6—8.
     $C_2$: Sixteen, because $2 \times 2 = 4$, $4 \times 2 = 8$, $8 \times 2 = 16$.

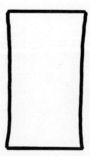

Figure 6-3.

(3)  T: What do you think this is? (pointing to Figure 6-3)
     $C_1$: A door.
     $C_2$: A glass.
     $C_3$: A window.

The teacher adds a handle to transform it into a mug or a pitcher and asks what the child thinks it is, what it contains, and what can be done with the contents. The child is expected to visualize beyond the immediate and the concrete. Language can be expanded and imagination stimulated by exercises such as these. Creativity can be encouraged by not placing restraints on a child's thinking. Any response is accepted since it reflects what the child is thinking (Grammatico and Miller, 1974).

A child's self-activity also divulges his stage of cognitive development. One may be seen sorting out, classifying, and organizing his environment, while another may be running around haphazardly from one activity to another without giving any sign of understanding how things go together. By watching a child in a free learning environment, a teacher can gain insights into what is going on in his mind and can guide him into paths that will lead to constructive activities that promote cognitive growth. Opportunity for freedom to explore must be part of everyday in the life of a preschool child as it should be for all learners. Language can accompany these explorations if the teacher is clever enough to pinpoint his thinking. For instance, a 5-year-old deaf child brings dishes to the play table from the shelf and sets them out with a ball on each plate. The teacher may say, "What is a ball doing here? We don't put balls on plates. Take it off and put it in the box where it belongs. We put cookies on plates, not balls." Or she might say, "I know this is a ball. Is this ball an orange? Is this ball an apple?" She waits for the child's response and upon learning it is an apple, she says, "May I eat my apple?" The two pretend to eat their apples. "Mmm, it's good. Can you say, 'Mmm, it's good.'?" Teachers of deaf children are faced with evaluating a child's thinking many times during the day. Becoming familiar with Piaget's periods of cognitive development can be most beneficial as a basis for understanding what is going on in the mind of a child and for making plans to exploit it.

## PLANNED EXPERIENCES AS THE BASIS FOR LANGUAGE DEVELOPMENT

Although the teacher must be ever vigilant in promoting thinking skills in the language program, most of the child's language will be derived from planned activities that have as their objectives not only cognitive development, but also social development and language development. The word *activities* implies an active participation on the part of the children and even of parents in planning experiences, and certainly active participation of the children in executing the plans. Imagine yourself as a friendly visitor entering a classroom of preschool deaf children 2 days before the Thanksgiving holiday and smelling a turkey cooking in an electric casserole on the teacher's desk. After an appreciative comment about the delicious odors engulfing the room, you might inquire about how this activity originated. The teacher explains that the activity was designed to give her three and four year olds the concept that a live bird had to turn into a carcass before it became a part of an edible feast. She felt that the children had not really understood the pictures of the first Thanksgiving that she had tacked up on her bulletin board. She wanted to make it clear that the Pilgrims had to go hunting to get their turkeys and we had to go to the store to get ours. Moreover, this was a good opportunity for the children to learn the names of the other foods, such as dressing and cranberry sauce, that she had prepared the day before while they had watched. The parents were also invited to share in the noon meal so that they could see how to teach vocabulary to their children at home. It was a gala affair and all the participants—the flushed and exhausted teacher, the appreciative parents, and the excited children—were happy about the occasion and called it a great success. There is no need to evaluate in detail this true story about one teacher's attempt to teach language to her preschool class, for its inappropriateness is all too apparent.. She seemed to be unaware that three and four year olds had little sense of distant past time, that they could read into pictures only what they knew, and that they learned best by doing and not by being passive bystanders. Perhaps you can think of a better way to achieve some of this teacher's objectives.

## AN INTEGRATED LANGUAGE ARTS EXPERIENCE

Now let us follow a group of preadolescent deaf children, ages 10 to 12, on a trip to the post office in a large city. These children had been corresponding with pen pals in another part of the country and had sent them a scrapbook of descriptions and pictures of themselves and their school, but it had never arrived. In their great disappointment they decided to find out what happened to their book. This sparked their interest in the United States postal service. They wrote a letter to the postmaster asking for a guided tour of the post office. In the meantime they went to the library for books and the teacher furnished them with pictures and charts illustrating the sequential steps in collecting, sorting, and delivering the mail. Early on in the activity, the children decided to make it the basis for another scrapbook for their pen pals.

Teaching is a business, and part of the business is the planning that keeps the machinery running smoothly. This teacher's overall plans for the integration of oral and written language with the reading program involved her inspecting all of the reading materials and visual aids available on the subject and selecting appropriate ones for her class. She chose books written at several levels of difficulty to meet the varying abilities of the children. She made a tentative vocabulary list exclusively for her own use. She noted the sentence structure and idioms used in the reading material with the intention of introducing them during the various discussions with the children. She knew that all the children needed more practice in constructing cohesive paragraphs and since they would be writing little essays for their scrapbook, she decided that the written form of language would be emphasized. Her goal was at least one paragraph for each child every day. In making her preliminary plans she left her options open for developing the syntactic structures listed in Grammar I. Final plans for the content of the activity were to be contingent on suggestions from the children, and the daily plans for syntactic development were to be based on observed needs as the activity progressed. All the language was to be individualized except for the syntactic difficulties commonly manifested by the group.

The children participated in deciding what to include in the activity. The books and visual materials immediately broadened the interests of several of the children. One of the boys became intrigued by the Pony Express and wanted to research the subject and write about it. Two of the girls were fascinated by postcards mailed to the teacher from foreign countries. They tried to locate the countries on the globe. They decided that they wanted to start a stamp collection. Some of the children had relatives living in other parts of the world so the parents were enlisted to tell the children stories about their cousins, uncles, and aunts whom they had never seen. This was a bonus indeed when they began to write compositions for the scrapbook.

In preparation for their excursion, the class got blanks to be filled out to trace their lost scrapbook. They had looked at filmstrips and books about the post office. They felt well prepared for the trip—or so they thought. On their routine but not very exciting tour, they finally arrived at the mail sorting area, a noisy place, so noisy that some of the children turned off their hearing aids. Suddenly one of the boys spied his deaf uncle at one of the zip code sorting machines and the whole place immediately became alive for them. All the workers were wearing headphones except the deaf man. This aroused their curiosity and they asked the guide, ''Hearing aid—what for?'' ''David's uncle no hearing aid—why?'' ''Is all man deaf?'' When they learned that the headphones were to keep the noise out and that the workers heard soft music through them, they were baffled. Then the questions really began to flow. ''Why is noise to make deaf?, Why am I deaf?,'' and many more. The teacher promised they would talk about the subject when they got back to school, but she was reinforced in her presumption that the children needed a great deal more information about asking questions. She gave questions first priority in her plans for teaching syntax.

When it was time to leave the post office at 11:30, the school bus that was to pick them up failed to arrive. After about 30 minutes, the children and their teacher began to get worried, so after consultation with each other about the solution to their problem, they made several telephone calls. After another hour's wait with no lunch in sight the teacher and her class were finally rescued. All afternoon and the next day, the delinquent bus got top billing in their thoughts and writing. Incidental but related experiences are as important as planned ones as sources of language acquisition. It does not really matter what the source is as long as it meets the criterion as useful for expression of a child's thoughts. Moreover, spontaneous use of language shows clearly a child's ability to produce it independently and is often an eye-opener to an alert teacher. A good teacher will make plans, but as in following a road map, will accept a necessary detour when it appears. However, it is not wise to rush off in all directions, but always to keep in mind that the shortest route to the final destination is the most efficient one.

The happy ending to this activity was a beautiful scrapbook for their pen pals, wrapped securely, addressed legibly, insured, and mailed. They had learned much more than planned—how much first class mail cost in comparison to other classes, how to weigh mail and to estimate its cost, how to insure a package, how to trace lost articles, how much 15 thirteen cent stamps cost, where Poland, Vietnam, and Mexico were located on the map, and even that deaf people could get jobs at the post office. It took 2 weeks more to complete the project than had originally been allocated to it. It was time to go on to something else. That something else was a unit on *Hearing and Deafness* agreed on by children and teacher and heartily supported by the parents who were invited to come to the final slide lecture the children had prepared. During the time devoted to this activity, a great many feelings came to the surface, a subject not usually included in a unit on science. It was an excellent time for parents and children to understand each others' feelings about the deafness of the children, and when these feelings seemed resolved and reconciled, the children were able to turn to other subjects with greater equanimity.

These particular units of study, the one related to social studies and the other to science, were not prescribed by the school's curriculum, but were complementary to it. If a teacher is mandated to follow a curriculum, it is still possible to use subject matter as the basis for an integrated language arts program which deals with the multifaceted aspects of language. Nevertheless, it seems most reasonable to develop speaking, writing, and reading skills within the framework of experiences that bring clear meaning to language and promote its immediate use.

## PROCEDURES FOR PRACTICING SYNTACTIC STRUCTURES

Despite the overall superiority of an experience-based integrated language arts approach, teachers find that children often require additional clarification of and practice in the use of syntactic structures beyond those provided within the experience itself. If they do, it becomes necessary to digress momentarily from the subject matter of the activity for special practice with those structures. As an example of how one teacher did this, let us go to the classroom of the children who were to take the trip to the post office. Early in the discussions with the children, the teacher noted that they were not using the present tense, third person singular_s morpheme in their spontaneous production of language, either oral or written. Two of the children were even using the base form of the verb for the past tense even though they had been exposed to the correct forms since the age of five. This indicated to her that (1) the children had never really understood the_s rule, (2) they had not had sufficient practice to stabilize the rule, (3) they had not learned the principal parts of common verbs of action, or (4) they had not distinguished between the past, which can be expressed by calendar or clock time, and the simple present, which has no precise relationship to calendar time. Present tense of verbs of action does include the present moment but also includes all of eternity as expressed in this sentence: *The sun rises in the east and sets in the west.* Its message is a generality. The teacher planned to explore all of these facets hoping to rectify misconceptions, clarify the semantics of the structure, and provide practice with the simple present tense of verbs of action. Here is her plan and an account of how she carried it out:

## A PLAN FOR CLARIFYING AND PRACTICING THIRD PERSON SINGULAR, PRESENT TENSE, WITH VERBS OF ACTION

The Class: Amy, Julie, David, Jerry, and Mark—ages 10 through 12. Two other children are mainstreamed and are not included in these sessions. The children's responses are indicated, respectively, as A, Ju, D, Je, and M.

Materials: Overhead projector; teacher prepared transparencies derived from available reading materials. The vocabulary was marginally familiar at the beginning of the activity, but the children had seen and used it sufficiently to account for its inclusion in the practice exercises.

Procedure: Five 15-minute daily lessons were planned for 1 week. The last day's lesson consumed 30 minutes. Each day the teacher filled in this general plan by considering the vocabulary to be used and the specific goals to be achieved.

1st day:   A.   Introduce the third person singular_s morpheme, present tense, through sentences found in reading materials.

           B.   Contrast first and third person.

2nd day:   A.   Generate the rule for the third person.

           B.   Contrast third person singular with third person plural.

           C.   Practice with a variety of verbs derived from the activity.

3rd day:  A.  Use a variety of appropriate optional adverbs with the present tense. Stress semantics of the tense.
          B.  Practice the adverbs as they arise in the children's sentences using first and third person singular.
4th day:  A.  Contrast present and past tenses using adverbs appropriate to each tense.
          B.  Practice the two tenses with sentences from the activity.
5th day:  Write compositions relating to the activity for the scrapbook.


### First Day

Children are seated at a half-circle table and are supplied with writing materials. Teacher projects on the overhead screen 15 sentences derived from the reading materials. A sample follows:

1.  A mailman wears a uniform to work.
2.  He begins work at 6:00 a.m.
3.  He sorts letters, magazines, and papers for his route.
4.  He ties the mail in bundles.
5.  He puts some of the mail into his leather pouch.
6.  A truck takes the extra mail to a mail storage box.

T:   Let's look at the verbs in these sentences. Jerry, what is the verb in Sentence 1?
Je:  wears (Teacher underlines the verb with two lines.)
T:   Right! (Each child has a chance to identify verbs in subsequent sentences.) How does each verb end?
A:   ssssssssss
T:   with an *es*. Can you say that, Amy? (She obliges.) Each verb ends with an *es*. (Teacher points to all the final *s'es*.) You all know Mrs. Korb. She's our mailcarrier. She delivers our school mail. We talked to her about how she spends her work day. She told us she got up at 5:00 a.m. every day. That's early, isn't it? I wonder what time you get up.
Je:  I get up at 7:30.
Ju:  I get up at 7:00.
A:   I get up at 7:00.
M:   I get up at 6:30.
D:   I get up at 8:00.
T:   You're lucky, David! David lives near school so he can get up late. Who can remember when Mark gets up?
Ju:  Mark get up at dik thirty.
T:   Let's hear those *s'es*, Julie. (Teacher says *gets up* and *six* for her.)
Ju:  Mark get up at six thirty.

T:  Please say *gets up*. Remember we must put an *s* on the verb when we talk about one person.

Ju: Mark gets up at six thirty.

T:  That's better. Now write in on your paper. (Each child has a chance to tell the rising time of every other child and to write it.)

T:  Who can tell me about everyone in the class. Don't look at your papers. If you like, you can tell me what time your mother and father get up, too.

C:  (Children do this part of the practice without error.)

T:  I liked your *eses*. Very good!


## Second Day

T:  Amy and Julie. Please tell us again what time you get up on school days.

A:  I get up at 7:00.

Ju: I get up at 7:00.

T:  Who can give me one sentence about Amy and Julie?

M:  Amy and Julie gets up at 7:00.

T:  You had a good sentence, Mark, but your verb was not right. We must say 'Amy and Julie *get up* at 7:00.' Do you know why?

M:  No.

T:  (Points to sentences she has written on a transparency: Amy gets up at 7:00. Julie gets up at 7:00. Amy and Julie get up at 7:00.) How many people are we talking about here? (Teacher points to: Amy gets up. . . .)

M:  One.

T:  How many people are we talking about here? (Teacher points to Julie gets up. . . .)

M:  One.

T:  How many people are we talking about here? (Amy and Julie get up at 7:00.)

M:  Two.

T:  Yes. (Displays yesterday's transparency.) How many people are we talking about here in Sentence 1, in Sentence 2, in Sentence 3. . . ?

M:  One.

T:  When we talk about one person or thing, what must we add to the verb?

M:  *ssss*

T:  Right! When we talk about two people or things, or more, we can forget about the *es*.

M:  I know.

T:  OK, we'll see! (smiling and challenging him) I hope all of you know when to add an *es* to the verb! Do you?

C:  (Nods in assent.)

T:  (Projects a set of 15 sentences, a sample of which follows:

1. Mail clerks sell stamps to people.
2. First class letters cost 16¢.
3. Post cards cost 11¢.
4. Clerks weigh letters and packages.
5. They put the correct postage on the packages.

T: David, how many people or things are we talking about in Sentence 1?
D: Many, all of them.
T: Yes, more than one. Is there an *es* on the verb?
Ju: No, no *es*.
T: Why not?
Ju: More than one, there is no *es*.
T: OK. When we talk about more than one person or thing we can forget about the *es*. Now, I'll read the first sentence: 'Mail clerks sell stamps to people.' Then I'd like each one to tell me what *one* mail clerk does. Amy, you begin.
A: Mail clerk sells stamps to people.
T: Your verb is right, but we must say, 'A mail clerk. . . .' (Teacher notes error in determiner for further special lesson with Amy.)
C: (Amy and class complete the list of sentences without error.)
T: We'll write all of these sentences when we finish the lesson. Let's go on now. I'm going to say a sentence about one person or thing and I'd like you to give me a sentence about several persons or things. Use the same verbs, please. (Teacher displays transparency containing 15 sentences, a sample of which follows.)

1. A parcel postman drives a truck.
2. He delivers packages to people.
3. He drives all over the city.
4. A clerk insures packages.
5. A letter to Mexico costs 16¢.

### Third Day

C: (Children zip through this exercise quickly with no errors in the verbs, although they have trouble with determiners, as in *Parcel postmen drive trucks*. Teacher decides that not only Amy but the whole class needs lessons to clarify use of determiners in statements of generality when the plural form is used.
T: I get up at 6:00 a.m. on school days. I get up at 7:00 a.m. on Saturdays, and I get up at 8:00 a.m. on Sundays. (Writes sentences on overhead underlining the optional adverbs as she goes along.) Jerry, tell me what time you get up on Sundays.

Je:   I get up at 8:00.
T:    Do you go to church on Sundays?
Je:   Yes.
T:    Tell me that in a sentence, please.
Je:   I go to church every Sundays.
T:    Almost right! We can say: 'I go to church Sundays,' or 'I go to church every Sunday.' (Writes sentences on overhead. Here is another noun-determiner situation that will have to be clarified later.)
Je:   I go to church every Sunday.
T:    Right. All of you, tell me where Jerry goes Sundays.
C:    (Children oblige in correct language varying between *Sundays*, *on Sundays*, and *every Sunday*.)
T:    Amy, do you go to church *every* Sunday?
A:    Sometimes.
T:    Do you go almost every Sunday?
A:    Yes, almost.
T:    Tell me that in a sentence.
A:    I almost go to church on Sundays.
T:    I'll help you. You can say: 'I go to church almost every Sunday,' or 'I almost always go to church on Sunday,' or 'Sometimes I go to church on Sundays.' (Teacher writes the sentences on the overhead for Amy and notes use of *on Sunday* and *on Sundays* to be clarified later.)
T:    Which one do you want to use? (Amy chooses: *I go to church almost every Sunday.*) Who goes swimming on Saturdays?
M/D:I do!
T:    Tell us that in a sentence.
M/D:I go swimming on Saturdays.
T:    Do you go swimming every Saturday?
M/D:Yes!
T:    OK, tell us that in a sentence.
M/D:We go swimming every Saturday.
T:    Julie, tell us what you do after school.
Ju:   I watch TV after school.
T:    Do you watch TV every day?
Ju:   Every day! I watch TV every day after school.
T:    Jerry, tell us what you do every Thursday after school.
Je:   I go to Boy Scouts every Thursday after school.
T:    Who can remember what we told about ourselves? We'll all have a turn.
Ju:   Jerry goes to church every Sunday. He goes to Boy Scouts every Thursday after school. Amy goes to church almost every Sunday. David and Mark go swimming every Saturday, and I watch TV every day after school.
T:    Good work, boys and girls!

### Fourth Day

T: Mrs. Korb brought us a letter yesterday from the postmaster. I hope you're happy about it. We can go to the post office next Tuesday. (Mrs. Korb is the school mailcarrier.) Mrs. Korb delivers mail every day except Sundays and holidays. She told us all about her work the other day. Who can tell us what she does every day? You start, David. (Teacher records children's sentences on a transparency as they say them.)

D: Mrs. Korb gets up at 5:00 a.m. every work day.

M: She goes to the post office in her car.

Je: She gets to the post office at 6:00 a.m. every day.

Ju: Mrs. Korb sorts her mail and puts it in her pouch.

T: My, those are good sentences. You haven't made any mistakes. Amy, it's your turn.

A: She drives to her route in her car. She puts some mail in her storage box.

T: Excellent. Let's have some more.

C: (Children oblige with a total of 18 sentences.)

T: Now, can anybody tell me what Mrs. Korb did yesterday? Not what she does *every day*, but what she did *yesterday*.

M: She brought us a letter from the postmaster.

T: Yes, of course. Do you think she got up at 5:00 a.m. yesterday?

M: I think she got up at 5:00 a.m.

T: Let's have some more sentences about what you think Mrs. Korb did yesterday.

C: (Children oblige with a long list of sentences, getting hints from the just completed transparency. A number of past tense verb forms were incorrect and errors were pointed out as they were made. Teacher noted that Amy and Julie needed most help with these forms and planned to give them special help on all verb forms in the near future.)

T: We don't have to say *yesterday* for every sentence. We must be sure to say it when we begin to tell something about what happened in the past. (The teacher records the past tense sentences attaching *yesterday* only to the first one.)

T: Do we say 'every day' to tell about the past?

C: No!

T: 'Every Sunday'?

C: No!

T: 'Every Thursday'?

C: No!

T: You're right! Very good!

## Fifth Day

T:  Today, let's write something for our scrapbook. How would you like to tell your friends about our mail-lady?

C:  (Children accede to the suggestion. After oral preparation for writing, the following compositions were chosen for the scrapbook:)

### Mrs. Korb, Our Mail-lady

We have a woman mailcarrier. Mrs. Korb uses a cart to deliver the mail. She smiles a lot and sometimes she whistles. She walks fast but she always waves to us. We like her very much.

### Your Letters

Every day we wait for Mrs. Korb. She comes to our school every day at recess time. Sometimes she teases us. She smiles and says, "No mail today." Then she shows us your letters. We love them. Please send more letters soon.

In Chapter 7 we will turn to the topic of writing compositions in some detail. These were included here to indicate how practice in syntactic structures can be integrated into the written language of deaf children.

Children can be guided very well in learning new syntactic structures or clarifying those not yet established by practicing them in patterns, a technique widely used in teaching foreign languages. You will notice that in the above plans, the teacher selected a simple pattern and a single known verb to introduce the—s morpheme. Then she had the children practice it in a slightly amplified pattern and with a broader vocabulary. She contrasted several related structures but always returned to the simplest one until she was sure that the children understood the limits of its use. Although the children's knowledge about the—s morpheme increased, there was still much more that they needed to learn about it. For one thing they must have practice using T/neg along with practice in moving the optional adverbs about as well as the preverb modifiers as in *My dad never gets angry at me* versus *My dad doesn't ever get angry at me*. And then there are all the question forms that relate to the present tense. Children cannot learn everything at once, but careful planning ensures that no aspect of any structure will be omitted or neglected. We will make suggestions for such planning in Chapter 8.

## ALTERNATIVES TO THE INTEGRATED LANGUAGE ARTS APPROACH IN TEACHING LANGUAGE

### The Fitzgerald Key

The procedure suggested in the above section is only one of a variety of ways in which teachers have tried over the years to teach syntax to deaf children. In the 1920s Fitzgerald (1926), a very creative and talented deaf woman, devised a scheme just for that purpose. It was a synthesis of the work of her predecessors, yet original and practical enough to be adopted almost universally in American schools for the deaf by the middle of the twentieth century. In essence it visualized the word order of English sentences within its six columns (Table 6-2). The first column is devoted to the subject of the sentence, the second to the verb, the third to the object, and the remaining three to the order of adverbs modifying the main verb. The Key was usually introduced to children at the age of 5 or 6. Although Fitzgerald did not eschew planned experiences or eliminate experiences as the basis for learning new structures, she did not stress them. The teacher usually selected a "language principle" from a language curriculum and taught it, clarifying its meaning from whatever sources she chose.

When a child originated language he had first to "speak in the Key," pointing to the correct columns as he spoke to be sure he got everything in the correct order. Then he restated his sentence in more rhythmic speech. He also wrote everything on special 22-inch wide Key paper to reinforce his oral production. Although the Key was brilliantly conceived, the practitioners who followed Fitzgerald tended to use it mechanically. For instance, a teacher who believed in "experiences" took her class to the circus every year. She would write a story about it, then cut it apart sentence by sentence, and had the children reconstruct it. After they had accomplished that, she cut the sentence strips into words and phrases and had the children place the resulting flash cards in the proper columns of the Key. Some children became very skillful in putting the puzzle together again, but somehow could not apply their skill to originating straight language. When the Key serves only as an end rather than as the means to straight language, it loses its value. It was a boon to teachers of the deaf before the days of modern linguistics, but today we have even better insights into language acquisition than the Key affords.

### Natural Language for the Deaf

During the 1950s two other approaches to teaching language to deaf children were described. The first of these was designated as the "natural" way to teach language, emphasizing the child's need to express himself as the basis for his language growth (Groht, 1958). This approach had been used at Lexington School for the Deaf in New York from the time of its founding. When a child needed a new word or structure to communicate, it was presented in the context of the situation requiring it. Then tutors offered alternate ways of expressing thoughts and ideas, thus relating new structures to those already known. Written language was a daily experience for all children. Miss Groht inspired hundreds of teachers and student teachers to emulate her procedures. She knew the English language thoroughly and also knew how to

**Table 6-2**

The Fitzgerald Key with Illustrations of Sentences Written in the Key

| Subject | Verb / Pred. Adj. Pred. Noun Pred. Pron. | Ind. Obj. | Dir. Obj. | Adverbial Modifiers of Main Verb | | |
|---|---|---|---|---|---|---|
| What: / Who: | | What: ( ) Whom: | Whom: What: | Where: | For—; How Far: / From—; How Often: / With—; How Long: / How: How Much: / Why: (if) | When: |
| Father | bought | me | a box of candy | | for my birthday. | |
| I | know | | that you have a dog at home. | | | |
| Jerry | likes | | to play with his dog. | | | |
| We | will go | | | to Chicago | on the train | this summer. |

From Streng et al., *Hearing Therapy for Children*. New York, Grune & Stratton, 1954.

127

teach it in developmental steps, though not all of her students could match her understanding and skill, so were often left floundering in a sea of unstructured language programs.

## Patterning

The second approach to emerge in the 1950s had its roots in procedures used in teaching foreign languages devised during World War II. Introduced at St. Joseph's Institute for the Deaf in St. Louis by Sr. Jeanne d'Arc (Barnes, 1958), it used patterns as the basis for language acquisition. It was linguistically based and generative in character. As an example, the request pattern might serve as the basis for language expansion. A child first learned to respond to such requests as *Come here*, *Get your chair*, *Help me*, or *Drink your milk*. As soon as he did, he was expected to make a verbal response before he reacted motorically. He was expected to say *I will* to the request *Help me*, or *I won't* to a negative one, as *Don't fall*. In like manner when he understood the *yes/no* question, he answered either *yes, yes I will/can/do/did* or *no, no I won't/can't/don't/didn't*. This prepared him to formulate sentences such as *I didn't cry* or *I won't tell* without further explanation, for he already knew the verb form and could use it in any newly introduced pattern. Language in this approach is based on constant communication between teacher and pupil and between pupil and pupil (Buckler, 1968).

There is no one best way to teach language, but it is my firm conviction that an approach which considers the child's cognitive stage of development and uses his experiences will be superior to any other as the basis for acquiring language. This puts a great burden on the teacher to be linguistically sophisticated, to be knowledgeable about the child's capabilities, and to be creative in planning opportunities for plenty of pattern practice to ensure that every deaf child achieves his highest potential in the standard usage of language.

## REFERENCES

Barnes Sr. Jeanne d'Arc: The development of connected language skills. Volta Rev 60:2, 58–65, 1958
Buckler Sr. MS: Expanding language through patterning. Volta Rev 70:2, 89–96, 1968
Fitzgerald E: Straight Language for the Deaf. Staunton, Va., The McClure Co., 1926; Washington, D.C., A. G. Bell Assoc., 1949
Grammatico LF and Miller SD: Curriculum for the preschool deaf child. Volta Rev 76:5, 280–289, 1974
Groht MA: Natural Language for Deaf Children. Washington, D.C., A. G. Bell Assoc., 1958
Streng AH: Syntax, Speech and Hearing, Applied Linguistics for Teachers of Children with Language and Hearing Disabilities. New York, Grune & Stratton, 1972

# 7
# Reading and Writing in the Curriculum

## ASPECTS OF THE CURRICULUM

School curricula during the last few decades have basically been societ-ally oriented. That is, children were expected to learn facts that were to help them understand the principles of social organization of our own and other cultures through the study of history and geography, and to learn the skills of reading, writing, and arithmetic to prepare them to absorb facts that were to make them good citizens and good workers. In the sixties and seventies modern curriculum began to place less emphasis on the learning of facts since there are too many of them for anyone to learn. Besides, facts can now be stored, retrieved, and transmitted by machines. It is more important to teach children where to find answers to questions than to memorize facts.

Today's curriculum concentrates on developing concepts and values that help an individual to deal with the facts that are abundantly available. Schools are becoming much more aware of the individual's personal and emotional needs, of his interests and values, and of how he learns. As a result the curriculum has become less structured. In many school systems individualized learning, open classrooms, and programmed teaching have replaced group instruction, lock-step promotion, and rigid grading systems in order to induce the kind of learning that will help children cope with the complexities of life.

It would not be feasible in a text of this kind to present a curriculum designed specifically for hearing impaired children. Hopefully, curricula for these children in segregated schools would reflect modern educational thought. Nevertheless, my predilection for a curriculum for all hearing im-paired children is one in which language and reading play an important part. A conceptually oriented curriculum based on recurring life situations would allow a child periodically to review vocabulary and language acquired at an elementary level, and continually to apply it and expand it with his maturing concepts. Only when language and vocabulary are constantly reviewed can they become part of his productive capacity.

We must regard everything that happens to a hearing impaired child to be an integral part of his curriculum. This is especially vital in the development and acquisition of language, for only through sensing and feeling can he "know." The scope of the curriculum thus becomes broad indeed. It includes knowledge about (1) the child himself, his sexuality, his personal identity, and his inner feelings; (2) health and nutrition, family relationships, and friendships; (3) the physical and chemical forces that impinge on him every hour of the day; (4) measurement; (5) money and its uses by consumers and government; and (6) work and recreation as fulfillment of personal and social needs. These are persisting life situations which affect a person in varying degrees from cradle to grave.

Some important concepts to be emphasized within the broad scope of the curriculum include interdependence of people and nations, origin of conflicts in families and nations, conservation of scarce resources, development and conservation of new sources of energy, ecosystems and man's relation to nature and the universe, technological growth and its effect on our lives and those of developing countries, population growth and control, morality and value systems, empathy with other points of view, concern for the social group and for loyalty, freedom, and equality. There is much to learn but there is a whole lifetime to learn it in. We need to make love of learning a part of the curriculum, too.

## PARTICIPANTS IN CURRICULUM PLANNING

In the past teachers were solely responsible for the content of the curriculum. Parents were considered interlopers if they expressed any opinions about what happened in the classroom. Today parents are encouraged to contribute to the school's curriculum by active participation in the planning. Likewise, children, given the opportunity for input, should be more eager to carry through plans that they helped make. But the teacher still has the heaviest responsibility in organizing and structuring the learning situation according to each child's cognitive level. Gone should be the days when she acted as lecturer or dispenser of facts prescribed by the curriculum while the children sat passively by, trying to be polite but very bored. In a stimulating environment, it will be the unusual child who will reject learning. It is the responsibility of the teacher to provide a classroom where the child may be an active participator in the learning process.

## READING IN THE CURRICULUM

Reading is not to be considered a subject within the curriculum such as geography, mathematics, or science. Rather, it is a tool whereby children can explore current ideas and events, gain insights into the past and into other cultures, and enjoy the flights of the imagination into the future and into the world of fairies and even monsters. Yet millions of persons in the United States depend on the media rather than on reading to learn about daily events and to satisfy vicariously some of their personal, emotional, and recreational needs.

If it is true that American children from preschool age through 13 years watch TV for as much as 5 to 7 hours a day, one can safely assume that there is little need or time for reading even if written material is available in the home. Schools, on the other hand, deal heavily with written material, for parents, despite their own devotion to the media, still expect their children to learn to read and write. Actually we live in a world where the printed word is still of considerable importance in our daily lives. As many as 30,000 books are added every year to the millions already in existence. About 2500 of them are directed to juveniles. To entice children to read, we must guarantee that there is some profit or satisfaction in it for them. They must discover the importance of the printed word and the joys and pleasure that go with reading.

Written language is different from the spoken language that we hear day in and day out. It is highly organized into complicated, standardized patterns, with pauses related to grammatical structures made evident by punctuation. It is often replete with metaphorical language and idioms, or loaded with vocabulary peculiar to the subject at hand, and frequently removed in time and space from the here and now. Spoken language is usually closer to its referents. Its unpredictable pauses are often punctuated by gestures, facial expression, and fillers such as *uh*, *you know*, or *I mean*. Intonation carries a great deal of meaning in oral communication. Thus we see that reading can not be simply a translation of auditory language to graphemic symbols. Instead, it involves learning an additional form of language through long hours of exposure and practice. Some children learn to read by themselves, but more require specialized instruction.

## STUDIES IN BEGINNING READING

For decades reading instruction traditionally began in the first grade when a child reached the magic age of 6½. This is no longer considered the definitive time when a child is ready to read. Rather than thinking about *a* readiness for reading, modern educators prefer to consider *readinesses* because children do not learn everything about reading at once. Children can learn some aspects of reading at an age considerably earlier than 6½, and others require further maturation and experience.

A great deal of time and federal money were spent during the 1960s in trying to discover the best method of teaching reading to normally hearing youngsters. The conclusion was that there was no one best way. Chall (1973) reviewed current research and concluded that among other things, better results in beginning reading seem to be achieved through a code-emphasis rather than a meaning-emphasis approach. It looked to her as though phonic skills were essential in helping normally hearing children to identify printed words. Despite the ambiguity of much of the research conducted during the sixties, a multiplicity of reading materials presenting highly structured steps for teaching phoneme-grapheme relationships appeared for teaching beginning reading. Most publishers of readers refer to these materials as being linguistically based, a term used loosely since only the phonetic aspects of the language are considered and structure is largely overlooked. A study of widely used basal readers reveals that even on the first level, all the language forms used by adults appear in them (Hargis, 1975b). The assumption is that the readers will understand the complicated syntax and the literary language employed by the authors.

Reading for meaning has not been entirely ignored by reading specialists. Although some psychologists believe that children under the age of 12 have difficulty in thinking in abstractions, it is very likely that children at earlier ages can interpret figurative language, providing the content of the material is within the realm of their experience. It appears that overall intelligence and general ability are factors most closely related to critical thinking, interpreting, inferring, and evaluating what is read. This, of course, applies to all of one's perceptions on a nonreading level as well. A person who cannot think critically about what he hears on radio or TV will also be unable to react to written materials in an incisive manner. Critical thinking is based on experience which involves noting likenesses and differences between and among a variety of experiences, categorizing, and classifying them and relating them to situations not immediately and directly experienced. Teachers can help children to develop their capacities to think by guiding experiences but not by presenting drills in reading comprehension.

## READING FOR HEARING IMPAIRED CHILDREN

At best, reading is difficult for many hearing children who understand and speak their native language. Imagine what it must be for those who hear only partially and who comprehend language only vaguely. Yet for children with hearing impairments, ability to read is very important. They have less access to the spoken word through the media than hearing persons do. Therefore they must often depend on the written word for gaining information and for communicating with others. Hopefully they will discover the pleasure of reading for enjoyment, too.

Pupils, ages 6 to 20, attending schools and programs for the hearing impaired in the United States are shown to achieve a reading grade placement of about 5.0 and a vocabulary level of 3.7 at age 16 (Gentile and Di Francesca, 1969). This does not mean that some children do not make scores equal to and even above their age levels, but on the whole the reading ability of the approximately 13,000 children in this study was retarded. The results support the 1946 findings of Pugh (1946) who concluded that children in schools for the deaf were retarded at all levels, especially in vocabulary and sentence meaning. Obviously not much has occurred in the intervening years to correct this deficiency. When we contemplate the causes for this general reading retardation, it becomes immediately clear that its roots go deep into the overall linguistic deficiency of hearing impaired children. Semantic as well as syntactic aspects seem to contribute equally to the problem.

## Reading as a Psycholinguistic Process

We actually know little about the reading process, but Smith (1971) offers some perceptive insights into the teaching of reading applicable not only to normally hearing children but also to deaf children. He views reading as a psycholinguistic process. He asserts that (1) reading is only superficially different from comprehending spoken language, (2) many skills employed in learning oral language can be employed in learning to read, and (3) the actual marks on the printed page are relatively less important than knowledge of language. What lies behind the eye is more important than what strikes the eye.

According to Smith, reading for meaning makes use of information both at the surface and within the deep structure of language at the same time using elements of semantic information and visual clues. Transformational rules appear to be the key to unravelling complicated structures. A series of short simple sentences is easier to process than one sentence containing several conjoined or embedded clauses. A reader must sometimes guess at the deep structure of complex sentences, and if he assumes the wrong underlying structure, he has to try another until it makes sense. In short, syntax plays an important role in comprehension of what is to be read. Teachers of the deaf know this only too well.

A good reader uses both syntactic and semantic redundancies in the language in order to eliminate some or all of the alternative meanings in a sequence of words. Syntactic knowledge duplicates visual and semantic clues.

For instance, in the sentence:

The woman bought a ———— of shoes.

the reader can replace the missing word by inserting the only one that makes
sense, namely *pair*. In the next sentence:

The woman bought a pair of ————.

the reader may anticipate *shoes*, *gloves*, or *pants*. When he sees the word
*gloves* in this sentence, he knows it is not *shoes* or *pants* if he has an elementary knowledge of the words that might fit into such a slot in this sentence.
Anyone who reads uses the visual information he receives to interpret sentences as a whole. Yet Smith (1971) minimizes the value of teaching phonics
in reading. To him, decoding is not transforming visual symbols into sound,
but transforming visual representation of language into meaning. Word recognition is not reading, for one does not identify individual words in fluent
reading. Smith views the teaching of phonics as a hope rather than a valid
technique for providing clues to the sounds of written words. For instance, in
the following pairs of words, the same combinations of letters produce different auditory effects: *wind-wind*, *read-read*, *shall-tall*, *father-fathead*,
*cough-plough*. Hundreds of rules are needed to identify new words by sound
alone, too many for any child to learn and remember. For profoundly deaf
children phonics will play a minor role, if any, in learning to read.

Smith (1971) further suggests that children can learn to read only by
reading materials within their experience and understanding, materials that
make sense to them. To read effectively, they should have a good idea in
advance of what they are reading. In short, they must have adequate background information about the subject at hand, familiarity with the semantic
requirements of the material, and knowledge of the language structures in it.
Having deaf children read aloud will not teach them to read. To read aloud
effectively, a person must really know in advance what he is to read, and then
he practices it. Even the President of the United States practices what his
speech writers have prepared for him so that he may present his views to his
audience with conviction and meaning. Reading aloud is an art, not a technique for teaching reading to hearing impaired children.

In light of the above comments, it is evident that the first reading matter
presented to a hearing impaired child must be based on his internalized language. It cannot consist of words plucked from a preprimer, such as *See what
I see*, but must be based on his actual experiences and written so as to reflect
his capacity to comprehend and use language.

A child who has not internalized the rules of basic sentence patterns
really cannot read, although he may be able to associate a written word with
an object or a picture. He is ready to read when he knows what a sentence is.

Then his reading matter must be controlled for semantic clarity as well as syntactic difficulty. It is the teacher and not the book publisher who prepares this reading material and in fact continues to so do for much of the child's early education. At the same time the child is learning the written form of his oral or spelled language. Although this approach differs from how a hearing child is taught to read, it seems the best alternative available to teachers of children with severe or profound losses.

For the young hearing impaired child who acquires his language through his ear as a result of early auditory stimulation aided by amplification, the process of learning to read should not differ much from that of any child who understands his native language, everything else being equal. Perhaps his vocabulary will be more restricted because he has not heard words used in differing contexts, because he has not been able to hear critical words above the ambient noise level, or because he is not familiar with metaphoric and idiomatic language. If this child is receiving most of his education in the regular school he will surely be exposed to phonics. He may need additional auditory training to alert him to the sounds of speech that his defective hearing normally eliminates. He may also need individual tutoring in reading to clarify the rhetorical aspects of language, but generally he should be able to survive in the mainstream of regular education.

### Teacher-made Reading Materials—Charts for Beginners

On the other hand, we must make adjustments for the deaf child who lacks ability to handle complex transformations, morphemic rules, phrase structure rules for nouns and verbs, and the numerous required deletions in written language, to say nothing about the semantic hazards that he faces. For him language and reading will be developing in tandem. The question of the order in which new language is presented differs in programs throughout the country. In some, children are introduced to it first through listening to and/or lipreading it; then they read it and finally speak it (the LRS approach). In another program they may listen, speak, and read; whereas in still another they may read first, then listen, and lastly speak. Whichever approach is used, it is wise to allow deaf children to see the written form of their motorically expressed language in close contiguity with it. The written form stabilizes the fleeting time-sequenced motor production of oral or spelled language and provides another means of associating symbols with events.

The responsibility to provide the proper form of the reading matter as well as its substance falls on the child's teacher. She must take cues from what the child tells her. She must record what he says or translate it using the correct structure as she sees it, but at all times reflecting the child's meaning.

For instance, if 5-year-old Laura comes in from recess escorting 4-year-old Kathie and says, "Mark bump . . . (pointing to Kathie) . . . fell down," the teacher may say "Oh, I'm sorry! Mark bumped Kathie. She fell down. Too bad!" The teacher proceeds to dust Kathie off and send her on her way. She then writes on the chalkboard:

> Mark bumped Kathie.
> She fell down.
> Too bad!

The teacher had observed the event so she was sure she was recording it correctly. Whenever there is a doubt about what a child is trying to report it is better to avoid recording it until the facts are checked. There is no use associating incorrect structure or vocabulary with an event unknown to the recorder. This teacher did contribute "Too bad!" to the embryonic paragraph in order to add a feeling tone to an otherwise drab account. She expanded the conversation with Laura to say, "I saw Mark bump Kathie. He didn't hurt her. He didn't look where he was going. Kathie didn't get hurt so we won't worry about it." She did not record this part of the conversation because it did not reflect Laura's intent in reporting the event.

Next, Laura's paragraph was transferred to a chart from the chalkboard and placed with other charts that had been accumulating for the past weeks. All the charts had been titled and illustrated by the children and were reproduced on 8 × 11 pages, bound into booklets and sent home to be read. Aloud? Silently? It would not matter because the language in the charts was the child's. Parents must be informed about the purpose of this type of reading material and must understand that it is prerequisite to reading in books.

The "experience-language-reading" chart must be attractive, well manuscripted, and properly spaced on a page. Charts may or may not be written in paragraph form. At first a single sentence should occupy a single line so as to present the sentence as an entity. Phrases should be kept together—noun, verb, or prepositional—for the same reason. Through this technique children should be assisted in reading sentences and phrases rather than words.

When actual paragraphs are used, the two-sentence paragraph is a good starting point. Later three- or four-sentence paragraphs may be constructed. It must be kept in mind that paragraphs have topic sentences and that only those sentences which are related to it in thought are to be part of the paragraph. You can easily see that the next chart is not a unified paragraph. If teachers can't write good paragraphs surely their children won't.

### Our Parakeet
Billy is a bird. He is a parakeet. Parakeets eat seeds. They drink water. Billy has blue feathers and a green tail. He can talk. He sits on a perch

and swings. Billy can say "Hi." We talk to Billy. The perch is in Billy's cage. We feed Billy. He can fly.

Try to reconstruct this set of sentences so as to make several good paragraphs. Discard or add anything you like to improve it. Perhaps you will need a new title, too.

Rush (1972) makes the following suggestions when writing for children with language deficiencies:

1. Keep sentences and paragraphs short.
2. The optimum length for sentences is 10 or 12 words. Intersperse short simple sentences with longer ones.
3. The opening sentence of a paragraph should be short and dramatic. The sentences that follow it must contribute to the topic and to the fluency of the paragraph. Read the paragraph aloud to see if the sentences follow one another in proper sequence. If they do not, rearrange them.
4. Vocabulary should be held within the range of the child's comprehension. Keep unfamiliar words at a minimum.
5. Use the active voice rather than the passive whenever possible.
6. Stumbling blocks to comprehension include conjunctions, pronoun referents, multiple meanings, and idioms. If there is doubt about the readability of a sentence containing a conjunction, cover up the conjunction. If the sentence meaning can still be derived from it, the sentence can stand as written, as in *The air was cool, _____ I wore my coat, and _____ you are cold, put on your sweater*. If you think the reader may have difficulty in discovering a referent for a pronoun, rewrite the sentence to avoid ambiguity. For instance, who is happy in the following sentences? *The teachers helped the students. They were happy*. What does *that* refer to in *The boys hid the treasure, but nobody else knew that.?*
7. There are no rules to follow in introducing multiple meanings and idioms. In beginning reading use simple language that the child is familiar with If idioms are used, the context can develop their meaning, but caution must direct the teacher in introducing them into reading material.

Children must become familiar with the meaning and use of punctuation marks: periods, commas, dashes, parentheses, exclamation and quotation marks, as well as with the use of capital letters. Later in books, children must be guided in interpreting charts, maps, tables, and graphs. Whenever appropriate, these aspects of written language are incorporated in teacher-made materials.

Direct quotations may be taught through the use of a modified experience chart. What a person said is recorded in a balloon and then transcribed into a sentence pattern. Eventually, the children may be asked to fill in a balloon from a text or write the contents of the balloon as a sentence or question. Figure 7-1 shows some charts illustrating the possible steps you might take to make direct quotation meaningful.

A series of language-experience-reading charts dealing with the use of pronouns in a paragraph can be constructed in which stick figures are substituted for pronouns. A pronoun is first used in the subject slot, later in the two object slots (direct and indirect), and finally in both. Plural forms in the nominative and objective cases are introduced when needed. Children can "read" these charts aloud since they are experience based. Possessive pronouns used as determiners can also be programmed into the materials in any order needed. (See Figures 7-1D and E.)

Another variety of chart is an important adjunct to the experience-language-reading chart. It is a bonafide *reading* chart, based on similar but not identical experiences recorded in the children's language charts. The vocabulary and syntax are all known to the children. It is written by the teacher so that the children must actually read in order to get meaning from written matter without help of illustrations. For instance, this chart was written to supplement Laura's chart about Kathie:

> Another Bump
> Eddie bumped Miss S.
> She didn't fall down.
> Eddie said, "I'm sorry."

The following chart is one to be read by the children who have the parakeet in their room. Jeff is an imaginary boy unknown to the class.

> Jeff's Bird.
> Jeff has a little yellow bird. It is a canary. The little yellow bird can't talk. It can't say "Hi." But the canary can sing. It sang for Jeff.

One of the major objectives of teacher-prepared material is to control syntax and vocabulary. A good rule to follow is to use only known syntactic and morphemic structures even if a limited new vocabulary is to be introduced, or to use only known vocabulary if a new structure is to be incorporated into the chart. A teacher should have some maneuverability in constructing material but must not deviate so far as to becloud the meaning for the reader. No more than one or two new words should be introduced in a running 50. The new words should be repeated several times if possible in the paragraph. Also, a new syntactic structure should not deviate too much from the known.

If children are to learn to read by reading, four or five supplementary charts should be prepared for each language experience chart. Some charts may be left incomplete, to be completed by a child or the group. Children read

Charts illustrating direct quotations.

A

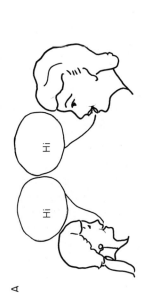

Linda said, "Hi!"    Miss S said, "Hi!"

B

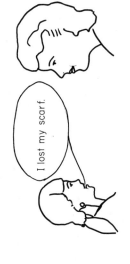

Linda said, "I lost my scarf."

"I lost my scarf," said Linda.

C

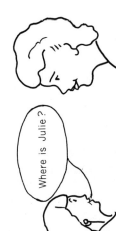

Linda asked, "Where is Julie?"

"Where is Julie?" Linda asked.

"Where is Julie?" asked Linda.

Figure 7-1. A introduces the direct quotation using only one form, as *Linda said, "Hi!"* In B an additional form is included. It places the quote first in the sentence. C displays three alternative forms for the quoted question.

139

140

Pronoun charts.

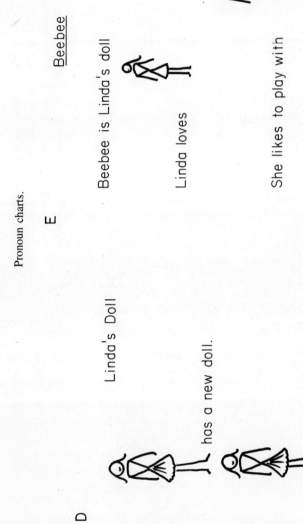

D

Linda's Doll

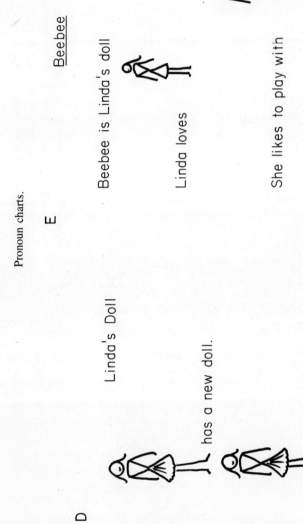 has a new doll.

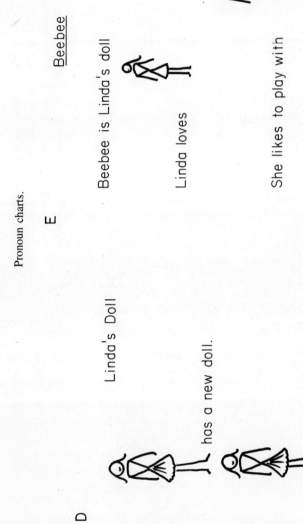 brought the doll to school.

E

Beebee

Beebee is Linda's doll

Linda loves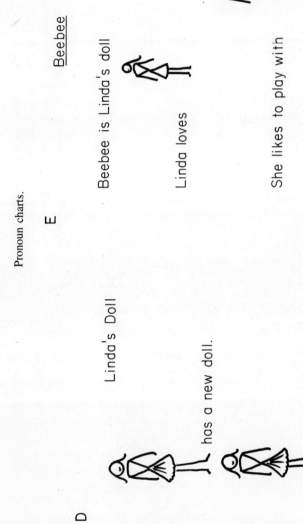

She likes to play with

She will make a dress for

Figure 7-1.  D & E: Children read charts by supplying pronouns in appropriate places.

these charts silently and summarize the contents, draw pictures to illustrate them, or dramatize them. Answering questions about them is perhaps the least desirable way of checking on comprehension, especially if the answers can be plucked directly from the sentences. Answering the questions "What color was the bird?" or "Can the bird talk?" brings no further insights to the child as to what he has read, and not much information to the teacher as to whether the child really comprehends the material.

## Teacher-made Materials for Advancing Pupils

As children progress through the grades, teachers will still find it necessary to prepare materials for them. These will include a wider and wider range of subject matter and will be based on planned class activities, field trips, science experiments, observations of natural phenomena, care of classroom animals and plants, films, TV programs, auditorium programs, dialogues for daily living, and dramatic skits. Some materials may be constructed to present a sequence of events, some to bring causal relationships, and some in which reading between the lines, or inferring, is required. Common idioms should appear in these materials in anticipation of the children's encountering them in books. It pays to scan books for colloquial language and idioms that can be naturally and easily incorporated in teacher-prepared materials.

It takes skill on the part of teachers to keep in mind all of the factors that contribute to the kind of reading matter that least interferes with the natural functioning of language. But if a child is to advance to reading syntactically complex and semantically weighty material in books, he must broaden his grammatical base and he must become familiar with the vernacular, and with colloquial and rhetorical language.

## Appropriateness of Commercial Reading
## Materials for Hearing Impaired Children

Parents will inevitably ask, "When will my child read in books?" and you will reply, "As soon as he can." Of course, the explanation cannot stop there. Parents and teachers alike must understand that books are written for children who know language. They know and use sentences and questions and the understand transformations, phrase structure rules, and morphemic variations of words in their spoken language. When an author produces a book for children, he keeps in mind children's interests, and to some extent their vocabulary and cognitive development, but he may pay scant attention to their background experience and practically none to the syntactic aspects of language itself. He assumes that his readers comprehend complicated, highly organized syntactic structures as well as colorful rhetorical language. In fact, he strives to make his writing colloquial and different from the dullness created by the use of plain, unadorned basic sentences.

Despite the abundance of reading materials, from textbooks to children's literature, very little of it is suitable for children with severe language delays. One solution to this dilemma is the linguistic rewriting of books. Although this is very time consuming, it does offer a better means of providing reading matter than that of producing entirely original teacher-composed manuscripts—or providing none at all. When it has been ascertained that a certain book is almost but not quite suitable for a child, the complex sentences are broken down into simpler ones. Where this is not possible because of semantic complications, sentences can be paraphrased. Known vocabulary can be substituted for idioms or colloquial language. Children read the simpler version first and then the original, comparing the two as they go along. Rereading such material is to be encouraged since children may assimilate the new vocabulary and structures without having to look up dozens of words in the dictionary or drill on language forms.

To read in books meaningfully requires a language sophistication far beyond what most six-year-old hearing impaired children possess. The paucity of their vocabulary contributes to this condition. It is estimated that a senior in high school has access to a vocabulary of about 15,000 words. This means that he had to learn at least 1000 to 1500 new words every year that he proceeded through the grades. A deaf child needs help and guidance in acquiring these thousands and thousands of words that have not only one but many meanings and that may be used idiomatically and figuratively.

Most of our common words, including prepositions, have multiple meanings. Let us assume that a child in the first grade can pronounce and identify the verb *make* in its infinitive form and in the past tense. He also knows its basic meaning of *to form or construct*. This word is used frequently in early reading material and could appear in sentences such as these which are paraphrased from a first grade reader.

1. Find the ones that *made* this rocket.
2. Don *made a picture of* his mother.
3. Don *made* a bargain.
4. Even when you *make a bad trade*, you have to stick to your bargain.
5. Don *made up* some stories.
6. "You have to *make* them *up*, Sue," said Don.
7. Soon Don had stories enough *to make* a book.
8. What *makes* you go so slow?
9. Don *made* the car go faster and faster.
10. The policemen *made* Don stop.

11.   The boys *made fun of* Don.
12.   Did that *make* Don *mad*!

The meanings of *make* in these sentences include the basic one of putting things together, but also composing in the mind, causing things to happen, and painting or drawing. In addition, the verb is used idiomatically in *make a bargain*, *have to make*, *make fun of*, and *make someone mad*. *Make* is also used in sentences containing other idioms as in *stick to your bargain* and *made fun of*. *Make* also appears in a variety of structures: as the main verb in simple sentences; as a verb in a relative clause and in an adverbial clause, in a question, and in an exclamation that looks like a question; as an infinitive; and as part of a double verb. Being able to pronounce *make* would not help a child know what it meant in these sentences unless he had experience with the specific meanings of all the vocabulary and idioms involved. If you look in a dictionary you will find that the definitions for *make* take up more than a whole column.

## GUIDING VOCABULARY GROWTH THROUGH DIRECTED STUDY

Since the vocabulary load in reading is very heavy, an intensive well-planned program of directed study of vocabulary, begun early in a child's school life, can anticipate as well as alleviate the burden somewhat. Vocabulary study focuses on the semantic aspects of language though never neglecting structure. Although the program anticipates the vocabulary used in books, vocabulary acquisition is integrated into the lives and experiences of the children. Here we must distinguish between the words a child uses in daily communication and those he understands. We no longer talk about *frocks*, but the word does appear in books. All of us adults understand more words than we use. Our written vocabulary may exceed our spoken one, but our reading vocabulary is usually the greatest of the three. Eventually the same should be true for the children we teach.

Although vocabulary for daily communication will be somewhat limited, it must be automatically retrievable. Vocabulary for reading will be extensive and must be organized for retrieval. A program of directed study will have as its goals: (1) a steady increase in the number of words that a child uses and understands, (2) clarification of a word's usage and of the dimensions of its features (how it can and cannot be used semantically and in grammatic structures), (3) knowledge of multiple meanings and idiomatic usage, (4) use of the dictionary, and (5) organizations of vocabulary for retrieval. A daily 20-minute period is the minimum time that should be devoted to this program.

The child's first words will come from his environment. They are usually concrete and picturable, as *dog, cap, milk, shoe, run,* and *fall.* Each word represents a category of things or actions, and when a child assigns the correct verbal symbol to the category, we know that he knows it. Everything, every action or attribute pertinent to the manipulation of his environment, must be identified and verbalized for him. It must be presented continually so as to ensure its retention.

## Noun Vocabulary

Let us direct our attention first to the noun vocabulary. Nouns can be classified as count and noncount nouns. Their difference must be noted since the use of determiners is dependent on this characteristic. The determiner system is a complicated one and every effort must be made to clarify its use when a noun vocabulary is under consideration. For instance, the following sentences contain only a few examples of the dozens of rules that a child must discover about determiners, or have clarified for him by his teacher:

*A* monkey peeled *an* orange. (Count noun/nondefinite articles: *a* and *an*.)
He three *the* peel on *the* floor. (Count noun/definite article.)
We bought (1) *the* fruit at (2) *a* fruit market. [(1) Noncount noun/definite determiner; (2) noncount noun used as a noun modifier with count noun/nondefinite determiner.]

On linen changing day in a school for the deaf, a young girl came to her dorm supervisor and said, "Big white broke" meaning that the sheet she had in her hand was torn. Although her utterance was creative and understood in the particular circumstance, it would not be clear if the receiver of the message were unaware of the situation which prompted it. Children must learn what nouns go with what verbs because of the restrictions placed on them by their use in sentences and by their features. Although we cannot say, "The sheet broke," or "The girl broke the sheet," we can say, "The glass broke," and "The girl broke the glass," or even "She broke her promise," and "She broke the record for the mile." The limits of a word's usage must be set and clarified in vocabulary study.

After a child accumulates a sizeable vocabulary of basic nouns, his attention may be drawn to the parts of the objects in his environment. For instance, he may learn that a car has a *seat belt, a door,* and *wheels,* but he is often unaware that his coat has *a pocket, a zipper, a collar, sleeves,* or *a lining.* In order to help him organize an accumulating number of words, we can start individual dictionaries for each child. Every basic word he knows is followed in this loose leaf dictionary by a page of parts, and the words are illustrated with pictures and sentences. At first, the basic word is assigned its place in the alphabet according to its first letter. Later the first and second or even third letter may enter into the task. Figure 7-2 illustrates several pages from such a dictionary.

As a child's intellect develops, he is able to see relations between several word categories in ascending levels of abstraction. *Apples*, *oranges*, and *bananas* may be classified as *fruit*; *peas*, *beans*, and *carrots* as *vegetables*; *fruit* and *vegetables* as *food*. Difficulty in understanding abstract words contributes greatly to inability to comprehend what is read. Hearing impaired children are known to be more deficient in the use of superordinate terms such as *recreation*, *clothing*, and *mass transit* than hearing children (Hughes, 1961). Yet they do use some. Because they don't know the differences between *pork*, *beef*, and *ham*, they overuse the term *meat*, and because they do not know the value of *pennies*, *dimes*, and *nickels*, they call all coins *money*. It is important that children learn hundreds of superordinate terms as well as their subordinate constituents. Usually these superordinate terms cannot be illustrated with pictures. Only other words will clarify their meanings. A separate section of a child's dictionary could well be devoted to this aspect of word study.

Many nouns are derived from other form classes of words such as verbs or adjectives, and even from whole sentences. For older children, the process of nominalization should become a part of vocabulary study. Nominalization is accomplished through use of both inflectional and derivational affixes. For example, from the verb *govern* we can create nouns by adding inflectional affixes, or morphemic endings, *-ed* or *-ing*, as in these sentences: *The rights of the governed must be zealously guarded* and *Governing is a serious business*. The addition of the derivational affix *ment* creates the noun *government*. [See Streng (1972) for more details on the subject of nominalization.]

For retrieval, these words may be classified by affix, by base word, or by any other organizing principle decided on by pupils and teacher and then recorded in an alphabetized $3 \times 5$ card file. Since derivational affixes can change the meanings of words, each word is illustrated with several sentences so that the limits of its usage can be established. The pupils must also learn the specific meanings of various affixes such as those implying negation (*anti-*, *in-*, *ir-*, *non-*, *un-*); direction (*ad-*, *cir-*, *up-*, *in-*, *re-*, *trans-*, *down-*); number (*bi-*, *tri-*, *quad-*, *oc-*); and agent (*-er*, *-or*, *-ist*, *-ian*). If pupils can discover the relationship of groups of words, they will have more access to meaning in reading.

## Verb Vocabulary

Verb bocabulary must also be organized for recall, and whereever possible coordinated with the noun vocabulary that the child is learning. Noun vocabulary can thus be reviewed in the directed study of the verb. Verbs can

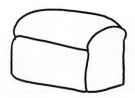

Mother baked bread on Saturday

I like raisin bread.

I like soft bread.

I put the bread in the breadbox.


### More about bread

a piece of bread

a slice of bread

I had two slices of bread for lunch.

I made a ham sandwich.

crust →

I like hard crust.

a loaf of bread

two loaves of bread

We bought two loaves of bread.

Figure 7-2.  Pages from a child's dictionary.

1 car

2 cars

3 cars

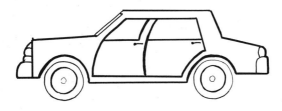

Miss S has a new car.

We went to the zoo in Miss S's car.

Two cars bumped.

### Parts of a car

tire    a tire

two tires

4 tires

Daddy had a flat tire

door/car door

I pinched my finger in the car door.

seat

I sat in the back seat.

I like to sit in the front seat.

seat belt

I put on the seat belt.

be classified as verbs of motion, states of being, those used in mental processes and modes of communication, verbs describing sight and sound and smell, and many more. A verb dictionary can be started soon after a child knows a few common verbs of action. Meaning is related first to human activity, then to animals, and finally to things in nature and to mechanical objects as they appear in his environment, as in:

| A boy can run. | A dog can run. | My watch is | The water is |
| A woman can run. | A bird can run. | running. | running in the gutter. |
| A little baby can't run. | A fish can't run. | The motor is running. | Your nose is running. |
| | | The electric meter is running. | Please wipe it. |
| | | | Tears ran down her cheeks. |

Other common verbs of action such as *fall*, *jump*, and *walk* can be treated in the same manner.

A special effort must be made in conjunction with auditory training to teach the vocabulary of words that convey sound, some of which will be within but many will not be within the child's experience depending on the type and degree of the hearing impairment. Books are loaded with words describing auditory effects. Loud sounds, for example, *bark*, *honk*, *scream*, *yell*, *shout*, and *wail*, can be associated with appropriate situations, but sounds such as *whisper*, *meow*, *peep*, *rustle*, *whine*, and *snore* can be dealt with only at a verbal level if a child cannot hear them even with amplification. Verb vocabulary can be organized around sounds that humans make, around communication, around sounds that animals make, and around sounds in nature: river sounds, sounds of the forest, of rain, of the wind, and many more. As an example, we may list sounds that humans make in order of loudness: *scream*, *yell*, *holler*, *wail*, *shout*, *call*, *say*, *murmur*, *whisper*. Animal sounds may be more generally organized, as in "A horse whinnies, neighs, nickers," and "birds caw, sing, peep, and cheap." "Water in a river may murmur, crash, and thunder (over a precipice.)" Any number of categories can be created according to the requirements of the situation.

Verb vocabulary can also be organized in regard to multiple meanings. Basic meanings, as well as meanings used in idiomatic expressions, will be included in this aspect of verb study. Verbs with particles should receive special attention. It is a good idea to scan books that the children will be reading to discover the verbs most commonly used in multiple ways and to incorporate them in the daily experiences of the children in anticipation of their reading them later. When a verb can also be used as a noun, as *fire* and *turn*, or as an auxiliary as *do* and *have*, distinction can be made in the examples provided. Here are records of two words from a child's dictionary which was started when the child was 6 and added to periodically. The child did his own recording as soon as he was able.

get (got, got, getting)

1. Billy got a new bike for his birthday.
2. John's got to (gotta) go home now.
3. He's gotta help his father.
4. I got cold waiting for the bus.
5. I've got a cold now.
6. Billy didn't get to see the circus.
7. Jerry got mad when Mark threw mud at him.
8. My Uncle Ned got married Saturday.
9. The robber got caught.

Note that Sentences 8 and 9 use *got* as a substitute for the passive voice.

turn (turned, turned, turning)

1. Turn around, Bill.
2. Turn on/off the light/water.
3. Turn the page/the key/the wheel.
4. We'll take turns.
5. Bob never got to take his turn.
6. The bus turned into the driveway.
7. The mice turned into coachmen.
8. The motor wouldn't turn over.
9. The leaves are turning color.
10. The light on the squad car turned.

Note that *turn* is used as a noun in Sentences 4 and 5 and with particles or adverbial complements in Sentences 1, 2, and 8.

## Adjective Vocabulary

It is more difficult to acquire meaning for adjectives than for nouns and verbs, since adjectives have a high degree of abstraction built into them. *Wide* is wide only in relation to the thing it describes: *a wide ribbon*, *a wide skirt*, *a wide street*, or *the wide, wide world*. Adjectives that describe feelings are an important class of adjectives for inclusion in a program of directed study of vocabulary for hearing impaired children. Most children learn too few to permit understanding of their own emotions. They use *good*, *bad*, *sad*, *cross*, *sorry*, *happy*, and *afraid* to describe everything from frustration and anger to joy and enchantment. Only a child knows what his inner feelings are, so one must be cautious in projecting his own feelings into the child's verbalizations.

Adults who witnessed the assassination of President Kennedy and watched subsequent events on TV felt devastated, deeply grieved, and even bereft. But some 8-year-old deaf children viewing the same events were unmoved. For them it was just another scene of violence, the kind that they had watched with fascination but not with concern many times before. Cognitive development, values, and attitudes influence how a child thinks about himself and others. Consequently, the acquisition of a vocabulary to express feelings will have to develop over a span of years and be refined as a child matures. Below is a suggested scheme for organizing adjectives to express feelings. Wherever possible, they are classified according to feeling tone and to intensity of feeling.

## How We Feel

pleased, delighted, happy, elated, high, ecstatic
surprised, amazed
blue, dejected, down, depressed
hurt, rejected
disappointed, frustrated
cross, upset, mad, angry, furious
afraid, frightened, scared, fearful
nervous, worried, anxious
embarrassed, ashamed
sorry, wretched
bored
envious, jealous
disgusted

English has a two-value system for its adjectives, so organization around opposites is feasible and popular. Although we have a few words that describe the midpoint between extremes as in *cold, warm, hot*, and *black, gray, and white*, there are no words that describe the midpoint between *fat* and *thin*, *big* and *little*, or *heavy* and *light*.

The limits of an adjective's use may be demonstrated in several ways. They may be practiced in the sentence pattern *NP + be + Adjective* and also in noun phrases as modifiers. For instance, we say, "You're a big boy now," but not "You're a large boy now," when we mean "act your age." Fine differences in the use of synonyms can be brought out through exercises designed for this purpose. Children can also be asked to select from a list the modifiers appropriate to a particular pattern as in I saw a(n)_____house/ movie/tree. They could chose from this list and also volunteer some of their own: *beautiful, big, clean, clever, deserted, dirty, exciting, fishy, funny, happy, high, interesting, little, long, old, old-fashioned, sad, sorry, tall*.

Since nouns also pattern as prenominal modifiers with nouns, they must be differentiated from adjectives only as they appear in a series. When they do they are the last in the series. We say *the log house*, *the old house*, *the old log house*.

The comparison of adjectives may also be included in directed study of vocabulary. Concepts underlying the comparative and superlative degrees should be introduced as soon as children can understand them and need them to express their ideas. This is also applicable to adverbs. Combing books for structures in which adjectives and adverbs appear will help prepare children for encountering them later.

A class of words which needs special semantic attention is the preposition. Although there are only about 60 simple and 25 double prepositions in English, their meanings are legion. They combine with common words to produce idioms and figurative language. In turn, the new combinations produce their own multiple meanings ad infinitum. Prepositions must be incorporated into the study of the verb phrase and the noun phrase as the child develops a need for expanding these aspects of his syntax.

One other class of words that a child should become familiar with prior to reading in books is the sentence connector. Unless a child has been introduced to such words as *then*, *just*, *just as*, *at last*, *at once*, *once*, *once again*, *once upon a time*, *but*, *so*, and *anyway* in teacher-prepared materials, he may have difficulty in ferreting out their meanings from contexts in more complicated environments (Hargis, 1975b).

## USING THE DICTIONARY

A dictionary is an indispensable reference book even for young children. Many attractive dictionaries are available for children from the first grade through high school. If this is so, you might wonder why you were urged to construct individual dictionaries for deaf children. The words in commercial dictionaries are not the most useful for the development of a vocabulary for everyday living. Moreover, when a child constructs his own store of words, he can better recall the contents, and can add more meanings as they accumulate through experience. His dictionaries are not to be discarded at the end of the school year, but are to be cumulative over a period of years until he is able to use commercial dictionaries effectively.

Children must learn the mechanics of dictionary use: estimating which fourth of the dictionary contains which letters of the alphabet, locating words by first, second, and third letter, and learning to use the pronunciation and syllabication keys. The introductions to children's dictionaries contain guides for acquiring these skills (Basic Dictionary of American English, 1962; Thorndike-Barnhart Beginning Dictionary, 1962).

Children's dictionaries can be useful in checking pronunciation, spelling, and syllabication of written words. When it comes to giving help in gaining meaning of new words, the dictionary has its limitations. Some definitions are circular. For instance, let us look up *tyrant*, a word from an easy social studies text. Depending on which dictionary you consult it may be defined as "a cruel ruler." If we look up *cruel*, we find it defined as "causing suffering to others, a cruel tyrant." If we look up *ruler*, we may find "1) one who governs, a sovereign, 2) a straight edged instrument used in measuring." We can eliminate #2, but to be sure we understand what a *ruler* really is, we look up *sovereign* and find three meanings, one of which gives us a clue. It says, "a ruler, monarch, a person in whom supreme power is vested." The language of this definition is not exactly simple, so we have come full circle ending up just about where we started.

When only two meanings are listed for a word, the probability is 50-50 that a correct choice can be made, but when a child has 10 to 20 meanings to choose from, his chances for a correct choice diminish greatly. Asking a child to look up a preselected list of unknown words in order to pick out the correct definition for a word in his reading lesson, for instance, is an impossible task if he does not know the context in which the word appeared. Asking him to memorize definitions is not only a meaningless, but a punishing task.

How then does a teacher go about helping children to use the dictionary to acquire new meanings? When you come across an unknown word in your reading, you use several strategies: you may try to pronounce the word for a clue, guess at its meaning from the context, or look at its prefixes, suffixes, and root if it is a polysyllable. If all of these fail, you go to your dictionary as a last resort, but always keeping in mind the context in which the word appeared. Children must be guided in finding correct meanings. Pictures and illustrative sentences are a big help in clarifying definitions, and dictionaries which contain these aids should be selected over those that do not.

Instead of the teacher's selecting a list of words from a reading assignment, perhaps the child should be asked to scan the lesson and make his own selection. Of course, there will be those children who don't know when they don't know the meaning of a word. It is then incumbent on the teacher to find out whether they do know the meaning in the particular context in which it occurs. Assume that from the following paragraph a child lists one or more of these words as unknown: *potter*, *clay*, *vessels*, *jars*, *contented*, *carriage*, *turquoise*, and *tassels*:

> Once upon a time there was a potter who worked hard all day long, making pots of clay. He made vessels for water and jars for grain. The potter was contented with his work until one day he saw the king ride by in his golden carriage. Servants held a sunshade of turquoise silk with golden tassels over him.

When the teacher discusses this paragraph with a child, reference to the flower pots on the classroom window sill should clarify the words *pots*, *potter*, and *clay*; *vessels*, and *jars* may be designated as synonyms of *pots*. Finally, the child consults his dictionary to verify the specific meanings for each word. In the same manner, the teacher may supply the word *happy* for *contented*, while the illustrations on the page would clarify the words *carriage*, *turquoise*, *tassels*, *sunshade*, and *servants*, even though the child had not designated them as unknown.

When familiar words appear in selections but their basic meanings are not applicable because they are used idiomatically or with another meaning, it may be necessary to rewrite whole paragraphs or even whole selections. In the following paragraph, the words *burning*, *outstanding*, and *crowing* may look familiar to a child. If the teacher asked him to look up these words, he could find three choices for each of them. Without knowing the context, he could hardly be expected to make the proper choice.

Could Falls High win the football game? That was the burning question. Falls High had an outstanding record, but the game was not going to be a walkaway for one team or the other. "So we mustn't start crowing yet," thought Dave.

The teacher might rewrite the paragraph in the following manner, substituting synonyms for probably unknown words and at the same time amplifying the meaning by adding explanatory sentences, and filling in inferential gaps. The synonyms are underlined for the children.

Could Falls High win the football game? That was the biggest, hottest question. Falls High had a very good record. The team had won all its games this year. The game was not going to be easy for Falls High or for the other team. "We don't know who will win. We mustn't think that we have won the game before it starts," thought Dave. (Or "We mustn't brag until we win," thought Dave.)

After the child reads the paragraph, he is directed to find the words in the textbook which mean the same as the underlined words in the substitute paragraph. Then he looks up those words in the dictionary and selects the correct definitions. Such practice is a necessary step in helping children to use their dictionaries effectively.

If too many unknown words are embedded in too many unknown structures, the reading level will obviously be too difficult for a child. The goal is to provide easy material within his known language boundaries. This presumes that the teacher must be thoroughly familiar with the child's capabilities to comprehend language of the kind found in books, that she knows how to judge the difficulty of a book's language if the book is to fit the child, and that she can write or rewrite at a particular level of difficulty.

## JUDGING AND SELECTING READING MATERIAL

The ideal approach to reading in books would be one in which a child was able to select his own reading matter suitable to his interests and ability. Despite the plethora of books for children, there are few, especially for young hearing impaired readers, that might match interest and language ability. An approach in which a child was required to read a school-wide adopted reading series, book by book, could very likely have the effect of inhibiting his interest in reading if every other word appeared in an unfamiliar setting and in material unrelated to his interest or background knowledge. Selection of suitable reading matter is critical to induce a child to want to read and to succeed in the process.

Readability formulas for judging and difficulty of books have been available for many years (Dale and Chall, 1948; Spache, 1953). They depend mainly on word count and length of sentences and words. Such information does not meet the needs of teachers who must deal with syntax as a major element in judging the appropriateness of books for deaf children. The Syntactic Complexity Formula (SCF), based on transformational grammar and on stages of language development, should be of significant assistance to teachers of hearing impaired children when guaging the difficulty of reading material appropriate to the interests and maturity of these children (Granowski and Botel, 1974). The formula can objectify the complexity of the language in a selection, although it does not intend to be a precise measure.

The SCF assigns a count of zero (0) to basic sentence patterns and simple transformations, and a count of 1, 2, or 3 to increasingly complex structures. Beginning reading scores could fall between 0 count and 3.5 or 4. According to the authors of the formula, the *Readers Digest* yielded an average complexity count of 6.8, and the *New York Times*, a score of 13.9 (Granowski and Botel, 1974). Table 7-1 is a slightly adapted form of the SCF in which two additional categories, verbal auxiliaries and contractions, have been included because of their significance to the understanding of language by deaf children. This adapted formula has not been substantiated by research, but it should still be valid in judging the readability of books and in serving as a guide in writing one's own original materials.

To use the formula, number the sentences. Encircle every structure that is to receive a count of 1, 2, or 3. Identify the designated structure with its proper number and its count value. Place the sum of the count value after the number of the sentence, as in the following example.

1(12)  1(12)

1.  2        George was a curious little monkey.

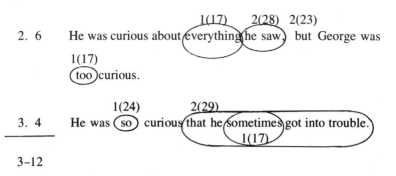

2. 6      He was curious about everything he saw, but George was

         1(17)
         too curious.

3. 4      He was so curious that he sometimes got into trouble.

3–12

Add the sums of the count structures and divide by the number of sentences to get the average complexity score. The complexity level of these three sentences is 4. When this formula was applied to the first 26 sentences of the story *Curious George*, taken from a second grade reader, it yielded a score of 2.5. (See page 162 of this chapter for this excerpt.) It is not enough to evaluate only one or two sentences in a selection, but the entire piece must be studied if its overall appropriateness is to be judged. The difficult sentences can easily be identified by their high scores and can be adjusted by rewriting if necessary.

## READING TESTS FOR HEARING IMPAIRED CHILDREN

In many school systems, standardized reading tests are administered to measure pupils' reading ability and to gather data for research. In some systems they are even used to make teachers accountable for what they have taught. Yet reading tests have limitations as do all tests of general achievement. These norm-referenced tests serve as instruments of comparison of large groups of children rather than as enlighteners of a child's real capacity to read, his motivation for and his interest in reading, or as predictors of his success.

Most of the widely used achievement tests are not standardized on hearing handicapped children. Neither the language of the test nor its directions are likely to be in the language that the children know. A score of Grade 4 on such a test may be more an artifact of the test construction than a true picture of a child's ability to read comprehendingly. With luck, he may be able to read with understanding at a second grade level. Standardized tests, whatever their value, cannot be used as a guide in planning a reading program for hearing impaired children.

Another kind of test, the cloze test, may better reveal the capacity of deaf

**Table 7-1**

Syntactic Complexity Formula

---

0-Count Structures

Sentence patterns—2 or 3 lexical items

    1. NP + V + (Adverbial): *Jim fell down. He cried.*

    2. NP + V + NP: *I ate the apple.*

    3. NP + be + Complement (noun, adjective, adverb): *It is a kite. That is funny. I am here.*

    4. NP + V + Infinitive Complement: *Jill wants to play.*

Simple transformations

    5. Interrogative, including tag-end questions: *Where is it?*

    6. Exclamation: *What a game!*

    7. Imperative: *Go to the store.*

Coordinate clauses

    8. Clauses joined by *and: She came and she stayed.*

    9. Non-sentence expressions: *Oh well!, Yes, And then*

1-Count Structures

Sentence patterns—4 lexical items

    10. NP + V + NP + NP (indirect object): *I gave him the book.*

    11. NP + V + NP + Complement: *We call him Rover.*

Noun modifiers

    12. Adjectives (*big, happy*): *I saw a funny show.*

    13. Possessives (baby's, Mary's): *Mary's dress is new.*

    14. Predeterminers (*some of, none of, six of*): *Two of the boys came.*

    15. Participles used in natural position as prenominal adjective: *boiling water*

    16. Prepositional phrases: *The book on the floor is mine.*

Other modifiers

    17. Adverbials including prepositional phrases, when they do not immediately follow the verb: *Bill threw the ball over the fence.*

    18. Modals: *could, would, must, ought, dare to, need to, have to;* and auxiliaries: *have, had, do, did, be + ing*

    19. Contractions for modals and auxiliaries: *I'd* for *had* or *would, He's* for *is* or *has, I've* for *have: I'd go if I could. He's been here.*

    20. Negatives: *no, not, never, neither, nor, n't*

    21. Set expressions: *once upon a time, many years ago, for instance*

    22. Gerunds used as subjects: *Jogging is popular now.*

    23. Infinitives when they do not immediately follow the verb: *I wanted to come.*

Coordinates

    24. Coordinate clauses joined by *but, for, so,* or *yet: I was sick so I stayed home.*

    25. Deletion in coordinate clauses—a 1 count is given for each lexical addition: *Julie and Jerry will finish or stay after school.*

    26. Paired coordinates—*both . . . and: Both Jane saw it and I saw it.*

---

**Table 7-1,** *continued*

---

### 2-Count Structures

27. Passives: *I was hit by the ball.*
28. Paired conjunctions—*either . . . or, neither . . . nor: Either she will go or I will go.*
29. Dependent clauses (adverb, noun, adjective): *They left before I did.*
30. Comparatives—*as . . as, same as, _____er than, more than, _____est: He is older than I am.*
31. Participles (*ed* or *ing* forms not used in usual adjectival position): *Running, John tripped. The dog, tied up, barked loudly.*
32. Infinitives as subjects: *To graduate is important.*
33. Appositives when set off by commas: *Mrs. Jones, my neighbor, is sick.*
34. Conjunctive adverbs—*however, thus, nevertheless,* etc.: *However, he returned the book .*

### 3-Count Structures

35. Clauses used as subjects: *What you do is your business.*
36. Absolutes: *The dance over, the group dispersed.*

---

Adapted from Granowsky and Botel (1974) with permission of the author and the International Reading Association.

children to read. It involves a simple technique that has as its purpose the measuring of readability and at the same time testing comprehension of the reader. Spache (1968) reports that the cloze test correlates substantially with standardized reading tests from the fourth grade to college. Moores and Quigley (1970) in a study using cloze procedures with deaf children found that their grammatical abilities, semantic insufficiencies, and limited vocabulary were clearly revealed by this technique. The information derived from a cloze test may be used to supplement the evaluation of books based on application of the Syntactic Complexity Formula. It can also contribute insights into a child's language gathered from oral and written samples.

The essential feature of a cloze test is the deletion of every nth word from a passage of 250 words. The most commonly used form, and the one recommended here, deletes every 5th word. Here are directions for constructing a cloze test:

1. Select a sample of about 250 words from a text you think suitable for a particular child. If you use a basal reader, you might choose a sample from near the end of the book.
2. Type the passage omitting every 5th word until you have 50 blanks, all the same length. Note exceptions in (3) below.

3.  Do not omit:
    a.  words from the first and last sentences;
    b.  the first word in a sentence (omit the following word instead);
    c.  proper nouns and numbers (omit the next word instead).

In evaluating a child's performance on this test, give each word a value of 2. Only the exact word is counted as correct. A child who scores less than 40 percent needs an easier book (Schoeller, 1973). The higher the score, the easier the book will be for the child. A score of 80 to 90 percent indicates an independent reading level, one between 40 and 60 percent an instructional level, and below 40 percent, a frustration level.

Some books do not lend themselves to evaluation by the cloze technique. For instance, it would be fruitless to use the following type of material for testing either readability or comprehension, for there is nothing readable or comprehendable about it. Therefore, this type of reading material should also be shunned in teaching hearing impaired children to read.

Look, look. Look, Don. See _____. See my car.
Go _____, go. Go fast. Go _____, car.
Look, look. Look, Jennie! See _____. See my bike.
See _____ go. See my bike _____ fast.

A few practice exercises based on known structures and vocabulary should precede the first presentation of a cloze test. A blackboard demonstration such as the following could prepare the child for the test. He should be encouraged to read the entire paragraph before filling in the blanks. He should be urged to guess at words he is not sure of.

A boy put on _____ coat and cap. He _____ outside to wait for _____ school bus. He waited _____ long time. He got _____ cold. Soon the bus _____.

The first portion of a cloze test based on *Curious George* (McKee et al., 1957), at a second grade reading level, is included below to show what a teacher might discover about a child's comprehension of book language beyond the score alone. This test was completed by our friend Julie, age 10 and deaf from birth, whose score on a reading achievement test was grade 2.1. She received a score of 34 percent on the cloze test, a score that indicated that the book was too difficult for her even at the instructional level. The first response in each blank was hers; the second is the correct response.

George was a curious little monkey. He was curious about monkeys (everything) he saw . . . but George was happy (too) curious. He was so tired (curious) that he sometimes got very (into) trouble.

George's home was in_____ a big tree. One days (day) as he sat in big (his) tree, he saw something move (new) and strange. It was a_____ man with a big black (yellow) hat.

George was very surprised (curious) about the hat. He looked and looked at it. A (The) man with the hat went (looked) up at George.

"That terrific (monkey) is curious about my monkeys (hat)," thought the man. "I'd will (like) to have him. I'll show (play) a trick on him and get him to come off (down) from that tree." The man sat down and took with (off) his hat. . . .

This cloze test revealed more of Julie's language deficiencies. In looking at the verb aspects of the entire test, it became apparent that she did not differentiate between past and present tenses, a fact already revealed in her production of language. She substituted form-class words, as a preposition for a verb and a pronoun when the word *going* was required in a verb phrase at the end of the test, not reproduced here. In the contracted verb phrases she responded correctly to *I'll*, but not to *I'd* (I'd will). In perfect aspects of verb phrases, both active and passive, she completed the blanks with an intensifier and a conjunction, indicating her lack of understanding of the syntactic and semantic connotations of the more complicated verb phrases.

Evident throughout the entire test was her lack of mastery of the double verb as in *took off*, *put on*, and *turn over*, especially when the pronoun *it* appeared between verb and particle. Idioms involving verbs, such as *took hold of*, *got into trouble*, and *played a trick* were obviously unfamiliar to her, thus interfering with the correct reconstitution of the text.

Before we could call our analysis complete, we would have had to look at determiners, conjunctions, intensifiers, infinitives, embedded sentences, and time phrases. And when it was all done we would have added important information to that collected from her oral reports and written compositions. We would note her strengths as well as weaknesses in the cloze test and use them for further language planning and book selection.

## PREPARING BACKGROUND FOR READING

When books are finally matched with each child's language ability, he may still need background information to understand their contents. For instance, in anticipation of the reading of fairy tales, or any literary work, a teacher might read the stories to the child or a group of children and encourage their dramatization. Thereafter the children should be better able to read them with understanding and pleasure. Historical subjects require a child to have a great deal of background information related to time and place. Hearing impaired children do not pick up this kind of information without considerable special teaching. It is often necessary to restrict reading to those sections of textbooks that relate to a child's personal or vicarious experiences until all background material is understood. It becomes obvious that reading a basal reader from cover to cover is not recommended if a child is not thoroughly familiar with all of the subject matter in it.

## THE READING LESSON

In real life people may read for sheer pleasure, for gaining information, for following directions in how to construct something, or even to fill out income tax blanks. When they read for recreation, they don't read for details. They remember only what strikes them as worthy of remembering. When they read for facts they may take notes or underline what seems important for further recall. Detail is significant only to settle arguments or to describe a sequence or a character. Readers frequently agree or disagree with an author's motives or with the polemics of politicians. Some may even respond by writing letters to the editor of the local newspaper. But who on earth is ever required to answer questions about what he reads after he leaves school? The message a young child gets when he has to answer questions day after day and year after year about everything he reads is that reading is for answering questions. A good library program may help dispell such misconceptions and should lead most children to want to read.

Nevertheless, children need guidance in learning to read. Early in their school reading experiences, they should become familiar with the vocabulary related to the book and its parts, as *cover*, *front*, *back*, *title*, *author*, *page*, *paragraph*, *sentence*, *map*, *graph*, and the like. They should eventually be able use the table of contents and the index if there is one. They must be helped to select appropriate meanings derived from context, to identify antecedents and pronoun referents, and to see time, space, and part-whole relationships. As they mature cognitively and their ability to read with comprehension increases, they must be guided in separating fact from fiction, in making inferences or reading between the lines where there are gaps in the text, in interpreting moods and feelings, in agreeing or disagreeing with what they read, in predicting outcomes and in distinguishing fact from propaganda.

In formal reading sessions, younger children may find it helpful to have a simple outline to guide them in reading after background material and vocabulary have been clarified. They may be asked to read to find out: (1) who did something (characters); (2) what they did (sequential development, causal relations, and the like); and (3) what happened (climax and results of the action). A more pertinent outline may be developed by the teacher depending on the specific selection to be read.

After the child has read the assignment, either paragraph by paragraph, page by page, or in its entirety, the selected material can be discussed to bring out salient points of information, feelings, and reasons for actions and their consequences. In the process the teacher may have asked many questions, but their function was reconstruction of the selection and not its reproduction. The questions will have tapped the child's background and been related to what he already knew and understood. In preparing the child to pick out topic sentences, the teacher does this for each paragraph for a long time before asking the child to do so. In like manner she summarizes paragraphs before asking the child to try his hand at summarizing. Then the child may use the study outline prepared by the teacher as his guide. After exercises such as this, or after dramatization of a story, it becomes obvious that routine answering of questions requiring reproduction of details in the story is anticlimactic and can easily be dispensed with.

Eventually the child will need to develop the skills of outlining and gathering information from various sources for purposes of writing reports or book reviews. Sharing what has been read can be satisfying to the reporter and beneficial to the audience. Such activities can also promote interest in reading and writing. When a child reads independently and voluntarily, we can be sure that this accomplishment will serve him well throughout his life.

## WRITTEN LANGUAGE

Children with severe and profound hearing impairments have to depend heavily on written language for communication. If a deaf person's speech is unintelligible, or if he uses only manual communication, he will have to write his message to those who do not understand him. Telecommunication devices over which a typed message is transmitted through telephone connections are being widely used in the deaf community, so schools are teaching children how to communicate through this medium (Romney, 1975). Anyone desiring to use these devices had better be fluent in composing meaningful messages on a typewriter. Typing should be a skill learned routinely in classrooms for hearing impaired children as early as the elementary school level.

Children are often observed busily writing during the day, copying news off of the chalkboard, answering questions or reading assignments, filling in blanks, copying definitions of new words into their notebooks, and a dozen other such activities. Teachers hope to keep children quietly busy while they are otherwise occupied. But "busy work" does not teach children how to write. What we are interested in is written communication which requires two participants, a transmitter of the message and a receiver. Without a reader, writing has no purpose.

For everyday communication, writing should be simple and direct. Grammar I, a very basic grammar, can serve as an adequate but minimal syntax for this purpose (Streng, 1972). Complex ideas can be expressed within the framework of a simple grammar by the use of a more abstract vocabulary. Every child should not necessarily be limited to using the simplest of grammars, but using a simple grammar well is preferable to using a garbled mass of words that carry no meaning at all to the reader.

In many schools for the deaf, the early morning "news" period is exploited as a means of teaching written language. Children are expected to produce news, to tell what has happened to them at home or in the world outside the classroom. Parents and parent surrogates are encouraged to prompt their child before he comes to school in the morning and to supplement his oral or gestured account with a written one of their own concerning the events to be reported on. It is assumed that both child and parents will profit from such a cooperative venture. Yet the news period as a means of teaching written language leaves much to be desired.

A child does not always have an interesting piece of news to report, so he may repeat a stereotyped version of what he knows is acceptable to the teacher, who usually is the sole recipient of his written news. If he reports something unfathomable to her, she may ask another child to interpret what he thinks happened and then put words into the child's mouth. Or a child may relate an excellent but fabricated bit of news as one seven year old did. He told a long story with a great many plausible details about his mother's having gone to the hospital to have her baby. It made beautiful written news. But when the teacher telephoned to the family that evening to congratulate them, the mother answered the telephone herself only to report that she was not due to go to the hospital for another month. By this time the child's imagined news had been put into "straight" language by the teacher, written on the chalkboard, corrected by the teacher, and copied into his Journal to be preserved for posterity. However, if any child had a genuine desire to write about an experience he had had, wherever it had occurred, it would be well to check out the questionable details before placing them in a permanent record.

Rather than using an hour or two for written daily news, the teacher could encourage a lively conversation of 15 minutes to satisfy the desires of all who had something to tell. The talk could range from "Show and Tell" and "Guess What I Have" to a report of a family experience, personal news of who hit whom, or news from the evening paper about a Little League Baseball game. Even though much of the talk might not be worth recording, an interchange of thoughts becomes valuable. It could develop a willingness to attend to what someone else was saying, something that not many hearing people do. Responding to what a person says with a question or a comment appropriate to the subject at hand should become a routine practice in the conversation period. The teacher's role during this period would consist of helping a child phrase a sentence if she knew he was capable of doing so, and reinforcing all who used good sentence structure. Besides, the period would serve as an opportunity for an ongoing evaluation of the child's ability to use language independently. The teacher would make brief notes of the language rules each child was violating and would later incorporate this information in the language building program.

As for the daily practice in writing, it could occur at any time during the day. It might take the form of writing a letter, keeping a diary—a secret one if the child so chose—and/or making a list of things to tell the family when school was over for the day. It could be a story about a picture a child drew or a report of a class trip, an accident, or an encounter on the playground. Every effort should be made to encourage a reverse flow of news from school to home, so that the parents are daily made aware of the child's progress in langauge as the teacher guides him in his acquisition of new vocabulary and structure.

As a child matures, he may choose a topic to report on, may write a book review, or may write directions for making an art object. He may interview a visitor or write minutes for a club meeting. In all these instances he must decide who his audience is and must gear his writing to it. The teacher should not ever be his sole audience. Writing to a pen pal, for the class or school news sheet, or for the school annual could serve as a stimulus for writing.

The mechanics of writing paragraphs—making margins, indenting, capitalizing, syllabicating, punctuating, titling—all require specific instruction. A group of 11 year olds who decided to write imaginative stories for a class of younger children learned all of these skills as they proceeded with their project. Over a period of several weeks they learned to jot down their thoughts in a primitive outline as they talked about them with their teacher, to write a first rough draft, paying attention to thoughts rather than form, and to revise and edit before they asked for help. They wrote at least three drafts before they typed their stories. They illustrated them and bound them into a booklet with a table of contents and a list of the authors. With great pride in accomplishment, they presented their book to their friends. They had discovered that writing was hard work but that it could be very satisfying.

An important aspect of writing is learning to edit. A teacher who goes through a paper with a red pencil does more to discourage a child than to help him for there is nothing more devastating to one's self-image than to face a sea of red marks on a paper. So why not teach a child to edit his own work as an integral part of the writing process? He will realize that everyone makes mistakes but that he must be responsible for revising his own writing as best he can. This may begin early. Before a young child writes a sentence on the chalkboard, it is assumed that he has already produced it orally or in written form. If he makes errors in writing it, attention may be drawn to one error at a time—a punctuation error, a spelling error, or a syntactic error. For instance, if a child omits a period, the correct form is provided by the teacher, and the sentence erased and rewritten in its entirety. If he forgets the period the second time, he is not reinforced until he repairs it himself. Eventually it dawns on the child that it is easier to edit than to rewrite, and before long he begins to be responsible for his own corrections. A misspelled word may be removed from the sentence and practiced until the child can remember it. Then the whole sentence is erased and rewritten. The same procedure obtains for syntactic errors as omission of morphemic endings or a required determiner. If a child views this procedure as punishment, it will not be an effective approach. He must receive praise for doing a good job of editing his own work and have a sense of accomplishment when he produces a well-formed sentence the first time.

The most important aspect of writing paragraphs or longer compositions is putting down thoughts and ideas in logical order. Children will have to learn to outline—to select major thoughts to be developed, and to use the outline in their writing. Teacher direction is very helpful at this stage when children talk over what they wish to say. If absolutely correct form is stressed, thought will be sacrificed. Thus the practice of rough drafting of paragraphs should be encouraged with editing being an important next step. Children are expected to reread their own papers first for form and make the corrections roughly before they consult the teacher about language and organization.

Editing paragraphs for language and vocabulary usage can be accomplished in several ways. Meaning takes precedence over structure so the semantic aspects must be attacked first. Idiomatic language or refinement of thought can be suggested after the teacher probes with the student just what he wishes to convey. Then the structure may be adjusted to convey clearer meaning. When the teacher is sure of the child's meaning, she may suggest alternative structures which more reasonably express the child's meaning. She may help reorganize and rearrange sentences, but all the time respecting the child's ideas. All composition work is individualized at the editing stage, although general principles in regard to mechanics may be taught as group lessons.

If spelling is taught as a function of writing, it need not be a stumbling block to written language. A child who has been exposed to directed vocabulary study will have learned to spell hundreds of words; he will have gained self-help dictionary skills, and he should not have to learn spelling from a spelling book.

Writing poetry could be a worthwhile and fascinating experience for hearing impaired children. It may actually be easier for them than writing prose, which requires that specified structural rules be followed. In poetic expression, structure is inconsequential. Thought expressed rhythmically or in striking visual form is what seems to make a poem. One need only glance at a page of modern poetry to find clues to what a poem is. Teachers who have helped children write poems have found it rewarding and so have the children.

Just as a child learns to read by reading, so he learns to write by writing. If a child has a real purpose for writing and a real reader to read what he has written, he will be motivated to write without too much prodding. An enthusiastic teacher can be an excellent catalyst in the process.

## REFERENCES

Basic Dictionary of American English. New York, Holt, Rhinehart and Winston, 1962

Chall J: Learning to read. In GA Miller (ed): Communication, Language and Meaning, Psychological Perspectives. New York, Basic Books, 117–126, 1973

Dale E and Chall J: A formula for predicting readability. Educ Res Bull 27:37–54, 1948

Gentile A and Di Francesca S: Academic Achievement Test Performances of Hearing Impaired Students, United States, Spring 1969. Washington, D.C., Office of Demographic Studies, Gallaudet College, 1969

Granowski A and Botel M: Background for a new syntactic complexity formula. Read Teacher 28:31–35, 1974

Hargis CH: Analysis of the syntactic and figurative structures of popular first grade level basal readers. Paper presented at Alice Streng Linguistic Symposium, University of Cincinnati, May 1975a

Hargis CH: Just, even and only: a lexicon of modifiers. Volta Rev 77:368–374, 1975b

Hughes RB: Verbal conceptualization in the deaf and hearing. Except Child 28:517–522, 1961

McKee P, Harrison ML, McCowan A, and Lehr E: Come Along. Boston, Houghton Mifflin, 108–111, 1957

Moores D and Quigley S: "Cloze" procedures in assessment of language skills of deaf persons. Proceedings of International Conference on Oral Education of the Deaf. Washington, D.C., A. G. Bell Assoc., 1363–1382, 1970

Pugh GS: Summaries from Appraisal of Silent Reading Abilities of Acoustically Handicapped Children. Am Ann Deaf 91:331–49, 1946

Quigley SP, Wilbur RB, Power DJ, Montelli DS, and Weincamp MW: Syntactic structures in the language of deaf children. Champaign, Ill., Institute of Child Behavior and Development, University of Illinois at Urbana-Champaign, 1975

Romney I: Deaf students use the telephone for the first time. Volta Rev 77:125–128, 1975

Rush ML: Writing for children with language and reading deficiencies. Volta Rev 74:492–501, 1972

Schoeller AW: Reading: help students to think, to learn. Instructor 55–56, 1973

Smith F: Understanding Reading. New York, Holt, Rinehart and Winston, 1971

Spache GD: A new responsibility formula for primary grade reading materials. Elementary School J 53:410–413, 1953

Spache GD: Contributions of allied fields to the teaching of reading. In Robinson HM (ed): Innovation and Change in Reading Instruction, 67th Yearbook, NSSC. Chicago, University of Chicago Press, 1968

Streng AH: Syntax Speech and Hearing, Applied Linguistics for Teachers of Children with Language and Hearing Disabilities. New York, Grune & Stratton, 1972

Thorndike-Barnhart Dictionary—Beginning Dictionary. Chicago, Scott Foresman, 1962

# 8

# Assessment and Planning for Language Growth

In Chapter 1 you were introduced to the Education for All Handicapped Children Act of 1975 (Public Law 94-142), which ensures each handicapped child between the ages of 3 and 21 a free public education if he needs one, in an educational program designed to meet his unique educational needs. Initially this program must take the form of a written statement arrived at by a team of evaluators that specifies instructional objectives and indicates what related services will be required to achieve these objectives. Each plan must include the child's present level of functioning as well as a statement of annual and intermediate goals that are to be reviewed as often as necessary but at least once a year to guarantee that the objectives are being met. Educators, parents, and, where appropriate, children must participate in developing the educational plan. Written assessments and detailed plans must be provided to implement the more general plans devised by the multidisciplinary team that first reviewed the needs of the child. Although these plans are to include all aspects of a child's education, we will confine our discussion in this chapter to the assessment of and the planning for the development and growth of language in the hearing impaired child. Since this is a technical task requiring a thorough knowledge of English grammar, not all parents will be able to participate in the formulation of the plans. However, they must be invited to participate if they so desire, and at least kept abreast of the objectives being set up for the child.

## FORMAL AND INFORMAL ASSESSMENT OF SYNTAX

Even if there were no laws to mandate assessment, it is only logical that planning cannot be done without it. Assessment is the first step in planning. It implies the collection of data from many sources. One kind of data is derived from the administration of formal language tests. Of the many available tests, most are limited to one specific aspect of language such as auditory comprehension, syntactic development, morphemic understanding, or vocabulary. These formal tests usually yield norm-based scores that do not actually reveal a child's functional use of language, but rather disclose how he performs in relation to a larger population. In 1976 Quigley and his associates (Quigley et al., 1976) published results of a research project based on a paper and pencil test, the Test of Syntactic Ability (TSA), that was designed to assess the development of syntactic structures in the language of deaf children ages 10 to 18. Subtests explored specific structures such as negation, conjunction, complementation, relativization, question formation, and certain aspects of verb usage. This test was prepared for research rather than for use in the classroom, so until easily administrable criterion-based tests are available, the only viable approach to assessment is the use of informal procedures for gathering specific and detailed information about each hearing impaired child's capacity to comprehend and produce language. Since syntax, along with sentence semantics, presents the greatest challenge to deaf children in learning language, these aspects should receive emphasis in assessment.

Parents and teachers have observed that deaf children at all ages seem to understand what is being said to them, yet they are unable to use "good" sentences. It is possible that situational context, facial expression, and gestures accompanying a verbal message play a major role in bringing meaning to the spoken word. Children get added hints from the stressed nouns and verbs in a sentence, but usually ignore the unstressed constituents such as determiners, prepositions, or verb auxiliaries. It is very likely that they fail to absorb structural meaning because what they hear and see is either partial or fragmentary. It is rather difficult to gather data on the actual knowledge a young child has about specific grammatical forms. He may readily respond to "Come here." Drink your juice," or "Find Jerry," in concrete situations that clue him into the meaning. One the basis of his response, one could assume that he was familiar with the request pattern. But if he is deprived of context, he may be completely nonplussed and unable to respond when mother says out of the clear blue sky, "Get Grandma's boots for her," or the teacher says, "Go hang up your coat." The child may know all the words but cannot get meaning from the structure in which they were used. Deaf children often confuse the two similar structures, *How old are you?* and *How are you?* They say, "I'm fine" in response to the first and "I'm 5" in response to the second. An incorrect response or lack of one in noncontextual situations may result from not having adequate vocabulary, not being familiar with a particular standard phrase structure rule or transformational rule, or not having generalized the meaning of a particular grammatical structure. As a consequence, assessing the ability of any child's comprehension of language requires insights into his capacity to understand not only word meanings but what he knows about structural rules and structural meanings.

## LEXICAL AND STRUCTURAL MEANING IN ASSESSMENT

Although lexical or word meaning and structural meaning are highly integrated in communication, in assessment it is necessary to separate the two. In the following sentences, a deaf child would need to know three lexical meanings of the verb phrases and the meanings of the three prepositional phrases beginning with *for* to understand the sentences.

1. The students signed expertly.
2. The students signed the song for the visitors. (for____: activity directed toward something)
3. The students signed up for the trip. (for____: intended destination)
4. The students signed out for the weekend. (for____: duration of time)

He could look up the word *sign* in a standard dictionary, but would likely not find the definitions for the idioms *sign up* and *sign out* there. He could find them in a dictionary of idioms if he recognized the verb phrase as having two parts. If he did not take structure into consideration, their lexical meanings could easily elude him. To recognize the meanings of the prepositional phrases, he would need to know under what conditions *for* could be used, even though he was able to comprehend that the phrase told something about the verb. These structures have closely intertwined lexical and structural meaning.

If we add some determiners and/or a verb qualifier to Sentence 1 above, the entire meaning of the sentence changes.

5. Few of the students signed very expertly. (Most of the group were not good signers.)
6. A few of the students signed very expertly. (Several of the group were good signers.)
7. Few students signed expertly. (Not very many students could sign expertly.)

From these examples we can see how important structure is to meaning. A deaf child does not consciously differentiate between lexical and structural meanings nor should he be expected to, but his teacher can and must if she is to have a clear picture of what he comprehends about syntactic structure. She can assure clarity by using familiar vocabulary when testing syntax, for only one aspect can be tested at a time.

## TECHNIQUES FOR ASSESSING COMPREHENSION

When a child has passed well beyond the two-word sentence phase in his expressive language development and can read sentences, it is possible to explore his comprehension through the written form of language. Quigley et al. (1976), using known vocabulary, utilized several techniques to test structural knowledge. They sometimes combined a test of comprehension with a test of production. For instance, a child was presented with a correct statement, as in *The girl looked at herself*, or an incorrect one, as in *I saw a boy who the boy wrote his name*. He was then asked to identify it as right or wrong, and to correct any error by rewriting it in standard English. A child might try to correct an acceptable grammatical statement because he did not actually understand the rules governing it; he might correct an incorrect statement but use a nonstandard rule to do so; he might consider a nonstandard sentence or question to be correct; or he might complete the task successfully. On the basis of the child's response, the assessor could determine whether he did or did not comprehend the rules being tested. Mastery of the rules would of course depend on their spontaneous use by the child.

A second technique that Quigley used explored the child's knowledge of synonymy. The student chose a statement from a group of sentences that had the same meaning as the prompt sentence or sentences as in this example:

John rode his bike. Mary rode her bike.
John and Mary rode her bike.
John and Mary rode a bike.
Mary and John rode their bikes.

An exercise of this kind is valuable in judging whether a child understands that a single meaning may reside in several related structures. It is important that deaf children realize that they too can express an idea using different structures, as in *He is not at home, He's not at home, He isn't at home*, or as in *I won't go unless you do, I'll go if you do*. When a child understands this principle, his language will be more flexible than if he were not aware of the power synonymy affords him in expressing himself. Teaching language through synonymy is highly recommended as a way to avert rigidity in a deaf child's language, so it is important that a teacher determine his competence in this regard.

Another technique, devised by researchers in linguistics, tests a child's ability to imitate sentences presented orally (Menyuk 1969). The rationale behind this procedure is that the young child beginning to learn language will be able to repeat a sentence if he is familiar with the rules used in the sentence. The forms he does not know are not imitated whereas those partially mastered usually emerge as paraphrases in his repetitions. Emerging structures are imitated only in the forms that the child understands (Whitehurst, 1977). When a child repeats only the last word or words in a sentence, he may be depending on memory alone, and may not comprehend the sentence at all. The deaf child whose language is in the emergent stage, as well it may be for many years of his life, will react much in the same way as a young hearing child does in his imitation responses. A sentence imitation task administered to a deaf child will yield additional information that could be valuable in the overall assessment. Bloom (1974) suggests that the evaluator check the child's sentence imitation responses against his spontaneous production to determine if the two are in conjunction. His independent production would then confirm or deny the results of the imitation task.

Julie, 10 years old and deaf from birth, responded to a sentence repetition task delivered through the auditory-visual mode as follows:

| Test Sentence | Child's Response |
|---|---|
| 1. A boy saw a robin. (5 words) | 1. A boy saw a robin. (5 words) |
| 2. A boy read a book about Pecos Bill. (8 words) | 2. A boy read a book Peco Bill. (7 words—meaning retained) |
| 3. A week ago a friend of mine came to visit me. (11 words) | 3. A week ago a friend come to visit. (8 words—meaning retained) |
| 4. A robin built a nest in a big tree in the back yard. (13 words) | 4. A robin build nest—tree—yard. (7 words—meaning not fully retained) |
| 5. When I was a little girl, I played with my dolls every day. (13 words) | 5. When you little girl, you play(ed) doll every day. (9 words—meaning retained) |
| 6. The mother robin sat in the nest while the father bird looked for worms. (14 words) | 6. I don't know. (When urged to try again after two more repetitions by the teacher, she said, "Too long.") |

This 5-minute exploration yielded considerable information about Julie's language comprehension. She could easily repeat five words verbatim and obviously understood the longer sentences, except for the last one, although she did not repeat them exactly. She had no difficulty with the transposed time clause introduced by *when* in Sentence 5, but she could not repeat the sentence containing the *while* clause even when it appeared in the regular post-verb position in Sentence 6. It is evident that she was not fluent in the use of certain prepositions or of some determiners. However, Julie used phrases like *a good story* in her spontaneous speech even though she failed to do so in Sentence 4. She regularly used *in*, *on*, and *under* without semantic error in her daily communication, but omitted them entirely in Sentence 4. She was unfamiliar with the idiom *play with* and she substituted one verb tense for another just as she did in her spontaneous usage.

## ASSESSMENT OF ORAL AND WRITTEN LANGUAGE PRODUCTION

The language a child produces independently and spontaneously is perhaps the most revelatory information that a teacher can collect. In a face-to-face unstructured conversation, a deaf child is on his own as far as language is concerned. He usually does not feel constrained by rules of syntax or phonology when he is intent on conveying a message. Listeners, on the other hand, may be faced with attempting to interpret the child's meaning through a haze of unintelligible speech, nonstandard syntax, and/or imprecise vocabulary. When this occurs, those who share the situational context with the child are likely to be most successful in gaining a sense of what a child is trying to say. If they do not succeed, they may ask another person familiar with the context to interpret for them before a meeting of the minds is achieved. It is important to realize that assessment can be based only on shared meanings. If you know what a child means when he speaks or writes, you should have a valuable source of information about his ability to produce grammatical structures independently. If you cannot decide exactly what he means, it is not possible to use that sample to assess his use of syntax.

Teachers should view all of a child's meaningful productions as a source of data for a continuing evaluation of his language. If a teacher gets into the habit of listening carefully at both meaning and structural level, she can begin to analyze the rules the child is employing. Perhaps she has noticed that a child has been misusing prepositions and decides to learn what the basis of his confusion is. She hears Billy say, "Mark kick to Eddie," "I told to Eddie 'Go home;' We went church this morning." She needs to gather more instances of his use of this one preposition before she can come to conclusions or plan lessons correcting his misconceptions about it. While she will set herself the task of continuing to look for *to* in his written and oral production, she may decide to explore his knowledge in greater detail through more analytical procedures. She may show him pictures of a mother kissing a baby, a boy hugging his dog, a boy kicking a football, and a batter batting a ball, in order to determine if the verb *kick* triggers the use of *to* or whether Billy has firmly in mind the concept of actor, action, patient in a sentence. If he says, "The mother kissed to the baby," "The boy hugged to the dog," and "The boy kicked to the football," she may feel safe in generalizing that he does not have the concept inherent in the basic sentence or that he is making an incorrect generalization about the use of *to* in that particular sentence pattern. But if he says, "Mother kissed the baby," "The boy hugged the dog," and "The boy kicked to the football," she knows that the verb *kick* is at the root of the confusion. A teaching plan will depend entirely on what a child needs to know about a particular structure. In turn, the teacher needs to know in detail what the child knows in order to plan intelligently. To do this she must gather enough samples to substantiate any hypotheses she may develop about a child's ability to produce that structure.

At the beginning of a school term, a teacher may want to discover quickly what language her pupils can produce. Since it is difficult to do two things at once, such as assess and teach simultaneously, she may set aside a special time during the first two weeks of the term to gather the first samples from her pupils. She will undoubtedly want to repeat the procedure any number of times throughout the year. These samples may be elicited in conversation between teacher and child, between two children, and between parent and child. Topics can be wide-ranging—what happened on the playground, in gym, in art class, at home, at Cub Scouts, at Junior Achievement; what was interesting in the news; fashions; and personal feelings about a subject of interest to an individual child. Pictures, filmstrips, and movies may stimulate a discussion if everything else fails (Muma, 1973).

A written record of all oral assessment sessions is mandatory if they are to serve as a resource for analysis and planning. No person alive can remember the myriad details that are contained in even a 5-minute conversation. To expedite the gathering of the data, it is most helpful to have assistance, both electronic and live. A teacher's aide, a volunteer, a student teacher, or better still a parent or sibling should be asked to participate in the evaluation even though a tape recorder or a videotape is used. The inclusion of a parent might restrain some children from performing normally, but when one does respond uninhibitedly, there can be dividends in the form of a deeper understanding on the part of the parent about the child's capacity to use language, a better communication between home and school and between parent and child, and a greater probability that the child will be held to high standards of production at home.

A tape recorder is a desirable adjunct in an oral assessment session. If a child's speech is not entirely intelligible, the teacher may want to stop him momentarily and ask him to repeat what he has just said, or intersperse his production with her own repetition of exactly what he said. If no tape recorder is available, the teacher will have to dictate verbatim to the assistant who must record not what the child meant but what he actually said. This is the least reliable kind of reproduction, but it is surely better than none. The best mode of recording a language sample is through the use of videotape. All the nuances of the session are preserved, including contextual clues, for in depth study at a later time by child and teacher alike (Muma, 1973).

Samples of written language are easier to gather than oral ones since the written form is procurable at any time without special monitoring. Written language, like oral language samples, can be based on incidents that have occurred within the context of mutual experience of writer and evaluator. Written "news" is not recommended as a sampling device because of the possible stereotyping of its contents and the probability that its meaning may be obscure to the assessor unless he is conversant with the events that inspired it.

From the time a deaf child can handle chalk or pencil, he usually is expected to write what he can say. Although his written language reflects what he knows about language, it is necessary to gather samples, both oral and written, to get a full picture of his ability to produce language. In comparing the compositions of hearing and deaf children, researchers have found the deaf to use many more words to express themselves than the hearing, but they employ a greatly restricted vocabulary and a less complex sentence structure (Heider and Heider, 1940; Myklebust, 1964). Myklebust found their sentences to be shorter and their style more rigid. In analyzing their errors he noted additions of unnecessary words, omission of words needed to produce standard English sentences, substitution of incorrect vocabulary items, and nonstandard word order. Observations such as these are helpful in alerting teachers to the kinds of errors they may find in their samples, but in an assessment our target will be to look at details of a child's grammatical production. Yet we must remember that structure is more than the sum of its parts. Meaning plays an integral part in any language analysis.

Now let us look at samples of Julie's oral and written language and use them as the basis for a more detailed evaluation of her capability to express herself spontaneously. She reported the following incident during a videotaped session in the presence of her mother, a teacher's aide in the school that her daughter attended. It was supported by gesture that made the meaning very clear. Julie was not coached before or after this session.

She had a glasses with brown (pointed to teacher's brown framed glasses). When we play outside with the ball, Glenda broke her glasses, yes. My brother (gestured that Glenda and her brother collided, the glasses were knocked off and broken at the nosepiece), yes, the glasses broke. My father put with glue on it; wait; black tape; table. (Gestured the entire procedure of holding the glasses together with the glue and tape.) Hold it, wait for one hour, then clean off. He told, ''Be careful. Cost lot a money.''

Later that day Julie was asked to write about the broken glasses. This is what she wrote:

My brother broke my sister glasses. My sister took her brown glasses to my father. My father put glue on side of glasses. And my father push together.
Then put tape on it and wait one hour or two hour. Then the tape off.
The end.

Julie

## A GUIDE FOR ASSESSING LANGUAGE SAMPLES

Before we try to analyze Julie's two productions, we ought to have a strategy for doing so. The following brief outline is based on the contents of Grammar I as outlined in Chapter 6, Table 6-1 (foldout), and which will serve as our guide in assessment.

1.  Estimate the overall semantic clarity. Does meaning come through? Is the vocabulary adequate? Is it used appropriately as to lexical meaning and structural meaning?
2.  Decide on the child's level of sophistication by observing his sentence structure. Does he use complete sentences, partial sentences, or one- or two-word sentences? How consistent is he? What patterns does he use? What influence does his vocabulary have on his use of structure?
3.  Observe the optional adverbs attached to the child's sentences. Is he using single adverbs, prepositional phrases, clauses? Is he using preverb modifiers and sentence connectors in written language? Is he observing order of adverbs? Is he transposing clauses to the beginning of the sentence?
4.  Observe the use of determiners in the noun phrases. Look at articles, possessives, and predeterminers, as *some of*. Does the child differentiate between count and noncount nouns in the use of determiners? Is he aware of the standard uses of the determiner? Does he use the definite determiner as a pronoun substitute the second time a noun is mentioned? Does he use prenominal adjectives or postnominal adjectives, such as prepositional phrases or clauses?
5.  Observe the child's use of pronouns. Does he adhere to rules for person, case, and number for personal pronouns? Does he use reflexives? Indefinite pronouns? How consistent is this use?

6. Observe which tenses and aspects the child uses. Does he have clear concepts about these tenses and aspects? Does he understand and use the standard morphemic rules used in verb phrases? Does he correlate tense and aspect with appropriate adverbial modifiers? Does he use modals? Does he use auxiliaries *be* and *have*? Is word order correct in her verb phrases?

7. Note all the transformations in his productions. Does he use only simple transformations? If so, which ones? Does he understand the limits of their use? Does he follow morphemic rules when required? What complex transformations does he use? Does he embed relative clauses, noun phrase complements, or questions?

8. Estimate his level of performance in reference to Grammar I and use this as the base for the expansion or correction of his language.

When there is doubt about a child's capacity to produce particular structures that appear in a sample, probing procedures can be set up that will test his comprehension and/or usage of these rules. His performance will then further clarify the need for including them in future plans.

## ANALYZING A LANGUAGE SAMPLE

There is no one best method for describing syntactic skills in any detail. Although some prepackaged forms on which to record a child's responses are available (Tyack and Gottsleben, 1974), it seems preferable for each teacher to devise procedures that suit her own preferences and needs. One procedure is to look at each sentence or sentence fragment that a child produces and rewrite it in standard English. For instance, Julie's oral sample can be treated in the following way. The italicized words indicate revisions and additions:

| Julie's Product | Standard Form |
|---|---|
| 1. She had glasses with brown. | 1. *Glenda has* glasses with *a brown frame.* |
| 2. (a) When we play outside with the ball, (b) Glenda broke her glasses. | 2. When we *played ball outside,* Glenda broke her glasses. |
| 3. My brother | 3. My brother *knocked Glenda's glasses off her nose.* |
| 4. Yes, the glasses broke. | 4. The glasses broke *at the nosepiece.* |
| 5. My father put with glue on it. | 5. My father put *glue on the two parts.* |
| 6. wait | 6. *He* waited *a while.* |

| 7. & 8. | black tape, table | 7. & 8. | *Then he put* black tape *around the two pieces and put them on the* table. |
|---|---|---|---|
| 9. | Hold it. | 9. | *He* held *them together.* |
| 10. | Wait for one hour. | 10. | *We* waited for one hour. |
| 11. | Then clean off. | 11. | Then *he took the tape* off. |
| 12. | He told, "Be careful." | 12. | He *said*, "Be careful." |
| 13. | Cost lot o' money. | 13. | *They* cost a lot o' money. (OK) |

By comparing Julie's language with the teacher's standard form, we can get a general idea about her performance. She produced two short sentences following the pattern NP + V + NP (1 and 2b), and two following the pattern NP + V (2a and 4), although in 5 she seems to have confused the two patterns. She used NP + V instead of NP + V + NP. She used more partial sentences than complete ones, omitting more subjects (in 6, 9, 10, and 13) than verbs (in 7 and 8). It appears that she lacked vocabulary to describe all the activity that occurred, as in 3, 4, and 5. This may have influenced the completeness of sentences 3 and 7. Yet in several instances she merely neglected to name the subject (6 through 11) because in her mind she had already identified her father as the actor, so why repeat his name? When her partial sentences were expanded, they fell into the two patterns she had used. Semantic errors can also be detected by rewriting as in sentences 1, *with brown* (frame), 2 *played with the ball* (*played ball*), and 12, *He told* (he said).

Although this technique yields considerable general information, we need a more detailed structural analysis in order to plan a remedial program and/or a developmental one. Following is one such procedure that has been found satisfactory for determining the structural aspects of a child's production. On single sheets of paper headed: (1) sentence patterns, (2) optional adverbs, (3) phrase structure rules—nouns, (4) pronouns, (5) phrase structure rules—verbs, and (6) transformations, each utterance in the sample is recorded under the appropriate rubric as *correct*, *approximated or partial*, or *incorrect*. It is as important to know what the child can produce as what he cannot, since his stabilized language will be the base line from which to make corrections and to expand his language. Table 8-1 contains a summary of the working sheet for Julie's two samples.

Julie's two reports of the same incident did not show wide variation in performance. She used a greater proportion of complete sentences in her written language than in her oral language. She followed rules of paragraphing and punctuation in the written composition. She used a restricted number of sentence patterns but the subject of her reports did not lend itself to the use of others. Her teacher realized the need for exploring her knowledge of the sentence patterns involving the verb *be* in subsequent sessions.

**Table 8-1**

Work Sheet for a Structural Analysis

| Structure | Use of Structural Rules | Examples |
|---|---|---|
| Sentence patterns | Correct: NP + VP | • . . . we play outside with the ball . . . |
| 20 sentences | | • The glasses broke. |
| | Approximated: | • 0 wait for one hour |
| | | • 0 wait |
| | Correct: NP + VP + NP | • . . . Glenda broke her glasses. |
| | | • She had glasses (with brown) |
| | | My brother broke my sister glasses. |
| | | My sister took her brown glasses . . . |
| | | My father put glue . . . |
| | Approximated/ partial: | • 0 Hold it. |
| | | • 0 Cost 0 lot a money. |
| | | • then 0 clean 0 off. |
| | | then 0 0 the tape off. |
| | | • black tape |
| | | • table |
| | Incorrect: | • My father put with glue on it. |
| Optional adverbs | Correct: | • . . . we play outside with the ball |
| | | • wait for one hour |
| | | My sister took her brown glasses to my father |
| | | . . . put tape on it |
| | Approximated: | My father put glue on 0 side of 0 glasses |
| | | Wait one or two hour0. |
| Phrase structure rules | | |
| NPs | Correct: Det + N | • the glasses, • the ball, the tape |
| | Incorrect: | a glasses |
| | Correct: Ø + N | Ø glue, Ø tape |
| | Correct: poss + N | • her glasses, • my brother, my father, • my father |
| | Incorrect: (careless error?) | my sister glasses |
| | Correct: Det + Mod + N | her brown glasses |

• Oral sample
o Omission

**Table 8-1,** *continued*

| Structure | Use of Structural Rules | Examples |
|---|---|---|
| Personal pronouns—personal | Correct: person, number, case | • She, • We, He |
| | Incorrect: number (questionable) | • Hold it, |
| | | Then put tape on it. |
| Phrase structure rules | Incorrect: (use in paragraphs) | My father... , My father... , My father... |
| Verb-tense | Correct: past tense | • broke, broke, • put, put, • told, took |
| | Incorrect: present for past | • play, • wait, • hold, • clean off, push, wait |
| | past for present | had for has |
| Transformations | | |
| T/conj. | Correct: S and S | And my father push together Then put tape on it and wait |
| | Approximated: | wait one hour or two hour |
| T/request | Correct: | • Be careful |
| T/Adv. clause | Correct: T/adv. clause shift | • When we play outside... |

Julie used optional adverbs quite consistently and correctly. Prepositional phrases of time and place were semantically and structurally correct except for one phrase in *Father put with glue on it.* In her written sample, she changed this form when she reported that *Father put glue on side of glasses.* She used *off* correctly as a verb complement in *clean off*, but also attached it to the noun in *tape off*, leaving a doubt as to whether she actually knows the structural use of *off* as a complement.

The structure of the noun phrase in Julie's language is still in an emergent stage. The phrase *a glasses with brown* turned into *her brown glasses* in her written paragraph. She employed her known language quite creatively in lieu of the void in her lexicon. She did not know the word *frame*, so she invented phrases to get her idea across. She demonstrated that she could construct NPs containing both post- and prenominal modifiers, although in both phrases immediately above there were errors. In the first she used *brown* as a noun and in the second she used *brown* in a noncolloquial sense. It is sometimes difficult but always necessary to determine if the vocabulary or the structure or both are the decisive factors in making an utterance standard or not.

In the samples and in Julie's sentence repetition task she made errors in the determiner system. She omitted determiners when she should have included them, as in *on side of glasses*. She failed to recognize *glasses* as a noncount noun even though she treated *glue* and *tape* as such correctly. She used the definite determiner *the* inconsistently, sometimes omitting it, as in *on side of glasses*, and sometimes including it where it was required, as in *the tape off*. The noun phrase is one of the most difficult for a deaf child to master and bears close scrutiny in assessment.

Pronouns in the first and third person singular and first person plural, nominitive case, seem well established. It is questionable whether Julie was referring to *glasses* or the *nosepiece* of the glasses when she used the pronoun *it*. Further sampling will be necessary in order to learn more about her knowledge of pronoun usage. She is obviously not conscious of the need to replace a noun with a pronoun after one reference to it, as evidenced in both her oral and written reports.

Since the incident that Julie reported occurred in the past, it seems logical that she should have used the past tense throughout her reports. She substituted the present tense form for the past form about 50 percent of the time when she did use a tense. Since *put* and *cost* have the same past and present tenses, they are excluded from the estimate. There is no doubt but that Julie will have to learn to differentiate between the use of the past and the present in further language learning. The lesson on tense in Chapter 6 (page 123) illustrates how her teacher clarified the differences between the two tenses and how she tried to establish the limits of their use.

The simple transformations that Julie used were the conjunctions *and* and *or*. She used them in semantically correct ways, although she did not use *or* in a correctly structured phrase. She has not yet learned the deletion rules that cover this structure. She used one clause, the time clause beginning with *when*, in a transposed position. These observations should be recorded and filed with all her other productions, past and future.

## KEEPING RECORDS

Assessment is perforce a continuing process. Dozens and dozens of samples will be necessary to gain clear insights into a child's language performance. Work sheets will pile up or be scattered about unless they are organized. One way to avoid chaos and to promote generalization is to prepare individual looseleaf notebooks in which work sheets are filed. If they are filed according to categories or headings, as Sentence Patterns, Phrase Structure Rules, and Transformations, blank pages may be included on which notes jotted down during the day on 3″ × 5″ cards or on a corner of the chalkboard can be entered. Each entry in an assessment should be dated. Internal organization will depend on personal preference. Some teachers might prefer to abstract the results of each analysis and transfer items to 4″ × 6″ cards stored in file boxes, one for each child. In any case, it is necessary to have easy access to information by organizing it. In the next section we will describe a card filing system that can serve the dual purpose of organizing the assessment and aiding in planning of individual language programs.

## INDIVIDUAL LONG-RANGE LANGUAGE PLANNING

Grammar I as outlined in Table 6-1, Suggested Sequential Acquisition of Syntactic Structures for Expressive Purposes for Hearing Impaired Children, may be viewed as a ready-made long-range plan covering a minimal number of essential grammatical structures for deaf children, and can be used as a general target for individual language performance. In preparation for making an individual language plan, each of the structures in Grammar I is elaborated and placed on its individual 4″ × 6″ card. Some teachers may find it helpful to consult with other references to support or increase their knowledge of the fine details to include on the cards. (Streng, 1972; Kretschmer and Kretschmer, 1973; Hargis, 1975, 1977; Praninskas, 1961). Since many school systems require that goals be stated as behavioral objectives, the following illustrations based on Level III of Table 6-1 will use that form. One card is prepared for each item. Here are a few random examples with headings derived from the outline we used in the assessment process.

*Sentence patterns*
    Child will use sentence pattern NP + VP + NP.
    Child will use NP + VP + NP + (Adv of time).
*Noun phrases*
    Child will use *a* with count nouns beginning with consonants and *ū*.
    Child will use *an* with count nouns beginning with *a, e, i, o, ŭ*.
    Child will use *some* with noncount nouns.
    Child will use *some* with plural count nouns.
    Child will use *ø det* with noncount nouns in statements of generality.
    Child will use *the* in referring to noun previously mentioned.
*Pronouns*
    Child will use third person singular masculine *he* as sentence subject.
    Child will use *him* as sentence object.
    Child will use *him* as object or preposition.
    Child will use *his* as a second genitive as in *That's his*.
*Verb phrases*
    Child will use NP + VP + NP with simple action verbs in the past
      tense.

Child will use adverb of place with intransitive verbs in NP + VP in past.

Child will use NP + VP + Adv complement + Adv of time, past tense.

Child will differentiate between use of transitive and intransitive verbs.

Child will use present tense of stative verbs in pattern NP + be + Locative Adv.

Child will use present tense, first person singular and plural in NP + be + Adj.

Child will use present tense morpheme in third person singular in NP + VP with action verbs.

*Simple transformations*

Child will use T/contr with modal *can* in T/neg as in . . . can't . . .

Child will use T/contr with *be* in first person singular as in I'm . . .

Child will use T/contr with *be* in third person singular as in He's . . .

As many as 200 or 300 cards could be written for Level IV of Table 6-1, depending on how detailed the preparation is. The cards can be duplicated so that a file can be compiled for every child in the program. Figure 8-1 illustrates two of the cards for Julie, whose assessment we have considered above. Provision is made on each card for the child's name, his Grammar I level, a specified syntactic category, a place to check off his ability to use the structures, and space to record samples from his assessment.

The cards are filed under one of three major divisions delineating the child's language as (1) stabilized, (2) approximated, and (3) not used. Subheadings in each division conform to the syntactic categories suggested in the assessment, as sentence patterns, phrase structure rules, and the like. Such an organization allows the teacher as well as parents and supervisory personnel easy access to the details of the child's current language competency and performance. Moreover, it allows for monitoring the growth of language simply by moving a card or cards from one section of the file to another without a great deal of paper work.

## FORMULATING THE INDIVIDUAL LANGUAGE PLAN

It is difficult to anticipate what or how much language a deaf child will learn in a specified time period. Even the wisest and most knowledgeable teacher may not be able to map out the exact details or the sequential presentation of structures for an entire year because much is dependent on variables not under control of pupil or teacher, yet it is essential to have a road map for taking the child from where he is to where we hope he will go. How fast he

| Name *Julie R* | Date | Performance Level |
|---|---|---|
| Level III<br><br>Transformations | 9/30 | ☐ Stabilized/Consistent<br>☒ Approximated/Partial<br>☐ Not used |

Performance Goal: T/infinitive as noun complement

Child will use inf after verbs like/want: I like to skate.

Assessment examples:

9/13● *I want to see "Zoom" tonight. (Se ✓ see for watch)*
9/17● *I want Amy ○ come to my house Saturday. (Sy.)*
9/18● *I like to sew a dress for my doll. (Se ✓ like for*
      *would like or want)*
9/24● *Mark like to play with checkers. (Sy - like for likes,*
       *Se ✓ play with for play)*

---

| Name *Julie R* | Date | Performance Level |
|---|---|---|
| Level IV<br><br>Transformations | 9/30 | ☐ Stabilized/Consistent<br>☒ Approximated/Partial<br>☐ Not used |

Performance Goal: T/infinitive as verb complement

Child will use inf after verbs of movement, go/come:
  We went to the store to buy some cake mix.

Assessment examples:

9/18 ● *My grandmother came ○ my house for baby sit. (Sy)*
9/23 ● *My family went to shopping Saturday. (Sy)*
9/27● *Jerry went to get a ball. (ok)*

●   Oral sample
Se √   Semantic error
Sy √   Syntactic error

Figure 8-1.   Samples from an assessment record.

reaches his destination will depend a great deal on the quality of daily instruction and the support he receives from his family at home.

As a guide for overall language planning, the following suggestions are offered:

1. Decide the base line from which to begin remediation or expansion of language by identifying those structures in Grammar I that the child uses consistently and correctly.
2. Identify those items about which the child has some knowledge but which are only approximated or partially correct. These should receive priority in daily planning since they may be amenable to early stabilization with a minimum amount of clarification and practice. The longer a child fails to acquire a correct rule, the more difficult it may be to change his usage.
3. List all the structures in the target level of Grammar I with which the child is unfamiliar.
4. Select a number of structures, averaging about two a week, for language expansion during the school year.
   a. Choose new structures that can be related to known structures as synonyms. For instance, if a child can use prepositional phrases and knows the meaning of *before* and *after* as in *I watch TV before supper*, and *I brush my teeth after breakfast*, the adverbial clause may be substituted for them as in *I watch TV before we have supper*, and *I brush my teeth after I eat breakfast*. The verb phrases *I will get*, *I'll get*, *I am going to get*, and *I'm going to get* can be considered as being synonymous. A child will have to learn the limits of their use as he practices them in sentences, but since he has deduced their meaning as synonyms, he can concentrate on their structural aspects.
   b. Select the simpler of two structures if there is a choice. It is easier for a child to learn the use of simple structures than the more complex ones. When he knows the meaning of *before* and *after* and can use them in prepositional phrases, he can then learn their use in adverbial clauses without question. If a child does not have control of T/do in negative statements, the chances are that he may have difficulty in formulating Yes-No questions which use that transformation and even more difficulty in learning the rule for *Wh* questions that require its use as part of a more complex transformation.
   c. Give high priority to those structures a child needs for expressing his thoughts and ideas. If they cannot be related to synonyms or to familiar structures in his repertory, an extended preparatory period is necessary to establish meaning as well as use. For instance, if the new structure is the *present perfect aspect*, it can be used freely and frequently in illustrations within the context of actual experiences, as in *When you've/have/finished your math, you may go to the library*.

*You've worked hard for a long time. Let's go outside now. John has been absent for three days. I hope he comes back to school tomorrow.* By saying it, spelling it, and writing it for the child, the teacher makes the child aware of the new structure's meaning even though he may still require considerable practice with it in order really to understand its use and to incorporate it into his language.

d.  Above all, keep in mind developmental sequences for children who are learning language. Refer to Chapter 4 and Chapter 6, Table 6-1, for suggestions that will ensure a firm foundation on which children can build their language.

Overall planning makes provision (1) for building vocabulary within the confines of known syntactic patterns, (2) for stabilizing those structures that a child approximates, and (3) for expanding his baseline production through the addition of new structures to known ones. When the overall language plan has at least been tentatively formulated, it is relatively simple to select those structures that should receive instructional priority. The selection for one child may not be the same as that for another. If a teacher is responsible for five children, she will need five different plans. Making five plans for five different children implies the individualizing of language instruction. This can be accomplished on a one-to-one basis or even in a group setting. For instance, in the group one child may be held for tense, another for use of prepositional phrases, and a third for correct use of pronoun reference after an initial introductory period which has clarified the meaning of the structure for the child. On the other hand, all the children in the group may require practice with the same structure. Although only one structure at a time should receive the focus of the child's attention, the teacher can still encourage individuals to incorporate almost-mastered constituents into their sentences.

A teacher must have a very thorough knowledge of each child's language in order to write instructional plans. Whether they are written with goals stated as behavioral objectives or in other specified terms will depend on local school regulations. Since most school systems are quite explicit about the writing of weekly block plans and daily lesson plans, this text will not go into details of how these are to be constructed. The important thing is to share the plans with all the persons responsible for the child's language growth and development. If a child is mainstreamed, the teacher of the regular class ought to be aware of his language needs. If he is in a rotating class in a residential school, every one of his teachers should be privy to his language needs. Language learning is logically an integral part of every math class, every social studies class, and every science class, and it cannot be ignored in favor of learning facts that may not be remembered longer than the time that it takes to forget them. Above all, the child's parents or parent surrogates must be familiar with the goals set up for the child so that they too can participate in helping him acquire better language. Only with constant guidance and support can a deaf child accomplish the somewhat overwhelming task of learning language. It is up to his teachers and his parents to see that he gets a fair chance.

## REFERENCES

Bloom L: Talking, understanding, and thinking. In Schiefelbusch RL and Lloyd LL (eds): Language Perspectives-Acquisition, Retardation, and Intervention. Baltimore, University Park Press, 1974

Hargis CH: Just, even and only: a lexicon of modifiers. Volta Rev 77:6, 368–374, 1975

Hargis CH: English Syntax, An Outline for Clinicians and Teachers of Language Handicapped Children. Springfield, Ill., Charles C Thomas, 1977

Heider F and Heider G: A comparison of sentence structure of deaf and hearing children. In Studies in the Psychology of the Deaf. Psychol. Monogr. #232, 1940

Kretschmer L and Kretschmer RJ Jr. (eds): Language Development Outline: A Guide for Clinicans and Teachers of Language Impaired Children. Cincinnati, Department of Special Education, University of Cincinnati, 1973

Lee LL: A screening test for syntax development. J Speech Hear Disord 35:102–112, 1970

Lee LL and Canter S: Developmental sentence scoring: a clinical procedure for estimating syntactic development in children's spontaneous speech. J Speech Hear Disord 36:315–340, 1971

Menyuk P: Sentences Children Use. Cambridge, Mass., MIT Press, 1969

Muma JR: Language assessment: some underlying assumptions. ASHA, 15:331–338, 1973

Myklebust HR: The Psychology of Deafness. New York, Grune & Stratton, 1964

Praninskas J: Rapid Review of English Grammar. Englewood Cliffs, N.J., Prentice-Hall, 1961

Quigley SP, Wilbur RB, Power DJ, Montanelli DS, and Steinkamp MW: Syntactic Structures in the Language of Deaf Children. Urbana, Ill., Institute for Child Behavior and Development, University of Illinois, 1976

Siegel GM and Broen PA: Language assessment. In Lloyd LL (ed): Communication, Assessment and Intervention Strategies. Baltimore, University Park Press, 1976

Streng AH: Syntax, Speech and Hearing, Applied Linguistics for Teachers of Children with Language and Hearing Disabilities. New York, Grune & Stratton, 1972

Tyack D and Gottsleben R: Language Sampling Analysis and Training, A Handbook for Teachers and Clinicians. Palo Alto, Ca., Consulting Psychologists Press, 1974

Whitehurst G: Comprehension, selective imitation and the CIP hypothesis. J Exp Child Psychol 23:23–38, 1977

# 9
# Beyond Deafness

A 1969 demographic study of hearing impaired children in United States schools and programs for the deaf reported that approximately 25 percent of those students had at least one handicap in addition to hearing loss, such as mental retardation, visual impairments, or motor problems (Office of Demographic Studies, 1970). With the passage of PL 94-142, the appearance of children with handicaps in addition to hearing impairment (the multihandicapped) may accelerate even more as educational programs for children with a wide variety of learning capabilities and styles become mandatory. In this chapter we will consider, first, some types of children whose major handicap is loss of hearing but who seem to have additional handicaps and second, possible program modifications which might help in planning for individual needs, such as changes in teaching strategies or manipulation of environmental conditions.

## DEFINITION OF MULTIHANDICAPPED

To clarify the term multihandicapped, we choose to differentiate between children whom some might term multihandicapped because of inadequate educational opportunities or because of social-cultural backgrounds which are divergent from middle class America, and those children whose problems are not environmental but intrinsic to the child. It is the latter group who are properly called multihandicapped, but unfortunately the former children are too often so designated. Deaf children with intrinsic problems may be labeled variously as having visual impairment, mental retardation, physical handicaps, social or emotional problems, language disorders, or learning disabilities. We favor trying to avoid such labels, however, turning instead to descriptions of behaviors and learning styles. The contemporary mechanism for focusing on described behaviors for clarifying each deaf child's needs and for suggesting management approaches employs evaluation teams who are charged with developing appropriate individual educational plans (IEPs) for all special children as mandated by federal legislation.

## IEP MANAGEMENT TEAMS FOR HEARING IMPAIRED CHILDREN

Under PL 94-142, each hearing impaired child must be evaluated by an IEP management team consisting of at least a representative from the local educational agency (LEA), the classroom teacher, and the parents of the child; it may also include any other professional deemed necessary for the development of a comprehensive but appropriate IEP. The management team has as its responsibility the development of an individual educational plan for each child assigned to it, specifying the needs of the child, the treatment plan that will meet these needs, statements of long- and short-term goals, and specification of methods for evaluation of the IEP's effectiveness in achieving these goals. We believe that in order to achieve such objectives, the audiologist and the school psychologist should routinely be included as members of each management team evaluating hearing impaired children.

The possibility of having more multihandicapped children in public school programs will require new approaches and instructional models. An expanded team of consultants should be available on an as-needed basis to ensure that fresh approaches to evaluation and to formulation of comprehensive IEPs for multihandicapped hearing impaired children will occur. This team of consultants could include ophthalmologists, pediatricians, physical therapists, clinical psychologists, child psychiatrists, speech pathologists, and psychoeducational diagnosticians familiar with the effects of mental retardation or learning disabilities.

Ideally, information from all appropriate consultants should be available before actual planning for multihandicapped children occurs. To ensure that help is available, it may be reasonable for local educational agencies to develop lists of community resources and special service personnel who are willing and able to evaluate multihandicapped hearing impaired children. If a pediatrician or psychologist without experience with deafness indicates that he would prefer not to attempt an evaluation, the teacher, with parental help, may be able to assist in the evaluation, thus encouraging a greater variety of resources. Deaf children should have the same access to diagnostic services as other children if the need arises. Education of the professional community to its responsibility to this group of children may be an invaluable contribution to the quality of care for all hearing impaired youngsters.

## Roles of IEP Management Team Members

The responsibility of the LEA representative is to see that the plan developed for each child has the support of the school system from which he comes since the school administration will have to provide the financial and personnel support to guarantee that the provisions of the IEP are carried out.

Participation of the parents is vital to the management team efforts. They can provide meaningful information concerning the child's functioning outside of school or of the evaluational setting. Such insights will aid other team members to understand the child's capabilities and reactions.

A qualified school psychologist can provide insight into learning patterns and strategies employed by children. Historically, the school psychologist has been seen as the individual who gives IQ tests. Such expectations must be changed, for a properly trained school psychologist should report on the strategies the child uses to gather information. Only when educational placement issues are at stake should he be expected to provide quantitative scores, which under PL 94-142 must consist of at least two sets of test results, both of which must take into account the child's linguistic and cultural background. The school psychologist can comment on whether the child's approach to problem solving is systematic or random, or whether the child requires more processing time than others of his age. Some children may require additional seconds to understand and react to information given to them. Knowledge of such a problem would allow the teacher to pace her instruction to ensure that processing problems are compensated for in the classroom. In order for the school psychologist to be a well-functioning member of the management team for deaf children, he must have experience and training with hearing impaired persons. Next to teaching professionals, the psychologist requires the greatest insight into deafness and its effects on learning and behavior to ensure that his observations have validity. Through no fault of their own, inexperienced psychologists may confuse behaviors attributable to deafness with abnormal behavior, resulting in recommendations or diagnoses that are faulty or misleading. A management team confronted with the inexperienced or improperly trained school psychologist should be prepared to provide in-service opportunities for him to learn about deafness and deaf children, or to encourage him to seek additional university-level work in deafness if available.

The audiologist's role on the management team should routinely include providing information on hearing levels, speech processing abilities or potentials, and personal hearing aid selection. In addition, he should be able to comment on the utility of group amplification systems for the classroom, provide guidance on classroom acoustics, and make suggestions on how to incorporate auditory experience into educational programming. It is important that the audiologist be an integral part of the team, to be available to explain test results which may include pure tone audiometry (both air and bone conduction), speech discrimination testing, impedance testing, special auditory testing, and detailed aided hearing measurement. If the child displays any active medically remediable problems, it should be the audiologist's responsibility to seek appropriate medical follow-up, as well as to perform regular monitoring to see if changes in auditory functioning have occurred. This monitoring is particularly critical if the child has any middle ear involvement in addition to sensorineural impairment. Impedance audiometry offers an easy method for assessing conductive mechanism function on even the youngest child. Audiological information should be reported regularly to the management team for purposes of revising IEPs. The audiologist should also be prepared to provide in-service lectures to parents and teachers to explain how to implement findings of audiological evaluations meaningfully into language development and educational programs. The audiologist should also be able to provide counseling sessions to parents, as well as teachers, on changes to watch for with introduction of amplification, the mechanics of hearing aid operation, and how to troubleshoot or identify problems of hearing aid malfunctioning. It is important, however, that the audiologist involve himself in educational matters only to the extent of his training, and in parent counseling—only as qualified by his education and experience.

The classroom teacher should be prepared as part of her role on the management team to provide information on the academic, linguistic, and social functioning of the child within the school setting. Such information is imperative for the realistic development of IEPs. Teachers, therefore, must be prepared to make critical observations and to become educational diagnosticians. The teacher's observational and diagnostic capabilities are particularly important since she may be required to initiate the special evaluations needed with multihandicapped children. It will probably be up to the teacher to report the behaviors that require special evaluation. It will generally be necessary for her to assist parents in following through with any referral recommendations made by the team, and it will almost certainly be up to her to implement the findings, usually without the benefit of supervision or monitoring. The teacher must assist the LEA to establish contacts with consultants who can provide diagnostic services to guarantee that important information will be obtained and then fed back for classroom modifications. Consultants are required to round out the type of information that would be useful to the management team. The types of additional consultative services that might be necessary to provide meaningful information about multihandicapped hearing impaired children vary according to the type of problems presented. The following sections will outline consultative services necessary to categories of children usually accepted under the rubric of multihandicapped. Each section will also include a discussion of some important management issues relative to that group of youngsters.

## THE VISUALLY IMPAIRED CHILD

Although most teachers will probably not encounter deaf-blind or deaf–low vision students, the hearing impaired child with some degree of visual deficit will appear frequently in classes for the deaf. In fact, the incidence of visual defects in school-age deaf children is approximately twice that or normal hearing children (Suchman, 1967; Maly, 1969). There are some genetic diseases in which progressive visual impairment (retinitis pigmentosa) is associated with progressive hearing loss. The possible implications of unde-tected visual problems in children who have to depend on vision for the majority of their learning are often treated rather casually. The management team must be sure that each hearing impaired child under its direction has complete visual screening, as well as medical examination of his eyes at regularly scheduled intervals.

Vision screening, which can be performed by a well-trained public school nurse, should involve not only checks for the major refractive errors (near sightedness, far sightedness) but observation of muscle balance func-tion, extent of visual field, and a careful tally of behaviors that could suggest visual problems such as thrusting of the head forward, tilting it to look at printed materials, squinting, rubbing the eyes, or confusion of some printed letters.

When children fail complete screening procedures, they should be re-ferred to the ophthalmologist. As the eye specialist, he can provide specific information on the visual acuity of each child, as well as appropriate prescrip-tions for lenses if necessary.

Having ensured that adequate visual testing has been accomplished and glasses obtained if needed, the management team, particularly the teacher, should pay attention to the visual environment and to presentation of visual information as well. There must be proper, soft, diffuse lighting in learning areas, with natural light used whenever possible. If a child is light sensitive or requires extra light, adaptations should be made.

Color and visual contrasts should be used widely. The teacher should avoid visual indigestion which results from making the environment too busy, but still try to enhance the contrast between the objects to be viewed and the background against which watching will be done.

Printed materials should be reviewed for size and contrast. Handwritten charts should not be placed on newsprint or other paper which allows felt-tipped markers to blur or bleed. Paper that is hard and shiny can be difficult to read from as well because of excessive reflective light.

The teacher must provide each child with time to see, to focus, and to learn visually, but must also ensure regular periods of visual rest, especially from fine visual tasks such as speechreading. Teachers must pay attention to visual health and visual environment since the deaf child's vision can never be treated too carefully, for there is evidence that even small defects in visual acuity can interfere with speechreading performance (Glaser and Berger, 1976).

## THE PHYSICALLY HANDICAPPED CHILD

Some hearing impaired children display motor and health problems that can interfere with their learning in school settings. It is advisable that all children be given complete physical examinations prior to their admission to school. This information should be made available to the management team so that adequate educational planning and adaptations can be made if necessary. When children begin to display behaviors which seem related to health such as sluggishness, excessive activity, and continual colds, referral should be made immediately to the family physician or pediatrician. For those parents that are unable to afford private medical care, it may be up to the management team to help the parent seek public health services when necessary.

Some children display motor problems that interfere seriously with their performance, such as cerebral palsy, congenital deformities, or spina bifida, whereas other children seem merely to have motor planning difficulties. Any child with atypical motor behavior should be referred for detailed evaluation. Both physical and occupational therapists might serve as consultants in this area. The physical therapist can provide information about how independent the child is or can learn to be, motorically. She may also provide ways to include mildly and moderately physically handicapped children more fully into the school routine through exercise and play programs, or how to reduce physical barriers to permit freer access to learning opportunities for the more severely impaired child. The occupational therapist should be able to provide information on the child's visual integration capabilities, specifically, how well the child organizes himself in his physical environment and how well he approaches and handles materials. For instance, if the child consistently overshoots objects in his attempt to reach for them, the team might solicit ways in which the occupational therapist can assist with selection and design of classroom materials to minimize such problems.

In Chapter 2 we discussed motor learning, which refers to learning necessary to execute visual-motor and proprioceptive types of activities with proper timing or coordination. Some hearing impaired children understand a considerable amount of spoken language but lack speech. That is, there is a clear discrepancy between their comprehension and their production capabilities. We are not referring here to the child whose speech is unclear, deaflike, or unintelligible due to profound hearing loss, but rather to the child who lacks any oral language production when it is clear that he is capable of language acquisition. These youngsters may have speech motor planning difficulties and require assistance in learning how to use their oral structures for the production of connected language. Such children often require non-naturalistic approaches to the development of speech (expressive oral language), which this book does not endorse for most children but which may be necessary for certain ones.

It is not possible to provide a detailed discussion of these approaches except that they generally begin with the teaching of individual speech sounds leading to eventual blending of a small set of phonemes into words. Once the child has acquired several words, there is instruction in organizing these words into complete thoughts or sentences. When blending is achieved, it is often possible to shift back to more naturalistic approaches. Once the child has learned basic motor planning as well as some things about the English speech sound system, he may move beyond the elements strategy to develop rule-induced language production. In application of an elements approach with children, we have found the best results when any speech sounds taught lead to production of words known to the child, especially words that can be used with real objects and actions. In this way the child can forge a relationship between the motor planning activities necessary for speech production and language forms which are already meaningful to him.

The reader is referred to material by Barry (1961), McGinnis (1963), or Monsees (1968) for detailed treatment of element approaches.

## THE MENTALLY RETARDED CHILD

Many hearing impaired children display difficulties in learning. It is often not an issue of whether they can learn, but rather how quickly and to what extent this learning occurs. Such children are often considered mentally retarded, which in this context is defined as children with developmental subaverage intellectual functioning who have an impairment in adaptive behavior. Adaptive behavior refers to an individual's adjustment to the natural and social demands of his environment, reflected in his maturation, learning, and social adjustment. Many mentally retarded children have characteristics in common with socially or emotionally disturbed or learning disabled children. Mental retardation can obviously coexist in a child with a variety of other handicaps, including deafness.

Like hearing impairment, mental retardation has been defined as a problem of degree, expressed in terms of a child's current status. Mentally retarded children often are divided into categories such as educable mentally retarded (EMR), trainable mentally retarded (TMR), and custodial mentally retarded (CMR). Although the last group is becoming somewhat prominent in special education, most hearing impaired children that the regular teacher encounters in classes for the deaf probably fall in the EMR or TMR categories. These two categories may be defined traditionally by IQ scores: 50 to 80 IQ range for EMR children, 30 to 50 IQ range for TMR children. It is clearly necessary, however, not to settle for the shortcut of a single IQ score, or to attempt to differentiate mental retardation from other childhood disorders such as childhood autism or organic brain damage. If a child is functioning on a subnormal level adaptively, he may accurately be called mentally retarded in his present condition.

We will confine our discussion to the child who is retarded in learning of language or school subjects, but whose learning levels are appropriate to his overall adaptive performance. In working with mentally retarded children, the teacher is reminded, first, that constant repetition and slow progress may be the rule. However, progress should be expected unless there is a concomitant language disorder, a topic to be discussed later in this chapter. It is imperative that mentally retarded hearing impaired children be provided with many exposures to the same material, but always in meaningful contexts. Second, the upper limit of linguistic achievement in mentally retarded hearing impaired children will not approach that of normally achieving children. Retarded children may not be capable of logical manipulations and finer semantic understandings usually expected from more capable children. The difficulty, however, is that one cannot be certain of the upper limits for mentally retarded children since only their currect status is really known. Management teams should not automatically expect failure or build it in to IEPs. Expectations should be flexible enough to allow for those slow learning children who will break the mold.

For mentally retarded children who have passed the developmental years, that is, those of upper elementary and high school ages, it might be useful to employ curricula that are practically oriented. Career education, focusing on persistent life experiences, should be stressed, leading eventually to vocational experiences and on-the-job opportunities. Language and academics should be geared toward preparing the child for living in the world, not for matriculating into college.

The primary management team members may be supplemented by a psychoeducational diagnostician familiar with mental retardation, who could aid in examining adaptive strategies of the child in maturational and social areas to assure that the hearing impaired child's full range of abilities is tapped, that programming choices are realistic, and that curricular changes are appropriate.

## THE SOCIALLY OR EMOTIONALLY DISTURBED CHILD

The emotional problems evidenced by some hearing impaired children are deep-seated and beyond the diagnostic skill of either teacher or school psychologist. In those instances, either a child psychiatrist or experienced clinical psychologist should be available to help interpret the behavior of the child and his family. Once an educational plan derived from such findings is devised, the teacher may require consultation from the school psychologist to assist her in implementing any recommendations for modification of classroom operations. Modifications could range from focus on interpersonal relationships, such as systematic programs for tolerance of physical contact, to restructuring classroom activities to ensure behavior control while maintaining educational progress.

Social awareness or contact is a set of behaviors which if elicited from children assures the teacher that the child is relating. Synder and McLean (1976), in discussing language learning, identify three important social prerequisites. To learn, children must have looking behaviors, smiling behaviors, and feedback behaviors. Looking behaviors are important, for unless the child is able to focus on objects or events without being distracted, he can not pay attention to the topics or materials being presented by the teacher. Appropriate smiling behavior is important since it allows the teacher to know that she is having some impact on the child. Feedback behavior is important because without it the child can not let the teacher know if he is attending. If these aspects of behavior are not established in a child, it makes language learning or any kind of school progress very difficult. Establishment of social awareness skills should be made part of any child's IEP if they do not already exist.

Social awareness skills can often be brought under control using behavior modification techniques. The teacher needs to specify the behavior she wants to establish and then to develop strategies that will encourage the desired behaviors. Shaping techniques may be used which involve accepting any gross approximation toward the behavior initially, and then gradually insisting on closer and closer approximations until the actual behavior is achieved. For instance, if the child's problem is a lack of eye contact, brief focus on the teacher's face may be acceptable initially. Once this goal is reached, actual eye contact for even a few seconds would be the next objective. Increasing periods of eye contact would then be encouraged, until finally normal looking is established. A variation on this theme to encourage beginning lipreading has been suggested by Donnelly (1974).

The reinforcement schedule is an important consideration in behavior management. The teacher must decide how frequently to reinforce the child's behavior to establish the desired response. In the beginning, the teacher might decide on 100 percent reinforcement. Occurrence of reinforcement must eventually be widely spaced, however, so that the child will come to accept the intrinsic reward of performing the behavior instead of relying exclusively on external reinforcement.

A second issue in behavior management programs is the type of reinforcers to be used. At least two types are recognized: social, that is, praise or patting the head, and tangible. The latter category is too frequently taken to mean consumable or food reinforcers. A hand vibrator, a brief breeze from an electric fan, and getting to blow a whistle are all tangible reinforcers which may assist initially in shaping behavior. The child must eventually come to accept the predominant type of reinforcement in society, that is, one's internal values or feelings as rewards, if the child is to operate independently of his teacher and family.

If a management team suggests the use of reinforcement techniques, then it is imperative that they specify the behaviors to be solicited, the reinforcement schedule to be followed, and the types of reinforcers that might be used initially.

## THE LEARNING DISABLED CHILD

Many children seem to have normal learning capacity but display behaviors that detract from or interfere with progress. Such children are often labeled as learning disabled. We prefer to avoid this type of label in educational diagnosis and to consider instead behaviors of children which may interfere with their learning. In establishing IEPs for children, one may need to emphasize establishing behavior control in order to facilitate academic and linguistic achievement. To assist in this process, it might be useful to have consultation from a psychoeducational diagnostician familiar with the problems displayed by learning disabled children. This person could aid in providing suggestions for behavior management techniques that could be implemented in the classroom.

In considering behaviors related to children identified as learning disabled, it is important to recognize those behaviors that are intrinsic to the child because of hearing impairment or internal learning problems, and those which are extrinsic to the child, and related to classroom operations.

There are some hearing impaired youngsters who have specific disabilities that influence learning styles. These children may be characterized as having difficulties in attention, in memory, in processing time, and in control of activity levels. Each of these conditions can influence the ability of any child to organize himself sufficiently to learn, and can affect the teacher's response to him as well.

## Attention Problems

From an earlier discussion of perceptual psychology, we learned of the importance of attention in the learning process. We learned that attention needs to be both active and selective. Some children have great difficulty in attending selectively. They become distracted by other objects in the environment or by irrelevant aspects of a task. In evaluating attention problems, one must be careful to distinguish between children with intrinsic attention problems and those who have learned to distract the teacher's attention when they are confronted with frustration. For instance, the child who in the middle of a lesson says *My finger hurt* or moves off to begin talking about another subject may be telling you *I don't understand what's going on. To protect myself, I'm changing the subject.* If such behavior occurs frequently, the teacher's presentation should be reviewed to determine if her lessons are too difficult, too demanding, or too boring for the students.

The child with an intrinsic attention problem is at best difficult to handle in a group setting. To reduce that frustration, the teacher should consider the possibility of providing this student with more individual instruction times throughout the day. Working in a group is a situation that any child should learn to tolerate, however. The following suggestions may help in that respect.

It is important that the child with an attention problem be seated near the teacher so that she can cue the child when to pay attention by pointing to objects or directing his focus to the relevant aspects of the task. It is best if the child's back is toward the open classroom, with group activities conducted in settings that have few distractions. When presenting materials, it is important that they be displayed one at a time directly in front of the child with the attention problem, and that other materials not currently in use be put out of the child's visual field. It is important to have materials prepared well ahead of time. The teacher who suddenly has to draw an extra picture or cut a piece of paper is providing an opportunity for the child's attention to wander to such a point that it might be necessary to repeat the entire lesson.

The language presented to this child should be geared to correspond, within reason, to his attention span. If the child is capable of watching for only a few seconds, language presentations should be short. Talking or signing beyond the child's attention span is not instructive for the child and may even be counterproductive if it gives him the impression that talking or signing is not for communication, but merely behavior that occurs in the classroom and can be ignored.

For individual work periods, the teacher might consider making a study area just for the child where he can do his work without distraction. It is important that this area not be used for punishment, but rather as an area for learning or for rest. Of course, one could effectively argue that all hearing impaired children need such consideration some time during the day. Individual scheduling should permit the child to have free access to his retreat area, both to enter and, after completion of tasks, to leave so that he does not acquire the feeling that he is being isolated from the class. If the teacher is considering the use of a study area, it is important that she plan the time the child spends there wisely. It should not become a place to do busy work, but rather a place to complete activities to which the child is having difficulty attending in the group setting.

## Memory Problems

From Chapter 2 we should recall the importance of memory in language learning. Memory functioning is facilitated by relating new information to old information so that each can be retained, recalled, and integrated into learning. In learning experiences the child must be constantly provided with environmental cues as to what should be retained and what can be disregarded. The more meaningful information is, the more likely he is to relate new learning to what he already knows.

Teachers of the hearing impaired note that some children do not remember information or linguistic forms from day to day, or even seemingly from minute to minute. Ability to remember and to recall information is a prerequisite to mastery of meaning and form in language. If an activity is devoid of meaning for the child, his ability to retain what he has learned is reduced. It is critical that materials be given to the child that have meaning to him. Many children who can't "remember" still seem able to retain information that the teacher considers incidental to the purpose of the activity. Despite the teacher's intent, the child has probably selected the most meaningful aspect of the event for him, which is why the information was retained.

Children with memory difficulties can often be helped to retain and comprehend through ensuring a rich learning context. The child may need help in learning to group or chunk information, especially if he has been encouraged to process language on a word-by-word basis, as a procedure for remediating his "memory" difficulties. Teaching strategies whose aim is item-by-item processing will often work against many children with memory deficits, for such strategies encourage fragmentation of language into so many units that the child's memory span is exceeded and his understanding of word relationships is not enhanced. Instead of item-by-item processing, the child with a memory problem should be encouraged to see sentences as containing larger units that can be processed simultaneously. Chunking aids the child in expanding the length of the unit being processed. The child can process three grammatical units instead of merely three words. Working with memory problems is difficult and may yield limited results. It is still important, however, to try to assist such children in achieving some success in use of symbol systems.

## Processing Time Problems

Another special category of child who requires attention is the student who needs extra time to process information. Among these children, the teacher may notice head nodding or lip or finger movement as if they are rehearsing what was said to them. Even then, a lag of several seconds may occur after rehearsal while the child tries to formulate an answer. It is important to note whether time does lapse before an answer is provided, so that such behavior can be managed by not overloading the child with more questions or information, but by allowing him the extra time needed to sort out and retrieve a response.

The only precaution, as indicated in Chapter 2, is that some delays in responding may occur for other reasons, such as an unwillingness to take chances. There are some children who have been so intimidated by the school atmosphere or the teaching styles of the staff that they will not risk answering questions or give information for fear of being penalized. With these latter children, it is not a case of providing additional processing time, but of building a trust relationship.

## High Activity Level Problems

Some hearing impaired children are described as having abnormal activity levels. Activity levels are often abnormal only in the eye of the beholder. The strain for any hearing impaired child of paying attention to minimal auditory information can not be underestimated. In addition, many hearing impaired children need to use vision and taction for ambient scanning as well as specific learning (Kretschmer, 1972) and as a consequence appear unusually restless. The child who is simply exploring his environment should not be confused with the child who cannot inhibit his behavior or who moves randomly through the environment instead of actively investigating it.

If an unusually active child is observed, one might ask first *Is he simply more active than I want him to be* rather than labeling him "hyperactive." In other words, is it a question of the definition of activity that is the issue or is his activity level a real problem to him and his learning? It might be useful if several people observe the classroom, perhaps even by videotape, to see if they can identify the child who is thought by the teacher to have unusual activity levels. Some children always have some part of their body in motion, which is highly annoying to some teachers but not to others. This motion probably doesn't interfere with the child's learning, and it may be an integral part of his style, especially if he is of primary school age.

A second consideration in defining activity level is the organization of the classroom itself. Few of us can tolerate chaos or confusion. If we are placed in a situation where uncertainty is the rule, many of us would react with increased, even random, activity. Does this make us hyperactive? If the classroom is unorganized and the classroom schedule unpredictable, this uncertainty can lead to increased activity levels in children. A properly organized, efficiently planned routine should characterize the classroom with some flexibility so that changes can occur when necessary or desirable. The teacher who is constantly faced with entire classes of "hyperactive" children, particularly when they have no previous history of unusual behavior, would do well to examine her own behavior to assess her contribution to activity levels.

If classroom organization (external factors) is not the cause of a particular child's activity level, then it is important to organize the school day to aid the child in learning internal self-control. A definite routine of activities should be established so that the high-active child knows what he should be doing at all times. It might be useful to preview the routines of each day by meeting with the child alone and going over the day's schedule. A schedule using color codes or pictures could be pasted near his desk if he has limited language. Any unusual deviations that are going to occur during the day should be discussed with the child ahead of time so that he knows what to expect. Otherwise, changes may produce uncertainty, a condition conducive to the eruption of high-activity behavior.

For a highly active child, a retreat area, such as that discussed in the section on attention, could be employed. If this approach is used, however, it is important to continue to include the child in group experiences so that he can learn to tolerate a variety of situations, some of which may be highly stimulating. Once the active child learns to control his behavior somewhat, he may still be prone to sudden bursts of energy, which in some instances can be quite violent. Usually physical signals, for example, dilation of the pupils, paling of the skin, or sudden jerking movements of the legs, precede such events. By devising ways in which energy can be dissipated, the teacher can use these signals to avoid destructive outbursts. The child's retreat area could be equipped with toys to punch or kick, or with just a mat for jumping. If the child appears to be agitated, the teacher can suggest that he go to the retreat area. Eventually, he can learn to go voluntarily as he needs to.

### Language Disorder Problems

One of the major complaints heard from teachers is that some children seem to have language learning difficulties. This usually means that even after extensive language instruction the child exhibits little or no linguistic understanding or performance. Such children tend to be quite upsetting to the teacher, for they seem normal in all respects except that they have difficulty formulating meaningful hypotheses about language. These children are able to communicate in that they gesture or demonstrate information to the teacher, but they do not acquire language, regardless of the mode of communication used. It can be seen that these children have the ability to attend and to remember. They usually can recall events from the past or even discuss ongoing events through pictures or dramatization. The difficulty is that they do not seem to attach a symbol, either oral or signed, to an experience.

From this description, it can easily be seen why such children are frustrating to teachers and other professionals. In Chapter 2 we learned of the importance of context in the learning process. Piaget, for example, comments that as children learn they interact with their environment, their context. The more information the child has about events which surround him, the more probable it is that the language he hears will have meaning. It is possible that children who are not learning language do not know how to use context to stabilize the language rules they hear or see. They probably require more contextual information than might be normal to assist them in learning language. For these children, removing learning from experience, using language alone to teach more language, memorizing dictionary definitions and patterns of sentences, or explaining and diagramming rules for syntax usage will be of little benefit. In developing IEPs for language disordered children, therefore, it is important that behavioral objectives focus on language programs that are incorporated into ongoing curricular efforts and that are tied to actual experience.

In addition to the management team, the speech/language pathologist might be consulted about children with language learning problems. As a communication disorder specialist, the speech/language pathologist may be able to provide important information relative to the development of communication in children. We must distinguish this consultant, however, from the more traditionally trained speech therapist, whose area of expertise is confined to speech and its disorders. The management team should certainly obtain consultation for the hearing impaired child with speech remediation needs. They should, however, explore with potential speech/language consultants their expertise with language learning problems before engaging such persons.

From a management point of view, following an academically oriented curriculum with language disordered hearing impaired children may be inappropriate since such curricula often do not make provision for maximum environmental or contextual support to learning, depending instead on abstractions away from reality. In many instances, particularly in the elementary grades and above, teachers use both language and pictures to teach more language with the expectation that all children will learn equally well. Such lessons for a child with minimal language or less than normal potential for learning language will certainly lead to frustration on the teacher's part and probably to a negative attitude toward school on the child's part. A better approach might be to modify instruction to focus on experiential units such as building things, setting up household tasks, or even repairing cars. If the child with language learning problems has strengths that are nonverbal in nature, then learning through doing has a special meaning. Language teaching even in the experiential approach should consist of constant repetition of specific language. To make this approach work, of course, the teacher requires a precise plan of the language to be presented, as well as notions about the appropriateness of the learning task for each child. For instance, a teenager should not make jello just for the sake of experience, but rather as part of some larger purpose such as planning a party for younger children or learning about quantities involved in food preparation. Too often the language level of the child leads the teacher to assume that the interest levels or social awareness of the child is limited as well.

Language learning research seems to indicate that some normally hearing children make initial progress in language learning, but plateau with distressingly limited performance levels in spite of adequate teaching and family support (Morehead, 1975). In hearing impaired populations, there are also some children who make rapid progress in learning single words and even in development of two-word combinations, but who do not progress beyond this stage, even after two or three years of good, consistent teaching.

From Chapter 4 we learned of research on normally hearing children which indicates that language learning may require the use of different strategies at different times. If this is true of normally hearing children, it certainly could also be true of hearing impaired children. For instance, for those children who fail to make the transition from two-word combinations to more complex sentences, it has been our observation that they use predominantly pronominal constructions. That is, they tend to focus on the functional relationships instead of switching to a use of both functional and grammatical relationships. Even earlier at the single-word level, children who are stalled in acquisition reflect a self-limiting strategy such as naming, which is one way to initiate language but is not the most productive route to acquisition of connected forms. Facilitation of language growth would better be accomplished by not reinforcing a naming strategy, but by focusing on action verbs, which according to linguists such as Chafe (1970) represent the core of connected spoken English. The teacher who is working with hearing impaired children having acquisition problems might begin the children with practice in comprehension and use of commands such as *Sit down* and *Run*. When some verb commands are mastered, the teacher might focus on verb plus direct object construction; on verb plus direct object plus adverb of location, and so on. Such an approach would aid the child in mastering the core of all sentences, eventually learning how the various grammatical units relate to one another. This approach although focused differently from a linguistic point of view is not unlike techniques of language instruction described in greater detail in Chapter 6 (Buckler, 1968).

## EXTERNALLY INDUCED HANDICAPS

There are two groups of children often identified as multihandicapped that are not intrinsically impaired. These two groups, educationally handicapped deaf children and culturally different children with hearing impairment, possess the ability to learn language normally, but due to external circumstances have failed to develop to their fullest potential. In most instances, the IEP management team can handle the needs of such children if their unique problems are recognized.

### Educationally Handicapped Children

Hearing impairment does have an effect on academic achievement and linguistic development such that most hearing impaired children require special services throughout their entire educational life. Despite this placement, many will still be linguistically handicapped adults. There are too many instances where achievement levels differ sharply from perceived or demonstrated ability. One of the causes of this disparity could be educational deprivation or mismanagement. Children may recieve special education, perhaps from preschool age, but do not have appropriate educational experiences because of outdated or inadequate curricula, or poorly prepared teachers. Although such conditions are becoming less frequent, many classrooms for hearing impaired children are still managed by marginally qualified persons. Many of these teachers have been regular educators or have worked in areas such as mental retardation or speech pathology, and then found their way into classes for the deaf, often because of administrative convenience. Some classes may even be manned by certified teachers of the deaf who have had inadequate teacher preparation or who have not modernized their teaching approaches.

Some communities establish single classrooms to house all hearing impaired children, a situation which often results in a group of nine or more children who range in age from 6 to 14 years, with hearing losses ranging from very slight to profound. Some children in such settings demonstrate no additional problems, whereas others may be multihandicapped. Guidelines (Mulholland and Fellendorf, 1968) for the establishment of day classes advocate that such programs be attempted only if a reasonable population of hearing impaired children exists. In those communities where a large population is not available, regional cooperation should be encouraged so that appropriate grouping and tracking can be established.

The single classroom program may be viable under certain circumstances, namely, (1) if no more than six to seven children are enrolled; (2) if most of the children can be mainstreamed; (3) if the teacher has assistance from older pupils in the school or class, or a teacher's aide; and (4) if the program can be organized so that the teacher has individual time with each pupil every day. Unfortunately, many of these conditions are not met in single class programs, so that many children often arrive at junior high school age with minimal communication and limited academic abilities.

These comments should not be interpreted to mean that large well-organized programs do not sometimes create educationally handicapped children. Children can be placed with a series of teachers who lack knowledge of how to work with deaf children, or who lack contemporary information, with the result that achievement is unsatisfactory. In evaluating children, it is necessary to take previous educational experiences into consideration to better understand present status and to plan future educational experiences.

Although invaluable time has been lost with many deaf students, it has been our experience that older educationally handicapped youngsters will respond to insightful teaching if it is geared toward their needs and is not demeaning. Language experiences that are organized as recommended for language disordered children, with an adjustment of topics and vocabulary to interests of older children, can result in language learning and in some educational growth. Presentation of basic sentences in naturalistic settings that emphasize appropriate prevocational topics can serve as the curriculum for educationally handicapped students. If basic syntactic and semantic relations can be acquired, which is usually the case, then work on more complex linguistic forms as well as advances in reading can still be attempted even late in the child's educational program. Educationally handicapped students never make up the time they have lost. However, instruction based on normal language acquisition sequences offers one positive way to try to achieve meaningful communication and minimum literacy levels.

## Socially and Culturally Different Children

As was indicated at the end of Chapter 2, it is no longer reasonable to describe American society as homogenous with regard to social, cultural, or linguistic factors. We have a variety of ethnic and linguistic differences within this country, to say nothing of easily recognizable economic differences. Many large metropolitan areas and portions of the Southwest and West are educating large numbers of bilingual students. For instance, as many as 30 percent of all students in the New York City Public Schools, and as many as 40 percent of deaf children in programs in that city have Spanish surnames (Correa, 1977). The majority of such bilingual children may have to learn English as a second language, through the school system.

There are an equal number of persons in our society who speak variations of English distinct enough to pose educational problems. Such language variations, if systematic and associated with a specific geographic, cultural, or socioeconomic group, are called dialects. Each of us speaks a variation of English, a dialect or idiolect conditioned by our linguistic, social, educational, and geographic experiences. These idiolects may be simple variations of so-called standard English, such as television broadcaster dialect or college professor dialect.

Good grammar or "proper" English is viewed as the standard by the majority of English speakers, a judgment which is socially, politically, racially, or economically based. Because nonstandard variations of English such as Black English are systematic and useful for communication among members of a particular segment of society, they must not be considered as bad, ungrammatical, or substandard, only different and less valued in certain communication situations. Although the evidence is equivocal, it has been argued that children who speak nonstandard English may suffer interference in their efforts to master educational material based on standard English (Baratz and Shuy, 1969; Bartel and Axelrod, 1973). The accuracy of such a viewpoint has not been proven conclusively. The important issue should be that regardless of the child's oral language usage, he must have opportunity to achieve mastery of printed English if his educational opportunities are to be equal to those of other children.

All children—deaf or normally hearing—come from a linguistic subgroup of the community. The type and use of language they are exposed to at home are not necessarily the type and use of language they are exposed to at school. This often results in the child's having to learn two languages, home talk and school talk. For many hearing impaired children, this may pose a serious problem, for they may be trying to learn the linguistic and communicative rules for two rather distinct systems. Their hearing impairment makes it difficult for them to learn either home or school dialect well. Not infrequently, poor, black, or non-English language dominant hearing impaired students are labeled multihandicapped when they may be perfectly capable of learning language and of being literate if the interference of language demands can be resolved between home and school.

PL 94-142 requires that all evaluations be appropriate to the child's linguistic background. For the child who comes from a bilingual or bidialectical home, any evaluation of his linguistic abilities will have to be cognizant of his language experiences.

Of course, it could be argued that children with significant hearing loss, by virtue of the severe nature of their impairment, are unaffected by language interference. Walton (1972) and Boutte (1975) both studied the linguistic environments and oral language usage of black hearing impaired adolescents from a metropolitan area. Both studies observed that black hearing impaired adolescents used a variety of oral Black English forms regardless of the degree of their hearing loss, but compared to normally hearing black adolescents, used more language forms that were deficient and not representative of either Black English or Standard School English. The linguistic environments of school and home were clearly different for all these youngsters. If such differences are ignored educationally, they can not help but interfere in some way with mastery of oral language, as well as the acquisition of literacy.

The management team that is faced with nonstandard dialectic environments for hearing impaired children who speak should make every attempt to assess which linguistic forms are a result of hearing impairment and therefore in need of remediation and which forms are more likely to be nonstandard dialectic forms not in need of remediation per se.

If the hearing impaired child's parents do not speak English or speak only fragmented English, one might consider whether as part of the IEP aiding the parents themselves to learn English would contribute to consistent communication patterns at school and home. The parents could be enrolled in evening classes in English, or the teacher might even suggest that she teach the parents along with the child. With nonstandard dialect speaking parents or non-English speaking parents, the issue of linguistic interference should be dealt with frankly, through the use of a well-qualified interpreter in the latter case. PL 94-142 mandates that information about their children must be conveyed to non-English speaking parents through the use of competent interpreting services. Regardless of the situation, the parents should be made to feel that there is no stigma attached to the language forms they use or which they wish their children to use.

American society through legislation is trying to assure appropriate publicly supported education as the birthright of every handicapped child, however divergent his adaptive behavior. Although legislation does not itself change attitudes, it does change funding and administrative procedures so that the classroom teacher and the parents will have the support necessary to identify and plan for each deaf child's learning differences, whether he is multihandicapped or not. In fact, the new emphasis in special education places those most neglected, the multihandicapped, highest in priority for assistance.

Teachers and school support personnel must expect to encounter a wide variety of learning and behavior styles in association with childhood deafness. Professional workers must expect, indeed be ready for, a challenge in planning for and teaching multihandicapped deaf children. The challenge is great, but not insurmountable.

## REFERENCES

Baratz J and Shuy R (eds): Teaching Black Children to Read. Washington, D.C., Center of Applied Linguistics, 1969

Barry H: The Young Aphasic Child. Washington, D.C., A. G. Bell Assoc., 1961

Bartel N and Axelrod J: Nonstandard English usage and reading ability in black junior high students. Except Child 39:653–655, 1973

Boutte J: A syntactical analysis of the oral language of 10 black hearing impaired and 10 black normally hearing adolescents. Unpublished masters thesis, University of Cincinnati, 1975

Buckler M: Expanding language through patterning. Volta Rev 70:89–96, 1968

Chafe W: Meaning and the Structure of Language. Chicago, University of Chicago Press, 1970

Correa G: Local community support for bilingual special education. Presentation, Council of Exceptional Children Convention, Atlanta, 1977

Donnelly K: Aural rehabilitation. In Donnelly K (ed): Interpreting Hearing Aid Technology. Springfield, Ill., Charles C. Thomas, 1974

Glaser R and Berger K: The relationship of artificially reduced visual acuity to speechreading performance. Ohio J Speech Hear 12:50–57, 1976

Kretschmer R: A study to assess the play activities and gesture output of hearing handicapped pre-school children. Cincinnati, Department of Special Education, 1972

Maly P: Screening for visual defects in hearing impaired children. Unpublished masters thesis, University of Cincinnati, 1969

McGinnis M: Aphasic Children. Washington, D.C., A. G. Bell Assoc., 1963

Monsees E: Structured Language for Children with Special Language Learning Problems. Washington, D.C., A. G. Bell Assoc., 1968

Morehead D: The study of linguistically deviant children. In Singh S (ed): Measurement Procedures in Speech, Hearing, and Language. Baltimore, University Park Press, 1975

Mulholland A and Fellendorf G (eds): National Research Conference on Day Programs for Hearing Impaired Children. Washington, D.C., A. G. Bell Assoc., 1968

Office of Demographic Studies: Additional Handicapping Conditions, Age of Onset of Hearing Loss, and Other Characteristics of Hearing Impaired Students. Washington, D.C., Gallaudet College, 1970

Snyder L and McLean J: Deficient acquisition strategies: a proposed acquisition framework for analyzing severe language deficiencies. Am J Ment Defic 81: 338–349, 1977

Suchman R: Visual impairment among deaf children. Arch Ophthalmol 77:18–21, 1967

Walton L: A description of the linguistic environments and the syntactic abilities of 10 black hearing impaired adolescents. Unpublished masters thesis, University of Cincinnati, 1972

# APPENDIX A
## Grammar I

Grammar I is a minimal grammar with which hearing impaired children should be able to express their actions and thoughts with sufficient clarity to make their needs and wants known.

### I. BASIC SENTENCE PATTERNS

- I.   $NP + V_1 (+ Adv_{p, m, t})^*$
- II.  $NP + V_t + NP (+ Adv_{p, m, t})$
- III. $NP + be + N (+ Adv_{p, t})$
- IV.  $NP + be + Adj (+ Adv_{p, t})$
- V.   $NP + be + Adv_p (+ Adv_t)$

### II. PHASE STRUCTURE RULES

1. *Noun phrases*
    - 1.1a.  Det + N
    - 1.1b.  Det → reg art
         [*a, an, the*]
         [gen]
         [dem]
    - 1.1c.  Det → <±def>
    - 1.1d.  Det → ∅

---

*p, place; m, manner; t, time.

      1.1e.  Det → dem
             *this, that, these, those*
      1.2.  Det + card + N
      1.3.  Det + N + Modifier
             (prep phrase from del rel clause)
      1.4.  Predet + Det + N
             *all of, some of*
      1.5.  Poss →
             [N's, -s']
             [of phrase]

2.  *Verb phrases*
      2.1.  VP → t + V
             [past]
      2.2.  VP → t + M
             [pres]
             [past]
             [*can*]
             [*will*]
      2.3.  VP → t + *be* + *-ing* + V
             [pres]
             [past]
      2.4.  VP → t + *have* + V
             [pres]
      2.5.  preverb + V

3.  *Adjectives*
      3.1.  Adj + N
      3.2.  Adj + N adjunct + N

4.  *Adverbs*
      4.1.  Order → place, manner, time


## III.  FEATURES OF THE LEXICON

1.  *Nouns*
     1.1  <± common>
     1.2  <±count>
     1.3  <±singular>
     1.4  <±possessive>
     1.5  <±abstract>
     1.6  <±animate>
     1.7  <±human>

2. *Pronouns*
    2.1   <±personal>
           1st, 2nd, 3rd
    2.2   <±singular>
    2.3   <±gender>
           M, F, N
    2.4   <±case>
           nom, poss, accus
    2.5   reflexive
    2.6   indefinite
3. *Verbs*
    3.1   <±transitive>
    3.2   <±progressive>
    3.3   <±catenation>
    3.4   v + particle
           v + complement
    3.5   inflec suffixes
    3.5a.  pres 3rd pers sing (*-s*)
    3.5b.  past (-ed) regular and irregular
    3.5c.  pres part (*-ing*)
    3.5d.  past part (*-en*)
4. *Adjectives*
    4.1   <±comparative>
           *-er, -est, more, most*
    4.2   <±catenation>
5. *Adverbs*
    5.1   <±preverbs>
6. *Prepositions*
    6.1   <±movement>
           <+time>
           <+place>

## IV. TRANSFORMATIONS

1. T/yes-no
2. T/negative
    includes T/*any* replacement for *some*
3. T/do
4. T/request
5. T/contraction

6. T/particle shift
7. T/adj shift
8. T/adv shift
9. T/wh- question
10. T/coordinating conjunction
    *and, but, or*
11. T/deletion
12. T/reflexive
13. T/factive clause
    *that* deletion
14. T/there
15. T/adverbial clause
    time, cause
16. T/for-to (+ deletions)
    NP complement of object,
    infinitive of purpose,
    complement of adjective
17. T/rel clause
    *who* or *that* embedded in object
    or last noun in sentence
18. T/rel pro (+ *be*) deletion
19. T/comparative
    Adj, Adv
20. T/passive substitute
    *got*

# APPENDIX B
## Grammar II

Grammar II is an advanced grammar which can be used basically for expanding the written expressive language of older children who are college bound or who show evidence of mastering Grammar I at an early age. Selections of items from Grammar II will be dependent on a pupil's need for expressing himself more clearly and more succinctly. Undoubtedly a more complex semantic component would accompany the development of Grammar II. This grammar requires considerable control over embedded noun phrase and verb phrase complements including all types of infinitive and question embedding. Grammar II, although encompassing a great many more transformations and phrase structure rules than Grammar I, is still a rather limited base for sophisticated writing since it does not deal with idiomatic or poetic expression. These aspects must be dealt with concurrently with growing syntactic competence.

### I. TRANSFORMATIONS

1. T/nominalization
   1.1a. poss + *-ing (his talking)*
   1.1b. N's derived from N, V, Adj + derivational suffix
2. T/indirect object
3. T/rel
   3.1. T/rel (introduced by *who, whose, whom, which*) embedded in subject, object and object of preposition as restrictive clause

3.2.   T/rel pro shift (when rel pro is object of embedded sentence)

3.3.   T/prep + rel pro shift

3.4.   T/rel pro deletion (when rel pro is not subject of embedded sentence)

3.5.   T/rel pro + *be* deletion

3.6.   T/rel (nonrestrictive clause)

3.7.   T/rel adv (introduced by *where, when*)

3.8.   T/rel pro replacement (for *that which, to that place, in that way,* and *at that time* with *whatever, wherever, however,* and *whenever*)

4.  T/embedded questions (introduced by *who, what, where, when*)

5.  T/extraposition

6.  T/*it* replacement

7.  T/wh- article replacement (as in *which* boy, *what* number)

8.  T/question tag

9.  T/neg (*much* replacement for *lots of*)

10.  T/subord conj (*if, unless, in order that,* etc. as needed for introducing adverbial clauses)

11.  T/preverb shift (intensifier)

12.  T/passive

13.  T/indirect discourse

13.1.   T/embedded NC (*that* after verbs such as *say, tell, declare, inform*)

13.2.   T/embedded inf (after verbs *tell* and *ask*)

13.3.   T/embedded NC (*if* after verb *ask*)

14.  T/verb agreement (tense sequence)

15.  T/deletion

15.1.   T/complementizer deletion

15.2.   T/conjunction deletion (in series)

15.3.   T/*it* deletion (from factive clause)

15.4.   T/pronoun deletion

15.5.   T/verb deletion (following modal or aux)

15.6.   T/*for* + N + *to* (from embedded sentence)

## II.  PHRASE STRUCTURE RULES

1.  *Noun phrases*

1.1.   Determiners

1.1a.   Preart + art + N

1.1b.   Preart + predet + art + N

1.1c.   Det + modifiers in series

      1.1d.   Det + N + deleted rel clause appearing as prep phrase
      1.1e.   Det + N + deleted rel clause appearing as *-ing* or *-en* verbal
      1.1f.   Det art + N + of + N (poss)
2.  *Verb phrases*
      2.1.   Active
      2.1a.  VP → t(pres/past) + M + *be* + *-ing* + V
      2.1b.  VP → t(pres/past) + *have* + *-en* + V
      2.1c.  VP → t(pres/past) + *have* + *-en* + be + *-ing* + V
      2.1d.  VP → t(pres/past) + M + *have* + *-en* + *be* + *-ing* + V
      2.2.   Passive
      2.2a.  VP + t(pres/past) + *be* + *-en* + V
            VP → t(pres/past) + *have* + *been* + *-en* + V
            VP → t(pres/past) + *be* + *being* + *-en* + V
3.  *Infinitive phrases*
      3.1.   positive active (*to say*)
      3.2.   *to* + *be* + *-ing* + base form (*to be saying*)
      3.3.   *to* + *have* + *-en* + V (*to have said*)
      3.4.   *to* + *have* + *been* + *-ing* + base form (*to have been saying*)
      3.5.   passive-positive
      3.6.   *to* + *be* + *-en* + V (*to be said*)
      3.7.   *to* + *have* + *-en* + *be*  *-en* + V (*to have been said*)
      3.8.   negative active: *not* + *to* + base form (*not to say*)
      3.9.   negative passive: *not* + *to be* + *-en* + V (*not to be said*)
4.  *Adjectives*: superlative followed by clause
5.  *Adverbs*: comparison of all adverbs
      5.1.   Preverb + V
      5.2.   aux + preverb + V

## III.  FEATURES OF THE LEXICON

<+ derivational suffices>
(added to N's, V's, and Adj's to produce new N's, V's, and Adj's)
<+ prefixes>
(added to N's, V's, and Adj's)

---

From Streng, A. H.: *Syntax Speech & Hearing*. New York, Grune & Stratton, 1972.

# Index

Abstraction, 31, 33
Acceptance, and mourning, 52, 53
Accomodation, 19, 20, 22
Achievement
  and ability, 203
  tests of
    norm-referenced, 155
    and planning, 155
    standardization in, 155
Acoustic method, 4
Action, use of, 83, 173
Actor–action–object, 75
Adaptive behavior, 194
Adjectives
  comparison of, 151
  as opposites, 150
  in Sentence Pattern IV, 150
  vocabulary of, 149
Adolescents
  Black English of, 206
  curriculum for, 103
    educationally handicapped, 204–205
    mentally retarded, 194–195

reading materials for, 141
topics for, in written English, 163
Affixes
  derivational, 145
  inflectional, 145
Age, of admission, schools for deaf, 1
Agent, use of, 75
Agent–action–complement relationship, 76
Agent–action–patient–location relationship, 84, 90
Agent–action–patient relationship, 76, 82, 83
American Asylum for the Deaf and Dumb, 1
American School for the Deaf, 1, 6
American Sign Language (ASL), 5, 60.
  See also Pidgin languages
  adaptations of, 5
  characteristics of, 92–94
  definitions of, 60
  in family communication, 62
  as instructional goal, 95

American Sign Language *(continued)*
  as primary language, 95
American Theatre of the Deaf, 92
Amplification
  aggressive use of, 61
  effective use of, 61
  and language learning, 61
  in parent-education program, 55
  as primary signal, 60
Anthony D, 5, 12
Anxiety, 100
Argument, in sentence, 77
Ask–tell sentences, 88
Assessment
  guide for, 175–176
  informal/formal, 168
  of language, oral/written, 176–181
  of language comprehension, 172
  and language planning, 168
  procedures for, 173
  record keeping in, 173, 179
  samples for, 175ff
  of sentences semantics/syntax, 168
  work sheets for, 178–179
Assimilation, 19, 20, 22
Attention
  difficulty with, 197
  to environmental speech sounds, 80
  to language, by infants, 80
  to language topic, 46
  in learning, 25–26
  to predicate of sentence, 46
  problems with, 197
  selectivity in, 24, 25, 197
  to sentence pattern regularity, 80
  in simultaneous communication, 26
  span of, 198
Attitudinal learning, 41–42, 99, 106
Audiograms, for evaluation, 63
Audiological services
  counseling parents and teachers, 190
  educational–audiological follow-up, 61
  electroacoustic assessment, 61
  hearing aid evaluation, 61
  hearing aid selection, 190
  impedence testing, 190

  trouble shooting, 190
Audiologist, 10, 53, 188
  responsibilities of, 190
  role on M-team, 189
Auditory global technique, 51
Auditory training, 3, 9, 80
Aural–oral approach, 5, 60, 62
Avila DL, 41, 43
Axelrod J, 205, 207

Baby register, 48–49
Bach E, 73, 95
Bailey N, 86, 95
Balfour G, 86, 87, 96
Baratz J, 205, 207
Bargaining, and mourning, 52, 53
Barnes JD, 128
Barry H, 193, 207
Bartel N, 205, 207
Basal readers
  judging suitability, 154–55
  language in, 132
  linguistic, 132
  school-wide series, 154
  selection of, 154
  selective reading in, 160
Base component, of grammar, 29
Base structure level, of syntax, 72
Bates E, 77, 96
Behavior
  adaptive, 194
  eye contact, 54, 195
  modification of, 16, 42
    as control, 107
    reinforcement schedules on, 196
    techniques, 195
Behavioral objectives
  in assessment analysis, 181
  and language disorders, 201
Behaviorism. *See* Stimulus–response
    (S–R) learning
Bellugi U, 30, 42, 94, 96
Bender R, 2, 6, 12
Berger K, 192, 207
Berko-Gleason J, 49, 67
Bilingualism

ASL and spoken English, 62
and deaf children, 62
in parent–school relationships, 206
in schools for deaf, 205
Black English, 205, 206
Blaton R, 89, 90, 98
Bloom L, 20, 42, 70, 75, 77, 82–84, 96,
171, 186
Book reviews, writing of, 161, 163
Bornstein H, 5, 12
Botel M, 154, 157, 165
Bound morphemes, 72
Boutte J, 206, 207
Bowerman M, 30, 43, 70, 81, 82, 84, 96
Brain, programmed for language
learning, 25
Brill R, 1, 6, 7, 8, 12
Brown R, 30, 43, 75, 84, 85, 96
Brunner J, 67, 146
Buckler M, 128, 203
Bureau of Education for the Handicapped,
105
Busy work, 161, 198

Calvert DR, 41, 43
Case grammar
actor, 75
agent, 29, 46, 75
beneficiary, 47
complement, 75
experiencer, 29
goal, 29
instrument, 29, 46, 75
locative, 29
mover, 75
object, 29
patient, 46, 75
temporal, 29, 75
Categorization
and classification, 20
comprehension of, 22
as requisite in thinking, 132
Causality, 23, 82, 87
Central Institute for the Deaf, 4
Cerebral palsy, and deafness, 2, 192
Chafe W, 72, 75, 96, 203, 207

Chall J, 132, 154, 165
Charts
characteristics of, positive, 136, 137,
193
direct quotations, 137, 139
experience–language–reading, 136
pronoun, 138, 140
reading, 138
Chicago Non-Verbal Examination, 31
Child psychologists, roles of, 188
Children
as active participants in learning, 24
as audience, 116
culturally different, 205
educationally handicapped, 203
hyperactive, 199–200
interests of, exploited, 141
language deficient, 84
language deviant, 37
mentally retarded, 193
physically handicapped, 192
preschool deaf, 24
socially disturbed, 195
visually handicapped, 191
Chomsky C, 88, 96
Chomsky N, 27–29, 43, 71, 72, 86, 96
Chunking information, 199
Clarke E, 81, 82, 86, 87, 96
Clarke School for the Deaf, 2
Classification, comprehension of, 22
Classroom
climate in, 99ff
discipline in, 107, 196
organization in, 200
retreat areas in, 198, 200, 201
self-control in, 107, 200
stimulating learning in, 102
Clauses. See Transformations
Cleft palate, and hearing, 2
Clinical psychologists, and education, 57
Cloze test, 155ff
and book selection, 159
construction of, 157
error evaluation in, 159
example of, 159
preparation for, 158

Cloze test *(continued)*
  scoring of, 158
Cognition
  characteristics of deaf, 31
  development of, 19ff, 27, 115, 141,
    150
  and language, 29
  tasks of, 19
  and universals, 28
Colleges for the deaf, 6
Columbia Institution for the Deaf, Dumb,
    and Blind, 6
Combinational meaning, in sentences, 75
Combs A, 41, 43, 107
Communication
  in ASL, 94
  dialogues
    barriers to, 50, 56
    breakdown of, 49
    in conversation period, 162
    importance of, 48, 50
    parents in, 50–51
    siblings in, 50
    teachers in, 51
  establishment of, 54
  exchanges, 84
  function of, 84
  and hearing aids, 54
  importance of, 50, 67
  modalities of
    aural–oral approach, 3, 5, 60
    fingerspelling, 60
    parent selection of, 63
    sign language, 5, 60
    total communication, 60
    unisensory approach, 5
  mother–infant, 48, 50–51, 59
  multiple purposes of, 85
  in one-way communication, 51
  in patterning approach, 127
  questioning in, 51
  styles of, 54
  teacher–child, 84, 128
  teacher–parent, 65
Communication component, of language,
    77

Communication patterns, of normal child,
    45ff
Complement, defined, 75
Complementation, 168
Complex sentences. *See also* Sentences
Composition. *See* Written language
Comprehension
  assessment of, 170–72
  as goal in programmed instruction, 106
  of languages, 80–81
  and production, 193
  and questions, 142
Concepts
  abstract, 17
  concrete, 17
  formation of, 31, 32
  higher-level, 18
  identification of, 27
Concreteness
  and meaning, 168
  of nouns, 144
  in symbol systems, 33
  in thinking, 115
Concrete operational period, 20, 22, 32,
    111
Conjoining, process of, 73, 87
Conor L, 63, 67
Conservation tasks, 21
  and deaf children, 31
  language for, 112
Consultants, to M-Teams
  child psychiatrists, 188
  clinical psychologists, 188
  occupational therapists, 193
  ophthalmologists, 191
  pediatricians, 188
  physical therapists, 193
  psycho-educational diagnosticians, 195
  speech-language pathologists, 201
Context
  and communication, 81
  and learning language, 201
  in reading, 160
  situational, 168
Conversational interaction, 162. *See also*
    Communication

Cooper R, 89, 96
Coordinated space, 82
Coordinating conjunction, 87
Copula, 85–86
Cornett RO, 3, 12
Correa G, 205, 207
Correction
    of speech, 101
    threatening/nonthreatening, 100
    of written language, 164
Corson H, 52, 67
Cued speech, 3, 4
Cultural learning, 41–42
*Curious George* (McKee et al.), 158
Curriculum
    concept development in, 130
    flexibility in, 103, 132
    for hearing impaired, 129
    participants in, 130
    persisting life situations in, 130, 194
    planning, 130
    reading in, 131ff
    scope of, 130
Custodial mentally retarded (CMR), 194.
    *See also* Mental retardation

Dale E, 154, 165
Dale P, 71, 79, 96
Davis H, 8, 12
Deaf child
    as information seeker, 70
    language learning of, 89
    in PL 94-142, 8
    and pragmatics, 78
Deafness, 1
    familial, 2
    as handicap, 52–53
    profound, 2
Deaf parents
    attitudes toward children, 62
    and education, of children, 63
    as minority group, 42
Delgado College, technical program, 6
Demographic studies
    of deaf children, 187
    of multihandicapped, 187

of reading achievement, 133
Denial, 52, 53, 77
Determiners, 144, 168, 180
Developmental stages of language
    acquisition, 47, 82, 84, 85, 110.
    *See also* Periods of intellectual
    functioning
Dialogues. *See* Communication
Dictionary
    for children, 151
    for idioms, 169
    and individual picture-sentence, 147
    use of, 151–153
Di Francesca, 5, 133, 165
Diptheria, and hearing, 2
Directed study
    of adjective vocabulary, 143
    goals of, 143
    of noun vocabulary, 143
    of verb vocabulary, 145–149
Discourse, defined, 72
Distinctive features, 24, 25, 27
Donaldson M, 86, 87, 96
Donnelly K, 196, 207
Dramatization
    as mode of communication, 201
    of stories, 159, 161, 162

Ear trumpets, 3
Editing, of written language
    by child, 163
    procedures for, 164
Educable mentally retarded (EMR), 194.
    *See also* Mental retardation
Education, of deaf, history, 2, 6
Education of All Handicapped Children
    Act of 1975 (PL94-142), 11, 64,
    167, 187–189, 191, 206
    aspects of, 7
    as civil rights law, 7
    due process requirements, 65
    individual educational planning (IEP),
    10
    interpreting services, 207
    least restrictive environment, 8
    and M-team, 10

Handicapped Children Act *(continued)*
  nondiscriminatory testing, 9
  parent counseling, 9
  psychological services, 9
  supportive services, 8–9
Eimas P, 80
Elementary and Secondary Education Act
      (ESSA), 7
Elements approach, in speech teaching,
      193
Embedding, process of, 88
Emotionally disturbed child, 195–196
Emotional needs of parents, 52
English, spoken, and deaf, 69
Entity, defined, 75
Ervin-Tripp S, 86, 87, 96
Ewing AWG, 41, 43
Ewing IR, 41, 43
Examinations
  audiologic, 9
  physical, 193
  visual, 191
Expansion, and language development,
      50, 51
Experiencer, defined, 75
Experiences
  and cooperative planning, 115
  and development program, 109
  incidental, 118

Farewell C, 45, 67, 79, 96
Features, of words, 29, 30, 75
Feedback
  and learning, 40, 195
  from muscles, 39
Feelings
  of child, about self, 41, 118
  of deaf parents, 52–53
  of hearing parents, 118
  vocabulary for, 149–151
Fellendorf G, 204, 208
Ferguson C, 48, 67
Fillmore C, 29, 43
Fingerspelling, 3, 60
Fischer S, 94, 96
Fitzgerald E, 126, 128

Fitzgerald Key, 125–127
Formal operational period, 20, 22
Frames, in program, 105
Free morphemes, 70
Friedman L, 93, 96
Friend JE, 106, 107
Frustration
  causes of, 197
  tolerance for, 100
Functional memory groups, 37
Furth HG, 20, 31–33

Gagne R, 16–18, 43
Gallaudet TH, 1, 2
Gallaudet College, 6
Generalizations
  over-, 81
  study of, 31, 32
  under-, 81
Genetics
  and deafness, 2
  and intellectual development, 19
Gentile A, 133, 165
Gibson EJ, 24, 25, 35, 43
Ginsburg H, 21, 43
Glaser R, 192, 207
Glasses, fixing, 55
Goal, in case grammar, 29
Goda S, 89, 96
Goldstein M, 4, 12
Gorell S, 91, 97
Gottsleben R, 176, 186
Grace Arthur Performance Scale, 31
Grammar. *See also* Case Grammar
  generative-transformational, 28
  as system, 29
Grammar I, 110–112, 117, 181
Grammar II, 213–214
Grammatico LF, 115, 128
Granowski A, 154, 157, 165
Granowsky S, 49, 67
Green EJ, 15, 43, 105, 108
Greenfield P, 83, 97
Greenstein J, 54, 67
Groht MA, 126, 128
Gustason G, 5, 12

Halle M, 71, 96
Halliday M, 85, 97
Handicapped
  educationally, 203
  linguistically, 203
  severely, 8
Hand signals, 3
Hard of hearing child, in PL94-142
Hargis C, 73, 97, 132, 151, 165, 181, 186
Harms R, 73, 95
Haycock GS, 41, 43
Hearing aids
  attitudes toward, 53
  developed, 5
  ear trumpets, 3
  effects of dysfunction, 61
  fitting of, 80
  parental use of, 63
  personal, 62, 63
  range of, 54-55
  use of, for communication, 54, 61
Heider G, 89, 97, 174, 186
Heider M, 89, 97, 174, 186
Hess L, 89, 97
Hiskey-Nabraska Test of Learning
    Aptitude, 31
Hoemann H, 91, 97
Home visitors, 56
Hood L, 75, 84, 96
Houston S, 72, 97
Hughes RB, 165
Huttenlocher J, 80, 81, 97


Idioms, 116, 131, 137, 141, 142, 148,
    151, 169
Imitation, and assessment, 171
Impedence testing, 190
Indexing, in ASL conversation, 93
Indirect discourse, 72, 88
Individual Education Plan (IEP), 10, 11,
    64, 181-184, 188-191, 194, 196,
    201, 206
Individualizing instruction, 106, 185
Infinitives. See Transformations
Ingram D, 84, 87, 97

Instrument, in case grammar, 29, 75, 82,
    83
Instrumental needs, 85
Intelligence
  boundaries of, for mentally retarded,
    189, 194
  standardized, 31
  tests
    of abstraction, 31
    of cognitive abilities, 31-32
    of reasoning, 32
International Congress of educators of the
    deaf, 3
Intonation
  in baby register, 49
  function of, 131
  in oral communication, 131
  patterns of, 80
  in word utterances, 89
Intransitive verb sentence, 73
IQ tests, 31, 194
Ivimey G, 90, 97

Jarvella R, 90, 97
Jenkins JJ, 37, 43

Kamii C, 23, 43
Kaplan E, 79, 97
Kaplan G, 79, 80, 97
Kendall School, 6
Kinaesthesia
  as feedback mechanism, 40
  and infants, 46
Kintgen E, 72, 73, 98
Klima E, 30, 42
Knowledge, 19
  and motor skills, 40
  relation to language, 22
Kretschmer RR, 24, 43, 90, 97, 181,
    186, 199, 207
Krossner W, 49, 67
Kubler-Ross E, 52, 67

Landes J, 45, 67, 79, 97
Langdon G, 42, 43
Language

Language *(continued)*
  assessment, 167
  as communication medium, 69
  components of, 69
  comprehension of, 70
  disorders of, 23, 37, 188, 203
  form and content, 71ff
  and knowledge, 22
  and logic, 23
  LRS approach, 135
  nature of, 70
  new forms of, 22
  oral, 39–40
  parameters of, 71–72
    morphophonemic, 71–72
    pragmatic, 71
    semantic, 71, 73
    syntactic, 71–73
  read, 132
  rules, 29, 70, 71, 201
  and school subjects, 185
  spoken, 69
  for thinking, 112–114
  universals in, 28
  written, 90, 131, 164, 174, 176
Language acquisition. *See also* Language
    development; Language learning
  and brain mechanism, 28
  by language delayed children, 201
  planning for, 181ff
  by retarded children, 193
  and syntactic structures, 118–124
Language development. *See also*
    Language acquisition; Language
    learning
  and disruption of development, 70
  and fantasy life, 85
  normal, 78ff
  Piagetian view of, 22–24
  program, components of, 55ff
  stages, 79, 86–87
Language instruction
  correction by mothers, 50
  planning for growth, 167, 181–183
Language interaction techniques
  expansion of, 50, 58

  modeling, 51
  prodding, 50
  prompting, 58
  questioning, 58
Language learning. *See also* Language
    acquisition; Language
    development
  approximation of rules, 70
  disorders of, 203
  emergence of, 30
  initial, 70
  and psycholinguistics, 27–30
  of rules, 29
  and teaching, 70
  theories of
    perceptual view, 26
    Piagetian view, 22
    psycholinguistic view, 27–30
    Skinnerian view, 17
Lavatelli CS, 19, 20, 23, 43, 44
Learning. *See also* Language learning
  and activity level, 199–201
  attention problems, 197–198
  attitudinal, 41, 99
  to classify, 17
  in classroom, 102–104
  climate for, 100
  conditions for, 110
  cultural, 41–42
  of disabled child, 196ff
  to edit, 163–164
  facts, 35–36
  grouping children for, 164, 185
  incidental, 25
  of infants, 79
  and language disorder, 201–203
  and memory, 33–36, 198–199
  motivation for, 16
  motor skills, 39
  processing-time problems, 199
  rule-generating capacity, 30
  social, 41, 106
  to speak, 39
  to swim, 39
  theories of, 15, 17, 21, 24–25, 27
Lee L, 186

Lenneberg E, 27, 44, 78, 79, 97
Lesson plans
  for optional adverbs, 120–124
  for third person singular, 118–125
  for use of copula, 101–102
Levin H, 24, 25, 35, 43
Lexical meanings, 73–74, 169–170
Lexington School for the Deaf, 126
Library program in reading, 160
Lightbown P, 75, 84, 96
Limber J, 86, 88, 97
Lindsay P, 24, 25, 33, 44
Ling D, 41, 44, 72, 97
Linguistics
  definintion of, 71
  code, 46
  and rewriting texts, 142
*Linguistics of Visual English* (Wampler),
    5
Lipreading, 2–4, 26, 37–38, 193
Local Education Agency (LEA), 1,
    10–12, 188–190
Locative, defined, 75
Long-term memory, 33–34, 38, 101
Lounsburg E, 61, 67
Love R, 89, 98
Lubinsky J, 90, 97
Lykos CM, 3, 12

Mainstreaming
  and children, 7
  and pragmatics, 77
Maly P, 191, 207
Manually-coded language
  *Linguistics of Visual English,* 5
  as pidgin systems, 60, 62, 93
  *Seeing Essential English,* 5
  *Signed English,* 5
  *Signing Exact English,* 5
Mathetic function, 15
Mavilya M, 59, 67
McGinnis M, 193, 208
McKee P, 158, 165
McLean J, 195, 208
Meaning
  combinational, 75

multiple, of words, 30, 152
  precedence over structure, 73
  of structures, 169
  and syntax, 85
Measles, and hearing, 2
Media
  centers, 6
  materials, 7
  for teaching, 104–105
  TV, 132
Memory, 33ff
  aspects, 33
  capacity for, of children, 34
  and chunking, 198
  defined, 33
  difficulties with, 198–199
  for facts, 35
  and language, 36–38
  limitations of, 28, 34
  for relative clauses, 88
  rote, 36
  for sentences, 37
Mental retardation, 188, 193–195. *See
    also* Retardation
  CMR: custodial mentally retarded, 194
  curriculum for, 194
  EMR: educable mentally retarded, 194
  TMR: trainable mentally retarded, 194
Menyuk P, 30, 36, 37, 44, 70–72, 80,
    86, 97, 171, 186
Metaphor, in reading, 131
Mignone B, 59, 67
Miller SD, 115, 128
Modeling, in language development, 51
Model Secondary School, 6
Moerk E, 45, 49, 50, 67
Monsees E, 193, 208
Moores D, 12, 157, 165
Morehead DM, 20, 44, 84, 97, 202, 208
Morphemes
  affixes, 28
  bound, 72
  change in, 111
  endings, 145
  free, 72
  for past tense, 38

Morphemes *(continued)*
  rules for, 72
  suffixes, 28
Morse P, 98
Moses K, 52, 53, 68
Mother–child interaction. *See also* Parents
  attitudes toward deafness, 54
  and baby register, 49
  characteristics of, 48–50
  communication with child, 48
  and contextual cues, 81
  and controlled reference, 46
  correction of child language, 50
  directing attention, 46
  discipline, 54
  and hearing impairment, 51ff
  maternal stimulation, 50–51
Motor ability, 39–41, 193
Mourning stages, 52
Mover, defined, 75
M-Team, 10, 11, 188, 194, 203, 206
Mulholland A, 204, 208
Multidisciplinary Team. *See* M-Team
Multihandicapped children,. 187–190
  cerebral palsied, 2
  cleft palate, 2
  definition, 187
  extrinsic causes of, 203
  intrinsic causes of, 187
Multiple meanings, 28, 29, 139
  of prepositions, 152
  in reading matter, 137
  and syntax, 142–143, 149
Muma JR, 173, 186
Mumps, and hearing, 2
Myklebust H, 89, 98, 174, 186

National Education Association, 105
National Technical Institute for the Deaf,
  6
Natural language, for the deaf, 126
Negation, 110, 112
  developmental stages in, 86
  and functional relationships, 84
  and parts of speech, 77
Nelson K, 81, 98

News
  in assessing child language, 174
  evaluation of, 162
  journals, 162
  reporting to parents, 163
  and teachers, 164
  written, 162
*New York Times,* difficulty of, 154
Nominalization, 145
Nonexistence, defined, 77
Norman D, 24, 25, 44
Northcott W, 57–59, 66, 68
Noun
  locative, 75
  phrase, difficulty of, 180
  as prenominal modifier, 153
  vocabulary, 144–145

Object, in case grammar, 29
Object constancy, 20, 82, 83
Objectives. *See* Behavioral objectives
Occupational therapists, 192–193
Odom P, 89, 90, 98
Oller D, 79, 98
One-word utterances, 110
Open classrooms, 129
Operant procedures. *See*
      Stimulus–response (S–R) learning
Operations, defined, 21
Opper S, 21, 43
Ophthalmologists, 188, 191
Oral approach. *See* Oralism
Oralism, 3, 5
Organizing sensory data, 24
Outlining skills, 161, 164
Oyer H, 56, 68

Parents. *See also* Mother–child
      interaction
  adjustment to deaf child, 52–53
  and children, communication, 64–67
  counseling, 9, 58, 63
  deaf, 62
  education programs, 57
  feelings of, 52–53, 57, 63, 66
  and infant programs, 55ff

as learners of English, 206
organizations of, 64–65
as participants, in curriculum
    preparation, 130
reaction to deafness, 52
as reinforcers of language, 17, 110
rights under PL94-142, 1, 9, 10, 63,
    167
as stimulators of language, 117
as teacher aids, 66
–teacher conferences, 65
as teachers, 70, 117
Patient, use of, 75, 83, 173
Patterning, described, 128
Pediatricians, role of, 188
Pen pals, 163
Perception, 19
    and learning, 24–26
    and psychology, 24–27, 99
    strategies and languages, 99
Perfetti CA 29, 44
Performatives, 78
Periods of intellectual functioning, 111
    concrete operational, 20, 22
    formal operational, 20, 23
    preoperational, 20–21
    sensory-motor, 20–21
Personal needs, and language, 85
Phillips J, 45, 68
Phonemes, defined, 72
Phonics, 18, 132, 134
Phonology, 29, 40
Physically handicapped, 188, 192–193
Physical therapists, 188, 192
Piaget J, 19–23, 26, 29, 31, 32, 44, 82,
    99, 104, 111, 112, 115, 201
Pictures, 104, 105, 119
Pidgin languages, 60, 62, 93
Pinter Non-Language Test, 31
Place, in case grammar, 29
Poetry, by deaf children, 164–165
Pollack D, 5, 12
Power DJ, 73, 98, 101, 108
Pragmatic function, 85
Pragmatics, 60
    concreteness, 77

description of, 77
development in deaf children, 91
performatives, 78
prediction, 77
presupposition, 78
propositions, 77
rule acquisition, 89
Praninskas, 181, 186
Predicate adjective sentence, 73
Predicate adverb sentence, 73
Predicate nominative sentence, 73
Predication, 47–48, 77
Preoperational period, 20, 21–22, 111
Prepositions, 77, 78, 151, 168, 172
Preschool children
    language acquisition in, 37
    learning communication, 84
    scanning behavior, 24
    vocabulary for, 112
Pressnell L, 89, 98
Primary signal, for hearing aid, 61
Probability tasks, 32
Problem solving, 31
Processing language, 30, 99
Prodding, and language development, 50,
    51
Programmed instruction, 105–106
Project LIFE films, 105–106
Pronouns
    difficulty with, 180
    teaching of, 138
Psychoeducational diagnosticians, 188
Psycholinguistics, 24, 27–30
Public Law 94–142. See Education for All
    Handicapped Children Act
Pugh G, 89, 98, 133, 165
Pulaski MAA, 19, 20, 22, 44
Punctuation, 137
Pure tone audiometry, 190
Purkey WW, 41, 43

Questions
    asked by deaf preadolescents, 117
    during conversation period, 162
    formation of, 112, 168
    function of, 160–161

Questions *(continued)*
 in one-word stage, 23
 priority in language development, 103,
  120
 simple, 110
 wh
  how, 23
  what, 23, 51
  what's that, 163
  when, 23, 103
  where, 23, 103
  which, 51
  who, 23, 51
  why, 20, 103
  yes–no, 51, 81, 84

Quigley S, 73, 90, 91, 98, 101, 108, 157,
  165, 168, 170, 186
Quotation, teaching of, 137–139

Rawlings BW, 6, 13
Readability formula, 154
*Readers Digest,* difficulty of, 154
Reading
 achievement of, 133
 aloud, by children, 134
 and background information, 134, 151,
  159
 charts, 135ff
 comprehension, checks for, 141
 in curriculum, 131
 easy, 153
 for facts, 133
 idioms in, 135, 137, 151, 153
 importance to deaf children, 132
 lessons in, 135, 141, 160
 and linguistic skills, 70
 materials for, 153, 154
 for meaning, 132, 133
 and phonics, 134
 as psycholinguistic process, 116
 readiness for, 131
 requisites for, 134
 retardation in, 133
 rhetorical language in, 135
 and semantic information, 135

 series, basal, 154
 stories, for children, 159
 and syntactic knowledge, 133, 134
 teaching to hard of hearing, 132
 transformational rules in, 133
 visual clues in, 132
 vocabulary load, 135
Reamer J, 89, 98
Reduplication, in ASL, 93–94
Reference, 17, 46–47, 83
Referential category, 83
Regulatory needs, 85
Rehearsal, 27, 28, 30, 35
Reinforcement, 19, 110. *See also*
  Stimulus–response (S–R) learning
 for correct written language, 164
 external, 199
 for good speech, 41
 schedule of, 196
 techniques, 199
Reinforcers, 16, 196
Rejection, 77
Relativization, 168
Repetition
 of language forms, 194
 in lipreading, 38
 of sentences, 37
 in S–R learning, 16
Report writing, 161
Representational thought, 20
Residual hearing, 55
Retardation. *See also* Mental retardation
 in language of deaf children, 31–33
 mental, among deaf children, 193–194
 in reading, 133
Retinitis pigmentosa, and hearing, 2, 191
Retreat areas, in classrooms, 198,
  200–201
Rochester method, of communication, 3
Romney I, 161, 165
Rosenstern J, 32, 44, 89, 96
Ross M, 62, 68
Rote learning
 of copula, 86
 of modulation, 85
 of verb forms, 38

Rules
  for behavior, 106
  for classroom interaction, 107
  higher order, in thinking, 18
  of language
    approximating rules, 86
    delayed acquisition of, 89
    deviant acquisition of, 89
    in linguistic code, 46
    mastery of, 86, 170
    morphophonemic, 70
    ordered, 28
    phonic, 18
    phrase structure, 89–90
    reduction, 90–91
    syntactic, 72
    transformational, 28, 73
  organized sets of, 18, 28, 73
Rush ML, 137, 165
Russell K, 73, 98
Russell WK, 101, 108

St. Joseph Institute for the Deaf, 128
St. Paul Vocational Institute, 6
Sarachan-Deily A, 89, 98
Scarlet fever, and hearing, 2
Schell Y, 61, 68
Schoeller AW, 158, 165
School annuals, 163
School psychologists, role of, 188, 189
Schools and classes for the deaf
  American Asylum for the Deaf and
    Dumb, 1
  American School for the Deaf, 1
  Central Institute for the Deaf, 4
  Clarke School for the Deaf, 2
  day classes, 204
  Kendall School, 6
  Model Secondary School, 6
Schumacher J, 17, 44
Seattle Community College, 6
Seeing Essential English (Anthony), 5
Semantics, 71–73
  aspects in reading, 133
  categories of, 46
  classifications

  nouns, 75
  verbs, 29, 46, 74, 75
clues in reading, 133
component of language, 29
idiomatic meanings, acquiring, 142
relationships, in case grammar
  actor or mover, 75
  agent, 29, 46, 75
  agent–action–complement, 76
  agent–action–patient, 76
  beneficiary, 47
  complement, 75
  entity, 75
  experiencer, 29, 75
  goal, 29
  instrument, 29, 46, 75
  object, 29
  patient, 75
  prepositions, 77
  temporal noun, 29
Sensory-motor area
  activity, 24
  data, organization of, 24
  experiences, 39
  period (Piaget), 20–21
Sensory storage, 33
Sentences
  basic, in natural settings, 204
  connector, 151
  frame for testing adjectives, 150
  one-word, 203
  patterns I-V, 72–73, 111–112
  repetition tasks, 1, 37, 89, 90
  simple, 110
  three-word, 85
  two-word, 203
  types, 90
Serial arrangements, comprehension of,
  22
Set relationships, comprehension of, 22
Shaping, 195–196
Sharp E, 23, 44
Sherman JA, 17, 44
Short-term memory, 25, 33–34, 37, 88,
  90, 101
Shuy R, 205, 207

*Signed English* (Bornstein), 5
*Signing Exact English* (Gustason et al.), 5
Sign language, 26, 30, 60, 92–95
Silverman SR, 8, 12, 41, 43
Simmons-Martin A, 51, 56, 59, 68
Simple sentences, 110
Sinclair-de-Zwart H, 23, 44
Single-word utterances, 83
Skinner B, 16, 17, 94
Slobin D, 28, 29, 43, 44, 78, 98
Smith F, 33, 34, 36, 44, 100, 104, 108,
    133–135, 165
Smith J, 83, 97
Snow C, 45, 68
Snyder L, 195, 208
Social interaction, 106
Social learning, 41–42, 44, 99
Socially disturbed child, 195–196
Social workers, 10, 57, 66
Source, in case grammar, 29
Spache GD, 154, 166
Spanish children, 95
Speech
    act, 40
    development, 40
    drills, 40
    improvement of, 40
    lack of, in handicapped, 193
    lessons, 102
Speech/language pathologists, 10, 188,
    201–202
Speech reading, 9. *See also* Lipreading
Speech therapists, 202
Spelling, 164
Spina bifida, 192
Spoken language
    lack of, in physically handicapped, 193
    and sign language, 92
    supported by gesture, 168
Standard School English, 206
Stark R, 72, 98
Stimulus–response (S–R) learning, 15ff.
    *See also* Reinforcement
    and behavior modification, 16, 42, 107,
        195, 196
    and deaf child, 16

    and environment, 18
    extension of, 17–19
    and memory, 35
    operant conditioning in, 16
    rehearsal in, 27
    reinforcement in, 19
Stout IW, 42, 43
Strategies
    for remembering, 34
        categories, 35
        pointing, 35
        rehearsal, 35
        sequential naming, 35
    for assessing language, 175–176
Streng AH, 72, 73, 98, 111, 128, 162,
    166, 181, 186
Structural meaning, 169–170
Subject–verb–object (S–V–O), 91
Subordinate conjunction, 87
Suchman R, 191, 208
Symbolic play, 19, 22
Symbolic system, 21
Synonymy, 170
Syntactic Complexity Formula (SCF),
    154, 156–158
Syntactic relationships, 71, 72, 85
Syntactic structures, practice with, 117ff
*Syntactic Structures* (Chomsky), 28
Syntax
    assessment of, 168–169
    definition of, 72
    importance of, 29
    levels of, 72
    testing of, 170
Systems of communication
    aural–oral, 3, 5, 60
    cued speech, 4
    manual
        alphabet, 3
        sign, 5
    manually coded, pidgin systems, 5, 60
    and recommendations for use, 95
    total communication, 60
    unisensory, 5

Tactile sense, 40, 61

Tape recorders, in assessment, 173–174
Teacher-aide, in assessment, 173
Teachers
  dialogues of, with parents, 66
  as educational diagnosticians, 190
  education of, 7
  as home visitors, 66
  and inadequacy of education, 204
  as lecturers to children, 130
  as members of M-Team, 180
  need for, 106, 109
  as parent counselors, 57
  patterning by, 37
  as planners, 181ff
  as providers of language environment,
    70
  role in parent education, 64
  and self-evaluation, 102
Teaching, as telling, 103
Telecommunication devices, 161
Television viewing, 131
Templin M, 32, 33, 44
Temporal adverbs, 122–124
Temporal nouns, 75
Temporality development, 82, 90
Tense
  morphenic aspects, 122–124
  omission by deaf children, 90
  present and past, compared, 127
Tervoort B, 91, 98
Testing
  informal, of language, 23
  psychological, 9
  of syntax, 170
Test of Syntactic Ability (TSA), 168, 170
Tests
  achievement, 155
  audiologic, 61
  cloze, 155, 157–159
  formal, of language, 168
  of intelligence, 31
  Piaget type, 31
  reading, 155
  vision, 99
Therapists
  occupational, 193

physical, 193
Thinking
  behaviorists on, 18
  building language for,
  critical, 132
  higher-level organization,
  perceptual restraints on, 22
  promotion of, 112–115
Thomas O, 72, 73, 98
Thompson W, 89, 98
Thorndike EL, 16, 44
Three-word combinations, 85
Time, in case grammar, 29
Tobin H, 89, 98
Tokens, in behavior modification, 16
Topic comment, 47
Total communication, 60
Tracy ML, 11, 13
Trainable mentally retarded (TMR), 194
Transformational grammar, 30, 77, 86,
    154
  base structure level, 72
  base sentence patterns, 73
  morphological component, 72
  phonological component, 72
  rules of, 28
  semantic component, 72
  syntactic component, 89, 90, 144, 172
  transformational component, 29, 30,
    72, 74
Transformations. See also
    Transformational grammar
  application, 73
  clauses
    before and after, 186
    sentences-final relative, 28, 88
  conjunctions, 86–87, 90–91
  deletion in, 74
  embedding, 74, 86
  infinitive verb complement, 88
  negative, 28, 86
  passive, 28
  rearrangement in, 74
  requests, 110
  semantic content of, 77
  simple, 110, 180

Transformations *(continued)*
  substitution in, 74
  types of, 77
  yes/no questions, 51
Transitive verb sentence, 73
Two-word combinations, 47, 82, 84, 85,
    110, 202
Tyack D, 176, 186
Typewriting, for deaf children, 162

Unisensory approach, to language, 5
Units of study, 121

Verb auxiliaries, 168
Verb–object relationship, 28
Verbs, 145
  predication, 77
  types of, 75, 90, 203
Vernon M, 31, 44
Vibrotactile device, 61
Videotaping, 200
  in assessment, 173–174
  in parent programs, 58
  for teacher self-evaluation, 102
Visual impairment, 188, 191–192
Vocabulary, 82, 110–112, 137, 143–145,
    160, 162
  abstract, 162
  adjectives, 149–151
  controlled, 142
  directed, 164
  function words, 82
  growth of, 143ff
  idomatic usage of, 143
  levels of abstraction in, 145
  load of, in reading, 152
  multiple meanings, 143
  new words, 110
  nouns, 144–145, 150–151
  organization for retrieval, 143
  of parts of objects, 160
  paucity of, in deaf, 142
  for reading, 142

  selection of, 115
  spoken/written, 143
  superordinate terms in, 145
  teaching of, 137
  verbs, 145ff
  word lists, 112
  in writing, 143
Vocational Education Act, 6
Vocational technical programs, 6, 194
Vorce E, 41, 44

Walton L, 206, 208
Wampler DW, 5, 13
Weber J, 89, 98
Wechsler Intelligence Scale for Children,
    31
West J, 89, 98
Whitehurst G, 171, 186
Wilbur R, 60, 68, 93, 94, 98, 165
Wilcox J, 89, 98
Word lists, problems with, 112
Written language
  in assessment, 176
  as communication
    letters, 163
    pen pals, 163·
    requirements of, 161
    in school papers, 163
    via telecommunication devices, 161
  and composition, 124
  correction of, 164
  of deaf children, 90
  individualized, 164
  mechanics of, 163
  as reinforcement, 135
  research on, 174
  and spoken language, 131
  topics for, 163

Youniss J, 32, 43

Zink G, 61, 68

abcdefghij
890128

**DATE DUE**

| | | | |
|---|---|---|---|
| APR 2 5 2009 | | | |
| 6-7-10 | | | |
| APR 1 6 2012 | | | |
| | | | |
| | | | |
| | | | |
| | | | |
| | | | |
| | | | |
| | | | |
| | | | |
| | | | |
| | | | |
| | | | |
| | | | |
| | | | |
| | | | |

Printed in USA

HIGHSMITH #45230

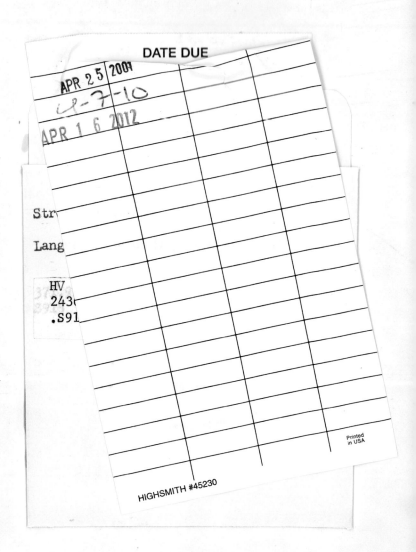

Str

Lang

HV
2430
.S91